SPARTANS

Ancient Cultures

These enjoyable, straightforward surverys of key themes in ancient culture are ideal for anyone new to the study of the ancient world. Each book reveals the excitement of discovering the diverse lifestyles, ideals, and beliefs of ancient peoples.

Published

In preparation

SPARTANS

A New History

NIGEL M. KENNELL

A John Wiley & Sons, Ltd., Publication

This edition first published 2010

© 2010 Nigel M. Kennell

Blackwell Publishing was acquired by John Wiley & Sons in February 2007. Blackwell's publishing program has been merged with Wiley's global Scientific, Technical, and Medical business to form Wiley-Blackwell.

Registered Office
John Wiley & Sons Ltd, The Atrium, Southern Gate, Chichester, West Sussex, PO19 8SQ, United Kingdom

Editorial Offices
350 Main Street, Malden, MA 02148-5020, USA
9600 Garsington Road, Oxford, OX4 2DQ, UK
The Atrium, Southern Gate, Chichester, West Sussex, PO19 8SQ, UK

For details of our global editorial offices, for customer services, and for information about how to apply for permission to reuse the copyright material in this book please see our website at www.wiley.com/wiley-blackwell.

The right of Nigel M. Kennell to be identified as the author of this work has been asserted in accordance with the Copyright, Designs and Patents Act 1988.

Library of Congress Cataloging-in-Publication Data

Kennell, Nigel M.
    Spartans : a new history / Nigel M. Kennell.
      p. cm. – (Ancient cultures)
    Includes bibliographical references and index.
    ISBN 978-1-4051-2999-2 (hardcover : alk. paper) – ISBN 978-1-4051-3000-4 (pbk. : alk. paper) 1. Sparta (Greece) – History. 2. Sparta (Greece) – History, Military. 3. Sparta (Greece)–Biography. I. Title.
DF261.S8K45 2010
938'.9–dc22
                                                            2009005158

A catalogue record for this book is available from the British Library.

Set in 10/12.5pt Rotation by Graphicraft Limited, Hong Kong
Printed in Singapore by Ho Printing Singapore Pte Ltd
I   2010

Contents

Illustrations

Map

Figures

Eurotas River

Limnai

Pitane

5
8
6
2
7
3
9

1

Mesoa

Kynosoura

4

Magoulitsa River

1 Hellenistic City Wall
2 Late Roman City Wall
3 Sanctuary of Artemis Orthia
4 Sanctuary of Poseidon Taenarius
5 Temple of Athena Chalcieocus
6 Chorus?
7 Agora
8 Early Roman Theater
9 Stoa

Map 1 The city of Sparta

Introduction

Spartans had disembarked from their triremes that day in 404 B.C.E. Now they stood on the soil of Attica, watching with the assembled crowds as imperial Athens' walls came tumbling down to the music of flute-girls hired for the occasion. The empire that had spread democracy at spear point, massacred whole populations in the name of preserving its freedom, and become an object of vilification to most Greeks was no more. Months of negotiations after the spectacular Spartan naval victory at distant Aegospotami on the Hellespont the previous year had only served to reinforce the Spartans' supremacy and confirm their position as the ultimate arbiters of any Greek city's fate. Sparta's popularity was also at its peak. It was a time when, as the historian Xenophon wrote, people thought "that freedom for Greece began on that day." The long and bitter Peloponnesian War was over. Sparta's position seemed unassailable.

But the Greeks knew that such successes as the Spartans enjoyed brought the danger of *hubris*, overconfidence in one's own abilities, which leads ultimately to *atê*, ruinous destruction. So it was with Sparta. Within the adult lifespan of a single man, the city went from undisputed leader of the Greeks to a bit-player on the regional scene, because of a single event – Sparta's stunning defeat by the Thebans at the battle of Leuctra in central Greece in 371 B.C.E. Stripped of the majority of their most productive farmland two years later, the Spartans had to endure the humiliation of seeing an independent city-state founded on that very land for their own former farm slaves by Greece's new great power. It was a blow from which Sparta never fully recovered.

How did this happen? How did such a successful military power collapse so rapidly? Was it just fate? Chance? The inexorable laws of history? What were the immediate factors in the years following Sparta's victory over Athens? Were there deeper reasons – characteristics, even flaws – embedded in the very fabric of Spartan society? These are among the questions about ancient Sparta that have intrigued historians for millennia, since the time of Aristotle in fact. Endeavoring to reach answers to them has gradually come to involve the weighing of a wide array of different sorts of evidence – literary, archaeological, epigraphical, and to an increasing extent in recent years, anthropological – to pierce the fog surrounding the notion of Sparta.

The Spartans of our imagination are familiar from films, novels, comics, and even certain history books. The men were ruled by iron discipline and an utter devotion to the laws of their city and the freedom of Greece; the women were more or less equivalent to the liberated women of modern times. These images of the Spartan way of life have been transmitted down through the centuries from the pens of ancient Greek and Roman writers through the scribes of the Middle Ages to the Renaissance humanists and thence to the scriptwriters, pundits, and novelists of the twenty-first century. It is a remarkably consistent picture that has stood the test of time. In recent years, however, the traditional view of Sparta has come under increasingly intense scrutiny as historians and archaeologists apply new techniques, perspectives, and occasionally even new pieces of evidence to the question of what it was to be a Spartan.

As a result, the long-standing consensus over the fundamental nature of Spartan society has begun to crumble. In its place, intense debate has arisen over each and every facet of what we thought we knew about Sparta and the Spartans. Even the very definition of "proper" Spartan history has changed as more and more specialists examine different aspects of post-classical Sparta. In other words, Sparta is "hot." But the ferment in Spartan scholarship has a downside. In no other area of ancient Greek history is there a greater gulf between the common conception of Sparta and what specialists believe and dispute. I hope that this book will help to bridge that gap by providing a survey of Spartan history from the city's origins to the end of antiquity that takes into account new specialist scholarship and places Spartan society into its wider Greek context.

I wrote this book using the first-class resources of the Blegen Library at the American School of Classical Studies at Athens, whose staff and faculty I thank. I am also grateful to Jutta Stroszeck, director of the Kerameikos excavations, for sharing with me the lastest results of her reinvestigation of the Tomb of the Lacedaemonians. Al Bertrand, Ben Thatcher, and now the team of Haze Humbert and Galen Smith of Wiley-Blackwell patiently watched over the book's long gestation, for which they have my deep gratitude. Finally, as ever, I acknowledge my debt beyond words to my wife Stefanie, my editor and best critic. *Corona vitae meae es.*

Ancient literary and epigraphical sources are cited according to the abbreviations in the *Oxford Classical Dictionary*, 3rd edn., 1996. All photographs are by myself, Nigel M. Kennell.

1

The Name, the Land, and the Sources

We begin with the name – or rather names – because, as with virtually everything connected with Sparta, what the city and its territory were called is more complicated than it first appears. There is a welter of names – Sparta, Spartans, *Spartiatai*, Laconia, Laconians, Lacedaemonia, and Lacedaemonians – each with a slightly different connotation and history. In the Classical period, the southern Peloponnese under Spartan control was commonly called *hê Lakônikê* (probably *gê*), "the Laconian (land)" (Hdt. 1.69.4; Thuc. 5.34.1). The territory we call Laconia was also referred to as *Lakedaimôn*. Unfortunately for clarity, the city of Sparta was also called *Lakedaimôn*, while the official designation of the Spartan state was *hoi Lakedaimonioi*, "the Lacedaemonians." In addition, the so-called *perioikoi*, who were free and lived in small civic communities around Laconia without enjoying the rights and obligations of full Spartan citizens, were often included among the Lacedaemonians as well. From time to time, the ambiguous designation "Laconian" (*Lakôn*) also crops up (e.g. Hdt. 1.68.2, 8.2.2; Thuc. 3.5.2). Thus, "Lacedaemonia" might designate either the Spartan civic center or all of Spartan territory, and "Lacedaemonians" could be Spartan citizens, the non-Spartan *perioikoi*, or a combination of the two. "Proper" Spartans, those adult males who maintained their commitments to the state, were *Spartiatai*, "Spartiates." Unlike *Lakedaimôn*, which has resisted etymological explanation, *Spartê* (Doric *Sparta*), is generally agreed to be connected with the verb *speiro* ("I sow") and mean something like "the sown (land)" – a suitable name for a newly founded community. The name is appropriate, as there is no archaeological evidence for settlement on the site before the early Iron Age. An exciting discovery in the early 1990s has added another layer to the history of these names. Excavations on the acropolis of Thebes in Boeotia uncovered a cache of clay tablets from the Mycenaean period, the Late Bronze Age (roughly 1400–1100 B.C.E.), written in Linear B. Several of these tablets mention men called either "the Lacedaemonian" (*ra-ke-da-mi-ni-jo*) or "the son of the Lacedaemonian" (*ra-]ke-da-mi-ni-jo-u-jo*), who may have played some role in cult activity. From these tablets, we now know that *Lakedaimôn* is the oldest geographical designation, dating back to the second half of the second millennium B.C.E., which inhabitants of Sparta may later have adopted in order to project an image of themselves as the guardians of the old Lacedaemonian heritage, a process underway by the eighth century.

The modern province of *Lakônia* is (very) roughly equivalent in its extent to ancient Lacedaemon. But present-day Laconians have to be content with the permanent loss of some of the most contentious real estate in ancient Greece – the Belminatis and the Sciritis, the uplands between the plain of Arcadian Tegea and the Eurotas valley, and the Thyreatis, in which the modern towns of Astros and Leonidion are located, not to mention the rich fields of Messenia, the economic foundation of Spartan might. Even without Messenia, though, ancient Laconia was vast in Greek terms, encompassing two major mountain ranges, Taygetus on the west and Parnon on the east, which terminate in the two large promontories of Cape Taenarum and Cape Malea. The forbidding east coast of the Malea peninsula, with few good anchorages, contrasts with the calmer waters of the Laconian gulf, around which lie a number of small coastal plains. Small to medium-sized towns cluster on them around the coast, many of them on or near the sites of ancient communities. The largest of the plains is that of Helos, where the river Eurotas flows into the sea, its sediments extending the land so much that the present coastline has little to do with the ancient. On the gulf's western side lies Cape Taenarum, known today as the Mani, an area with a fearsome reputation for its rugged landscape and population.

The heart of Laconia is the valley of the river Eurotas, which flows from mountain springs in the north before entering the Laconian gulf through the southern marshland. The almost sheer fastness of Taygetus provided raw materials such as animals for the hunt and probably some timber, but little opportunity for settlement, while on the opposite side of the valley Parnon's gentler slopes cradle many upland and coastal plains that could, and still do, support modest-sized communities.

Communication between these towns themselves and with Sparta has until recently been quite difficult, however. The paving and expansion of roads over the last few decades has made travel much quicker within Laconia, but the mountainous terrain still imposes long detours. In antiquity, the sense of isolation in communities several mountain passes and many kilometers away from the Eurotas valley must have been strongly felt, making the fact that ancient Laconia remained unified for so many centuries all the more impressive.

The Spartan heartland extended outwards from the banks of the Eurotas in a valley approximately 12 km wide at its greatest extent and 22 km long. Formed by a massive subsidence before the Pliocene era (more than 5.332 million years ago) and subsequent erosion on the valley's sides accompanied by flooding by the sea, the valley floor was covered by marine deposits, which were in turn overlaid by fans of alluvial sediment. Soil derived from this layer was the basis of agriculture in the region during antiquity. Fertile and well watered both by the Eurotas itself, one of the few Greek rivers that still flows during the summer, as well as by streams flowing from Taygetus, the valley today produces abundant crops of olives, citrus, and a variety of vegetables, using large-scale irrigation.

1.1   The Eurotas river south of Sparta

In antiquity, agriculture may have been hampered by the ridges formed by erosion and the several prominent hills that break up the terrain, though the question of how much the present landscape of the Eurotas basin resembles the ancient does not have a clear-cut answer. Recent research indicates that the deposit of sediment throughout the Mediterranean took place sporadically over an extended period from before the Bronze Age down to about a century ago and was probably due to single catastrophic events like earthquakes or flash floods rather than to climate change or even human activity. The landscape of Laconia has thus been in continuous flux, with some areas disappearing under flood sediment and others turning into cliffs from sudden erosion or slumping of parts of hills. The intense earthquake that hit Sparta in 465/4 B.C.E. likely had profound effects on the surrounding landscape.

The valley today is shut off from the sea by a line of hills, known as Vardounia, which springs from Taygetus on the west and ends at the course of the Kourtaki near the modern village of Krokeai. The main ancient and modern route through these hills reaches the port town of Gytheum on the Laconian gulf, which was Sparta's major maritime outlet. The dramatic topography of the northern part of the Eurotas valley, where the two mountain ranges draw together, is best appreciated on the modern highway to Sparta, which after climbing slightly to leave the Tripolis plain and threading through the rocky uplands

1.2   The Eurotas valley from the north

1.3   Sparta and Taygetus from the Menelaeum

descends rapidly along the western foothills of Parnon to the valley floor, thus affording a magnificent view of the valley, with Taygetus' southern peaks towering over.

Modern Sparta spreads out from several hills clustered around the southeastern extremity of a long spur of Taygetus. The river Eurotas flows by on the east, its tributary the Magoulitsa describing a great arc to the south, while the hills of the ancient acropolis and Palaikastro to the north form natural boundaries which even today constrain the city's sprawl somewhat. Refounded on the site of its ancient predecessor, the modern city has disappointed those who dreamt of uncovering major archaeological finds, validating the Athenian historian Thucydides' prediction of Sparta's potential as a major destination for archaeologically inclined tourists.

> Suppose, for example, that the city of Sparta were to become deserted and that only the temples and foundations of the buildings remained, I think that future generations would, as time passed, find it very difficult to believe that the place had really been as powerful as it was represented to be.
>
> (1.10.5)

In Thucydides' time, Sparta probably did look unimpressive compared to Athens. Spartans lived scattered into separate settlements called *obai*

("obes") or "villages." Four obes were located around the hill forming the acropolis. Limnae ("Marshes"), probably the oldest inhabited
area of the city, was situated along the western bank of the Eurotas
and derived its name from the high water table in that area. To the
west and north of the highest point of the acropolis, where the Roman-
era theater can be seen today, was Pitane, apparently Sparta's most
desirable neighborhood. The locations of Mesoa and Cynosura are less
definite, but most specialists would place them side by side to the south
of the acropolis. Amyclae, a community about 5 km to the south of
the city, is usually considered to have been incorporated into the city
as an obe in the eighth century, though the only direct evidence for its
obal status is Roman in date (*IG* V.1 26).

Of all the buildings, monuments, and sites in ancient Sparta, only three
can be identified with any certainty – the sanctuary of Artemis Orthia
beside the Eurotas, the temple of Athena Chalcioecus ("of the Bronze
House") on the acropolis, and the early Roman theater just below it.
Outside the city proper some sanctuaries have been excavated, while
a recent surface survey has considerably enlarged our knowledge but
also raised some unexpected but vitally important new questions. On
the whole, though, Laconia remains remarkably underexploited in
archaeological terms. Only since the 1990s, for instance, has systematic
excavation been carried out at the site of one of Sparta's dependent
communities, Geronthrae – a project that has the potential to nuance
significantly our present picture of Sparta's relations with its dependent
communities.

This brings us to the literary sources. Constructing a history of
Sparta is bedeviled by two complicating factors – the lack of a corpus
of writings by Classical Spartan authors that might illuminate the inner
workings of Spartan institutions and the mindset of Spartans themselves
and the existence of a large corpus of writings by non-Spartans claiming to do just that. This is the famous "Spartan mirage," through which
the image of the historical city gradually became transformed through
the work of philosophers, biographers, historians, and romantics into
that of a radically unique state unlike any other in Greece and often
in seeming contradiction to fundamental laws of human behavior.

The image of Spartan uniqueness fostered the preservation down to
our time of remnants of poetry from as early as the seventh century.
The fragments of the Spartan poet Tyrtaeus (F1-24 West[2]), along with
the partial survival of poetry by his contemporary Alcman, represent the
largest cache of primary literary evidence for Sparta from any century

in antiquity. Tyrtaeus' poems are mainly concerned with encouraging young Spartans to fight vigorously in the lengthy and harrowing conflict with their neighbors, the Messenians, and are consequently of major importance in dating the Spartan wars of conquest, as well as in providing information on martial ideology (F10, F12 West[2]; cf. F11, lines 4, 23–9). Another important fragment seems to have been composed at a time of social unrest connected with the war and may be closely related to one of the earliest surviving Greek constitutional texts, the so-called Great Rhetra (F4 West[2]). If Tyrtaeus' poems conform to our expectation of what Spartan poetry was like, Alcman's do not. His poetry reflects a sophisticated society reveling in the good life: Song, dance, physical beauty, splendid textiles, and the brightness of gold figure prominently. The most significant surviving poem of Alcman's, on a papyrus found near Saqqara in Egypt in 1855, is a song for a chorus of maidens (*Partheneion*), participating in a dawn ritual of re-clothing an image of a goddess, perhaps to be identified as Artemis Orthia (*PMGF* F1). Archaeological finds, notably from the shrine of Orthia itself, also attest to a love of luxury, humor, and even frivolity in the early Archaic period that hardly jibes with the dour, militaristic Spartans of the ancient (and modern) imagination.

A gap of about two hundred years separates Tyrtaeus and Alcman from our next major source, Herodotus of Halicarnassus, who completed his *Histories* around 425 B.C.E. Herodotus' immediate subject, the repulsion of two Persian assaults on Greece in 490 and 480/79 B.C.E., led him to a wide-ranging oral inquiry (*historiê*) as to the underlying causes of this ancient "clash of civilizations." Whenever an area first comes into contact with a major eastern power, either the Persians or their predecessors, in the course of his narrative Herodotus uses the occasion to supply background information on the history and culture of the peoples dwelling there. Croesus of Lydia's appeal to Sparta for aid against the Persians in the sixth century (1.65–77) is just such an occasion, when Herodotus provides an outline of early Spartan history and we first encounter what later became essential elements of the Spartan mirage – a terrible period of unrest ended only by the divinely sanctioned constitutional and social reforms of the legendary lawgiver Lycurgus (1.65–6). Sparta's leading position during the later sixth century and its command of the coalition of Hellenic states in the 480/79 war against the Persians meant that Herodotus often had occasion to sketch the historical circumstances behind incidents preceding and during that war. As a consequence, Herodotus is our major, and indeed our only source for most Archaic Spartan history. But history in the narrow modern sense was only one of Herodotus' interests, so he also describes certain Spartan social customs. His catalog of the privileges enjoyed by kings in peace and war and life and death ranks among the more valuable accounts of Spartan institutions surviving from antiquity (6.56–9). Once seriously impugned, Herodotus' claim to be presenting material gathered from personal autopsy and word-of-mouth inquiries of oral sources is now overwhelmingly accepted. Sometimes we can even glimpse traces of social or political tension behind the accounts he collected. A case in point concerns Cleomenes I, who, when first introduced is described as behaving as "the most just of men" (3.148.2), only later to be characterized as "without restraint, actually a maniac" (5.42.1). The conflicting perceptions of the long-dead king perhaps reflect family or, more likely, political differences among Herodotus' informants.

In Herodotus' younger contemporary Thucydides, author of the account of the Peloponnesian War, we meet a different sort of historian altogether. Thucydides' subject, a war being fought as he researched and wrote most of his book (1.1, 5.26.1), differed profoundly from that of Herodotus, the great conflict of a previous generation that had fast acquired quasi-mythic dimensions. His approach to the task of communicating the results of his research also differs. Instead of recording several versions of a story, at letting the reader decide between them, Thucydides sifted through his material to find what he saw as the truth (1.22.2). When he does admit the existence of alternative versions of events, it is to show them up as misconceived or plainly false. For instance, without naming him, he alludes to Herodotus' assertions that the Spartan kings cast two votes in council and that there was a contingent of troops "from Pitane" (1.20.3) in order to affirm their falsity. His twenty-year exile for losing Thracian Amphipolis to the Spartan general Brasidas in 424/3 (4.104–8, 5.26.5) allowed him access to the city and its inhabitants. At Sparta, he was able to read the inscription above the tomb of Pausanias, victor of Plataea (1.13.4) and the sight of its unremarkable public buildings must have inspired his famous statement, quoted above, that Sparta's and Athens' architecture were almost inverted reflections of the two cities' power and influence (1.10.2). He also appears familiar with significant distinctions of social class among the inhabitants of Laconia, and knows something of Spartan legislative procedure. Thucydides penetrated the secrecy of the state sufficiently to uncover the story of the "disappearing" of two thousand helots (4.80.3–5), though the veracity of this event has recently been doubted. Thucydides knew Sparta and strove to be as accurate as possible, though even he fell victim to the allure of the Spartan mirage, when he repeated one of its shibboleths – that the Spartan way of life had remained completely unchanged for four hundred years (1.18.1). Other early flickerings of the mirage have been discerned in his statement that the Spartans were the first to adopt a modest lifestyle in which the wealthy differed little from the rest of the population (1.6.4).

Our next major source, Xenophon, presents yet another contrast, since for a significant portion of his adult life he was a soldier, and apparently quite a good one. Born in the later fifth century, perhaps around 430 B.C.E., Xenophon lived through the bloody, confusing years following the defeat of Athens and the establishment of Spartan hegemony, only to see Sparta itself laid low by the disaster at Leuctra in 371 B.C.E. and the subsequent humiliation of Thebes' invasion of Laconia. He died sometime after 356/5 B.C.E., in the decade after Thebes' brief hegemony ended at Mantinea (362 B.C.E.), when the shadow of Philip II was beginning to lengthen over Greek affairs. Among his literary productions are two items of paramount importance to the study of Sparta – his *Hellenica* (*Hellenic Affairs*), the history of the rise and fall of Sparta from 411 to 362 B.C.E., and the *Constitution of the Lacedaemonians*, the only study of Spartan public and social institutions to survive intact from antiquity.

Much denigrated in the past as an unworthy successor to Thucydides, Xenophon's skills as a historian have recently undergone intense reevaluation. In particular, Xenophon's supposedly pro-Spartan bias has been reinterpreted as a focus on Sparta's actions both good and bad in order to illuminate the pitfalls of grasping at political domination. Still, the *Hellenica's* failings have resulted in scholars' often resorting to the fragments of another fourth-century historian, Ephorus, who based his narrative on the almost completely lost work of an anonymous figure known as the Oxyrhynchus historian. Despite its drawbacks, the *Hellenica* provides a unique glimpse into Spartan internal affairs through the eyes of a privileged outsider. Even more information is provided by the short *Constitution of the Lacedaemonians*, in whose 15 chapters Xenophon tried to account for Sparta's eminence as a result of their laws and customs in peace and war. Written at some date between 394 and 371 B.C.E., the *Constitution* presents Spartan institutions in an overwhelmingly positive light, except for the fourteenth chapter which Xenophon devotes to a bitter denunciation of the current

Spartan lifestyle. This chapter's jarring tone, so at odds with the rest of the book, has led scholars to question whether its present location in the *Constitution* is correct and even to propose that it was added later by a disillusioned Xenophon after the defeat at Leuctra in 371 B.C.E. But most now believe that the chapter is where Xenophon originally wanted it, which raises the interesting question of the *Constitution's* relationship to the contemporary reality of Sparta. Xenophon's emphatic denial in chapter 14 that in his time – he twice uses the word *nun* ("now") – the Spartans held to the Lycurgan line points to the preceding account being at least partly idealized and colored by nostalgia. In all likelihood, Xenophon never experienced a Sparta living in harmony with all the features of the Lycurgan system he describes in the *Constitution*, if indeed Sparta ever did.

A massive thirty-book universal *History* written by Ephorus of Cyme (*c.* 405–380 B.C.E.) was also influential in antiquity. Ephorus' work was well known and used as a source by many later authors. It is preserved only in fragments, although large sections, apparently quoted verbatim, appear in Strabo's *Geography* and in the *Bibliotheke* of Diodorus Siculus, another Roman-era author, where they provide much information about the very early history of Sparta and Laconia. Care is needed, however, since Polybius accused his predecessor of distorting the image of certain Spartan institutions (Polyb. 6.46.10).

In Plato (*c.* 429–347 B.C.E.) and his pupil Aristotle (384–322 B.C.E.) we encounter the first and only complete extant works in which Sparta appears as an object of political and philosophical inquiry. Allusions to Spartan constitutional and social practice run like a thread throughout Plato's works, a legacy of his intellectual apprenticeship in the pro-Spartan circle of Socrates. Plato did not undertake a thorough, systematic analysis of Spartan society. That was not his aim. Rather, he approvingly noted many aspects worthy of emulation, such as respect for the old and authoritarianism, while sometimes leveling criticism, for instance against what he saw as an over-emphasis in citizen training on inculcating physical courage alone. The virtues of Plato's Sparta far outweigh its faults; thus, in the *Republic* it appears as an example of the second-best type of constitution, lacking just a little of the best (yet unrealized) constitution, that of aristocracy (*Resp.* 545a–c). As a timocratic constitution, Sparta's still possessed admirable features – obedience to the law and a distaste for agriculture among them (*Resp.* 548d). But the cancer of individualism had already begun to infect the body politic in the form of greed for wealth and lust for military glory, which leads to obsessive militarism and secret accumulation of riches, in defiance of the law (*Resp.* 547e–548b). Timocracy inevitably degenerates into the next lower type of constitution, oligarchy. The failings of the timocratic state echo criticisms of contemporary Sparta, especially as regarding the display of wealth, about which we have already noticed Xenophon complaining. For Plato, as for Xenophon, the city of his day had declined from its pristine state under the laws of Lycurgus, but the philosopher, unlike the soldier-historian, viewed all decline as inexorable and not a problem peculiar to Sparta. Sparta figures most prominently in the *Laws*, Plato's latest work, in which a trio of travellers in Crete discuss the laws for a new city called Magnesia. As they traipse on, they propose and argue over the right sort of constitutional arrangements for Magnesia, drawing heavily on perceived Spartan precedents for the training of citizens, and the role of music and gymnastics. Plato was no uncritical fan of Sparta, however: he acutely finds a fatal flaw in the Spartan tendency to elicit good behavior from its citizens through compulsion rather than persuasion and education (*Leg.* 666e).

Compared to Plato's approach, Aristotle's treatment of Sparta is motivated more by taxonomy than idealism. In the *Politics*, he shows how the human good, discussed in the *Nicomachean Ethics*, can be attained through the practical science of political theory. Aristotle collects previous theories of the best state, along with examples of political and constitutional practice from contemporary states, and subjects them to analysis. Sparta, as a much-praised exemplar of the best sort of constitution (*Pol.* 2.3.10 [1265b]), one that is a mixture of oligarchy, monarchy, and democracy, is a natural focus of his attention. Thus, the *Politics* contains a wealth of references to specific Spartan practices, which Aristotle either praises or (often) condemns. The number and specificity of these descriptions may well be a result of the research carried out for *The Constitution of the Lacedaemonians*, part of a research megaproject to examine the constitutions of major Greek states (and Carthage), of which only the *Constitution of the Athenians* now survives. Aristotle is interested in classifying Sparta's constitution correctly and investigating the city as it existed in the later fourth century rather than in using it as a model for the perfect state. He makes a useful though acerbic guide. His assessments of the procedure for electing ephors as "childish" (*Pol.* 2.6.16 [1270b]), the power of Spartan women as detrimental to the state (*Pol.* 2.6.5 [1269b]), and Spartan citizen training as overemphasizing savagery (*Pol.* 8.3.3 [1338a]) are well known.

But he also praises the training system for being under state control (*Pol.* 8.1.3 [1337a]), notes that the Spartans, because of their training, are said to be good judges of music (*Pol.* 8.4.6 [1339b]), and provides the surprising information that fathers with three or more sons were exempted from military service (*Pol.* 2.6.13 [1270b]). Aristotle regarded the Spartan constitution, so admired by theorists, as fundamentally flawed – the very reason for the city's fall. In contrast to the essentially positive viewpoint of Xenophon and Plato, Aristotle saw the laws of Lycurgus as harboring the very worm of Spartan decay. He did not consider contemporary Sparta's reduced standing as a sign of decline from an earlier pristinely Lycurgan state either because of wilful abandonment of the laws or due to an immutable law of corruption. Failure was built into the system by the decisions of the lawgiver himself: "And yet it is clear, since the Spartans now no longer have an empire, that they are not fortunate, nor was the lawgiver a good one" (*Pol.* 7.13.12 [1333b]).

After Aristotle, the next extant source of any substantial relevance to Sparta is Polybius (*c.* 200–*c.* 118 B.C.E.), who wrote his history of Rome's rise to superpower status after 146 B.C.E. In his famous comparison of Rome and Sparta as exemplifying types of the much-sought-after mixed constitution, Polybius represented Lycurgus as the rational guiding force behind Sparta's traditional laws. But his immediate concern was with the more recent history of Sparta, especially its revival under king Cleomenes III and the later career of Nabis, Sparta's last king (or tyrant) and enemy of Rome, which prepared the ground for Sparta's unhappy membership in the Achaean League and her subsequent role as the *casus belli* for the conflict that resulted in Rome crushing the League and establishing permanent control over Greece. The parts of his history that survive in Greek and the large section which lie behind Livy's Latin version provide us with a vital, albeit selective, picture of the city during its last years as an independent actor.

A few chapters of the *Geography* written by Strabo of Amaseia during the reigns of Augustus and Tiberius shed spots of valuable light on Sparta in the early years of Roman rule. His reference to the constitutional settlement of Laconia after the fall of Nabis in the early second century B.C.E. provides information found nowhere else (8.5.5), while our understanding of the fate of Gaius Julius Eurycles, Sparta's ruler in the later first century, depends to a great extent on Strabo's text (8.5.5). Short though his account is (8.4.10–8.5.7), Strabo has also provided much fuel for debate on Sparta's history and social institutions in the Classical period, because he preserves Ephorus' version of the origin of the helots (8.5.4) and, alone of ancient writers, refers to an important pamphlet of King Pausanias (8.5.5).

The influence of Plutarch of Chaeronea (c. 42–c. 120 C.E.) on perceptions of Sparta endured for centuries. His voluminous output of biographical, philological, and philosophical works made him one of the most significant shapers of early modern political and historical thought. His Spartan lives – of Lysander, Agesilaus, Agis, and Cleomenes, and especially Lycurgus – as well as collections of notable sayings supposedly by Spartans, represented Spartan society as disciplined, obedient, focused on physical culture, and deeply conservative, an image that remains powerfully affecting even today. As a biographical subject, Lycurgus presented a nearly insurmountable problem – he almost certainly did not exist. Even in antiquity, debate accompanied every aspect of his life and activity, leading Plutarch to admit, "concerning Lycurgus the Lawgiver absolutely nothing can be said that is beyond dispute. His ancestry, his foreign travels, his death, and above all his activity concerning the laws and the constitution, all are reported differently. And there is the least agreement about the chronology of the man's life" (Lyc. 1.1). On the other hand, Plutarch could draw upon a rich, but varied, "biographical" tradition about Lycurgus that had developed since the Classical period, as historians and other writers elaborated and conjectured from meager evidence when they did not simply invent plausible details. Thus, the part of the *Lycurgus* purporting to describe his life and political activity is outright fiction, based on the work of these lost writers who constructed a life for their subject that would account for the received image of early Sparta. Plutarch's Sparta of the eighth century B.C.E. comes dressed in late Hellenistic garb, complete with palace intrigue (Lyc. 3.2–4), a coup (Lyc. 5.5–9), and – the most obvious anachronism – silver and gold coinage (Lyc. 9.2).

Of greater, though not indisputable, value are the passages ostensibly reporting Lycurgus' constitutional and social reforms, beginning with the document known as the Great Rhetra (Lyc. 6.2). All the famous institutions of Classical Sparta are on display, endowed with a pronounced Platonic cast: the Gerousia (Lyc. 5.11–14); the ephorate, considered by Plutarch as post-Lycurgan (Lyc. 7.1–2), equal distribution of land and banning of precious-metal coinage (Lyc. 8–9), common messes (Lyc. 10, 12), and physical education for girls and inducements for marriage (Lyc. 14–15). Plutarch then describes in some detail the citizen training of young male Spartans (*Lyc.* 16–19.5) and lists various worthwhile Spartan sayings that prove its efficacy (*Lyc.* 20). The later chapters of the *Lycurgus* are also the source for such mainstays of Spartan scholarship as the method of electing members to the Gerousia (*Lyc.* 26), intramural burial (*Lyc.* 27.1), and Spartan abuse of the helots, including the infamous Crypteia (*Lyc.* 28.2–13).

Apart from the *Lycurgus*, Plutarch wrote two other biographies of Classical Spartan figures, Agesilaus and Lysander, about whose existence there is no doubt whatsoever. Because of the prominence of these two figures in the events that shaped Greece from the end of the Peloponnesian War to the disaster at Leuctra, Plutarch's narratives have special importance, as he drew on sources other than Xenophon, whose idiosyncratic approach has so frustrated historians. Plutarch's narratives thus often serve to correct or supplement deficiencies in Xenophon's. His other Spartan biography is the joint one of the reformer kings Agis IV (reigned 245–241 B.C.E.) and Cleomenes III (reigned 235–220/19 B.C.E.). Drawing principally on the work of the Athenian historian Phylarchus, who was contemporary with the events he describes, Plutarch fashioned a dramatic narrative of reformist zeal confronting deeply entrenched, and corrupt, special interests. Despite its obvious bias, which is due more to Phylarchus than to Plutarch himself, the *Agis and Cleomenes* provides a few glimpses into life in Hellenistic Sparta. Rounding out the Spartan-centered content in the Plutarchan corpus are the collections of sayings attributed to famous Spartan men and women (*Mor.* 208a–242d), among which is also an odd set of passages on various customs commonly called the *Laconian Institutions* (*Mor.* 236f–240b). The sayings of famous Spartans belong to a flourishing and popular Hellenistic genre of quotations called *apophthegmata*, in which edifying, moralizing, or just amusing sayings were attributed to well-known historical figures. The first collections of Spartan *apophthegmata* seem to date from the early third century B.C.E., while the latest historical figure to appear in them is Agis IV (*Mor.* 216c–d).

After Plutarch, Pausanias is the most important Greek writer of the imperial period to contribute to our knowledge of Sparta. In his *Periegesis*, Pausanias provides a complex and richly textured picture of Greece, its cults, festivals, monuments, and thriving local traditions at the middle of the second century of our era. Pausanias' utility as a guide for archaeologists has long been acknowledged, but only relatively recently have his aims as a writer been recognized, let alone appreciated. Pausanias describes a Sparta brimming with monuments attesting to its great past: the stoa built from the spoils of the Persian Wars, adorned with figures of Persians that held up the roof in place of columns (3.9.3); the Aphetaid road, on which Odysseus raced for the hand of Penelope (3.12.1); the cenotaph of Brasidas and the graves of Leonidas and Pausanias the victor of Plataea (3.14.1) among many others – so many, in fact, that Pausanias was at a loss to describe them all (3.11.1). Unfortunately, as I have noted earlier, only a tiny handful of these have been identified with any certainty.

Unlike Plutarch, obviously, his aim was to describe the contemporary city, but Pausanias was also concerned with situating the sights he described within their historical context. In so doing, he preserved fragments of earlier historians' work that would otherwise have been lost. He in fact begins his fourth book, on Messenia, with a lengthy digression on that territory's conquest by Spartans in the Archaic period. Negligible though its evidentiary value may be, the account preserved by Pausanias provides a useful insight into how the later Messenians constructed their past at a time when elite Greeks conventionally defined their place in the contemporary world almost exclusively in terms of their Archaic or Classical history. His introduction to Book 3, on Sparta and Laconia, is sounder, due for the most part to its being largely derived from Herodotus, whose style of historiography strongly influenced Pausanias' own.

In addition to the literary sources, inscriptions can play a small and unevenly distributed part in constructing Sparta's history. It is true that surviving epigraphical texts from the Classical period can be counted almost on the fingers of one hand. Official documents relate exclusively to what we would call foreign affairs, including one of the best known Spartan inscriptions, the Spartan War Fund. Among the private inscriptions is the single victory dedication from the sanctuary of Artemis Orthia that dates from before the Roman period (*IG* V.1 255) and a series of inscriptions from the sanctuary of Poseidon on Cape Taenarum, the southernmost tip of Laconia, that attest to the freeing of Spartan slaves (*IG* V.1 1228–33). The best known inscription erected by a private individual is the lengthy stele of Damonon (*IG* V.1 213), in which he records his victories and those of his son in a variety of chariot races and other athletic events in local festivals throughout Laconia.

Epigraphical evidence comes into its own during the Roman period, when the literary sources largely evaporate. A few fragmentary decrees (e.g. *IG* V.1 18–20) are supplemented by inscribed careers (*IG* V.1 31–47; *SEG* 11 476–501), catalogs of magistrates (*IG* V.1 48–212; *SEG* 11 502–647), and many honorific inscriptions for civic worthies of both sexes (*IG* V.1 455–613; *SEG* 11 761–70), all of which provide us with a wealth of prosopographical information. For instance, thanks to these documents, we know the names of far more women from the Roman period than from any other period of Sparta's history. Since the honors recorded by these texts are couched in a highly evolved, richly encoded language of praise common throughout the Greek East, much of the dynamics of civic life can be discerned through these inscriptions. Most important, however, is the series of dedications found at the Orthia sanctuary, erected by victors in contests of the Roman-era citizen training system, the *agoge*, which constitute the largest concentration of evidence for this sort of institution in the Greek East outside Athens. The texts accompanying the iron sickles that were the prizes in the contests enable us to reconstruct the workings of this important public institution in more detail than at any other time.

From all these texts, fragments of texts, artifacts, and barely visible remnants of material culture scattered over almost a millennium, the historian's task is to construct a Sparta that is consonant with the surviving evidence and to people it with Spartans who, with any luck, are more than historically determined ciphers or philosophical allegories.

2

Sons of Heracles

Spartans knew who they were and where they came from. They were Dorians. Their ancestors had conquered Laconia as part of a massive expedition led by the descendants of Heracles himself several decades after the Trojan War. They had Tyrtaeus' word for it:

> For the son of Cronus himself, husband of beautifully crowned Hera,
> Zeus, granted to the Heraclidae this city,
> with whom, leaving windy Erineus,
> we arrived at the broad island of Pelops.
>
> (F. 3 West,[2] lines 12–15)

These lines are the earliest surviving expression of a cycle of stories Spartans and other inhabitants of the Peloponnese told to explain who they were, why they spoke they way they did, why they worshipped certain deities, and why they had certain public institutions in common. They were all descended from the men of Doris by the river Erineus in central Greece who had helped the Heraclids attain their rightful inheritance and been rewarded with mastery of the Peloponnese. The story of the Dorian invasion, or more accurately, the Return of the Descendants of Heracles (the Heraclids), shaped the Spartan sense of identity more than that of any other population group in the Peloponnese.

According to Diodorus Siculus (4.57–8), after Heracles' death and apotheosis on Mount Oeta his sons went into exile in Trachis in central Greece because of the enmity of Heracles' old nemesis, King Eurystheus. When Hyllus, Heracles' eldest son by Deianeira, and some of the others grew up, they had to leave Trachis, again under pressure from Eurystheus, now king of Mycenae and nursing an unremitting grudge against Heracles' progeny. Since no other city was willing to risk Eurystheus' wrath, the Heraclids and their friends ended up in Attica, where they were allowed to settle at the town of Trikorythos in the northeast above Marathon. Later, when all Heracles' sons had reached manhood, Eurystheus led an army into Attica against them but was killed by Hyllus as he attempted to flee. The Heraclids now seized the opportunity for a full-scale invasion of the Peloponnese. They were met by Atreus, the new king of Mycenae, and his Tegean allies at the Isthmus of Corinth. Hyllus proposed a duel between two champions to prevent excessive bloodshed, on condition that if he won, the Heraclids would take over the Peloponnese; if he lost, they would withdraw and stay away for at least fifty (according to Diodorus) or one hundred years (Hdt. 9.26.2). Echemus, king of the Tegeans, took up the challenge and killed Hyllus. Respecting the agreement, the Heraclids withdrew back to Trikorythos. After fifty years, so Diodorus tells us, the Heraclids would return. Unfortunately, his narrative of those events is lost.

Apollodorus' version of the tale (2.8.2–4) is somewhat different, indicating that Ephorus is probably not his ultimate source. He says the Heraclids succeeded in conquering all the Peloponnesian cities in a first invasion attempt before being driven out by a plague and taking up residence at Marathon. Learning from the oracle of Delphi that the Heraclids could return when the third crop ripened, Hyllus waited three years before making another attempt. After a lacuna, in which Hyllus' death in the battle at the Isthmus may have been related, comes a reference to Orestes as "king of the Peloponnesians" and to another, evidently later, battle in which Aristomachus, Hyllus' grandson, also met his death. Apollodorus next reports that the Heraclid Temenus and his brothers, the sons of Aristomachus, went to Delphi where they received the same apparently futile oracle as before. When they reproached the god for causing their forebears' failure, Apollo replied that they had misunderstood. The "crops" were not literal, but human generations and, apparently referring to another oracle, the "narrows of the sea" meant the sea to the right of the Isthmus (in other words, from the Delphic point of view, to the west). Suitably enlightened, Temenus amassed an army and readied ships in Locris, west of Delphi, at the place later named Naupactus. While waiting to cross the Gulf of Corinth, Aristodemus, father of Procles and Eurysthenes, was killed, perhaps by divine agency, and the whole expedition wrecked by storm and famine because of an act of impiety – murdering a seer – committed by a great-grandson of Heracles. Once they had patched things up with the relevant divine powers by banishing the murderer, waiting another decade, and hiring Oxylus, ancestor of the kings of Elis, as a replacement prophet, the Heraclids assembled another amphibious force and (finally!) achieved success. They conquered the Peloponnesians, slaying Tisamenus, son of Orestes, in the process. Among the casualties on the Heraclid side, Apollodorus singles out Pamphylus and Dymas, the sons of the Dorian king Aegimius, who evidently led a contingent of Dorian allies. Now masters of the peninsula, the surviving Heraclid leaders – Temenus, Procles and Eurysthenes, and Cresphontes – divided the conquered land up amongst themselves by lot. Argos went to Temenus, Laconia to Procles and Eurysthenes, and Messenia to Cresphontes. Thucydides dated the conquest of the Peloponnese by the Dorians and Heraclids to eighty years after the Trojan War (1.12.4).

The story is nothing if not convoluted. The Heraclids took two attempts to gain their objective, if Diodorus described only the successful invasion in the lost portion of his text. Apollodorus, on the other hand, likely described as many as four separate attempts to invade the Peloponnese. Also remarkable is the obscurity of the Dorians' role, considering this is supposed to be the charter myth explaining the Dorian predominance south of the Isthmus. Where are the Dorians, then?

They can be found in Pamphylus and Dymas, sons of Aegimius, himself the son of Dorus, and king of the Dorians, whose realm was near Mounts Ossa and Olympus, in the region called Hestiaiotis. Later expelled, they wandered, according to Herodotus, first around the Thessalian plain, finally making their way south to Dryopis, later named Doris and considered to be the Dorian metropolis (Hdt. 1.56.3, 8.31). They settled there in the region also called Erineus. Their connection with the Heraclids came about through Aegimius' adoption of Hyllus, alongside his natural sons Dymas and Pamphylus, as part token of his appreciation for Heracles' aid in vanquishing the oppressive Lapiths, the other part being the gift of one-third of the kingdom, which Aegimius was to keep in trust for Heracles' sons (*FGrH* 70 F15). In a speech he wrote in the *persona* of Archidamus III, the fourth-century political pundit Isocrates has the Heraclids living with the Dorians after the death of Eurystheus (*Archid.* 17), providing a convenient context for Hyllus' adoption. A problem exists, however: Hyllus' adoptive brothers Dymas and Pamphylus were killed in the final, successful assault that supposedly took place fifty years, a hundred years, or three generations later. This glaring chronological discrepancy reveals the adoption motif as a device to link two separate mythic traditions.

Argos has reasonably been proposed as the origin of the richer, more prominent Heraclid story. The genealogical connections were developed more fully there than elsewhere: while Spartan kings traced their ancestry to Heracles, his genealogy in the Argolid went back through his great-grandfather Perseus all the way to Zeus. Only the Argive royal house was named after a Heraclid, Temenus. Only Argos, according to an oracle mentioned by Isocrates, was theirs by right of inheritance (*Archid.* 18). Messene, in contrast, was spear-won land that Heracles entrusted to Nestor after he had conquered the city to avenge a cattle theft. Laconia was theirs by gift, because Tyndareus gave it to Heracles in return for being restored to the throne and because, as an offspring of Zeus, Heracles was related to Tyndareus' own sons, Castor and Pollux (Isoc. *Archid.* 18–19). Thus, compared to their clear links with Argos, the Heraclids' connections to the territories of Laconia and Messenia look contrived.

The Dorian narrative itself seems to be a composite of several different elements best exemplified in Herodotus' description of the Dorians' wanderings and the various places in central Greece that were proposed as their original home. The connections between the historical Dorians and their supposed ancestors are also rather tenuous, as in the case of the three Dorian tribes – Hylleis, Dymanes, and Pamphyloi – whose namesakes never made it to the Peloponnese, and one of whom, Hyllus, was not even a Dorian by birth. In addition, the tribal name "Pamphyloi" transparently means "People from all the tribes," a strong signal that it was an artificial creation. Within the narrative as we have it today, no Dorian character actually does anything apart from Aegimius, whose adoption of Hyllus provides a link between the two groups. The sole "act" of the only other named Dorian characters, Dymas and Pamphylus, is to die in the invasion. All in all, the story of the Dorian arrival in the Peloponnese, which was attached at some point to that of the Heraclids' return, is drastically underwritten. It is quite possible that the stories of the Heraclids and Dorians were developed independently in the Argolid and in Laconia respectively before being adopted and combined by peoples throughout the Peloponnese who adapted them to their own needs. The prominence of the Argolid in epic tradition probably explains why the Heraclid story overshadowed that of the Dorians.

This is what the Spartans evidently believed about their past. How much counts as history? The question leads to one of the most important ongoing debates among historians and archaeologists – what caused the end of Bronze Age civilization in Greece? What the Greeks called the Age of Heroes (Hes. *Op*. 155–65) corresponds roughly to the later second millennium B.C.E., the Late Bronze Age, also known today as the Mycenaean period, after the site of Mycenae north of Argos. Mycenaean civilization flourished from the sixteenth century to about 1200–1180 B.C.E., when palaces throughout mainland Greece and Crete were destroyed by fire within a relatively short period of time, perhaps a generation, and never permanently reoccupied. Though the Mycenaeans were not united in a single state, their culture was dominant for centuries over the islands of the Aegean, including even Crete, which they conquered in the later fifteenth century. Mycenaean artifacts found in the Middle East, Egypt and Anatolia, as well as non-Greek items found at Mycenaean centers indicate that they were part of extensive and active trading networks that spanned the eastern Mediterranean and beyond.

As regards Mycenaean Lacedaemon, it is very probable, on the evidence of the Theban Linear B tablets, that *Lakedaimôn* signified a region rather than a town. Whether that region corresponded more or less with the Lacedaemon of the Classical period is at present unknowable, but the topography of Laconia tells against it. Just as likely would be a collection of smaller competing "powers," each centered in the various farmable valleys and coastal plains dotting the Laconian landscape, the most significant being associated with the fertile lands of the Eurotas valley. Since decades of excavations under the modern city have uncovered only a few prehistoric sherds, most archaeologists accept that Bronze Age Sparta could have been located on or near a prominent ridge to the southeast that towers above the Eurotas and where a complex of buildings, called mansions by their excavators, has been found next to a later shrine dedicated to Helen and Menelaus. The dimensions of the structures and the quantity of the finds at the Menelaeum site are the most impressive of Laconia's Bronze Age sites, but are nothing like those found at palace sites elsewhere on the mainland. On the other hand, the complex may originally have been larger before parts eroded down the hillside, and jars imported from Crete as well as clay sealings for storage jars testify to its local importance. A less likely contender for a Mycenean administrative center is the site of Pellana, northwest of modern Sparta, where the excavator has claimed to have discovered the palace of Menelaus and Helen. Clay sealings found in excavations at Geronthrae (now Geraki) suggest that the acropolis of that community also had an administrative function in the Bronze Age, while the extensive remains at Agios Stephanos in the Helos plain on the Laconian Gulf show that community's prosperity and extensive trade links but are insufficient to identify it as a political center.

A few kilometers further south of the Menelaeum are the remains of a tholos tomb that contained two gold cups with repoussé representations of the capture and taming of wild bulls dated to the fifteenth century B.C.E., now known as the Vapheio cups from the name of the nearest village. Between the Vapheio tomb and the Menelaeum site, on the eastern height of a low but prominent hill that runs off to the west, is a sanctuary to an unknown Mycenaean female divinity where an important sanctuary of Apollo Amyclaeus and Hyacinthus was located in the Classical period. The proximity of the three sites – Amyclaeum, Vapheio tomb, and Menelaeum mansions – suggests that the Mycenaean heartland of Lacedaemon was the central part of the Eurotas valley, as it was in the Classical period and still is today. This identification has been strengthened by the recent discovery of several graves in the area of modern Sparta known as Psychiko, quite close to the Menelaeum, which contained gold grave offerings comparable in date to those found in the Grave Circles at Mycenae.

After a period of decline, the Menelaeum underwent a revival towards the end of the Mycenean period, in the later thirteenth century, and enjoyed trading contacts with the Argolid. The period of prosperity was short lived, however. In the twelfth century, after the Menelaeum houses were finally destroyed, squatters later took up residence among the remains, producing pots that were quite different from those previously used. Known as "Barbarian Ware" or, less tendentiously, "Handmade Burnished Ware," the pottery found in the post-destruction levels was not made on a wheel like its Mycenaean predecessors and had a much coarser and darker colored fabric than the light, fine-grained clay used in the pots from pre-destruction layers. The same style of pot, also found at other destroyed Mycenaean centers, was taken to indicate that a new ethnic group had made its way into the Mycenaean world. Questions naturally arose – was this evidence for the Dorian Invasion? Was it proof that the stories of the Return of the Heraclids contained a kernel of historical truth?

As new archaeological data accumulate and old results are reassessed, what happened at the end of the Bronze Age is becoming clearer, though many important questions remain unanswered. First, although major Mycenaean palaces were all apparently destroyed by fire, there is much debate over whether this was a result of hostile human activity in every case. The destructions may have taken place within a short space of time, archaeologically speaking, but could still have spanned thirty years or more and been due to a variety of reasons. A spate of natural disasters such as earthquakes, famines, and epidemics, external threats such as that posed by the mysterious "Sea Peoples," internal strife, or even revolution by an oppressed peasantry have all been proposed as factors in the fall of Mycenean civilization.

For some time, "Barbarian Ware" was widely thought to support the theory of a massive incursion of outsiders into the Greek world, probably from the north, who after putting the Bronze Age palaces to the torch settled in the ruins and made the sort of pottery they were familiar with. However, as "Barbarian Ware" has now been found at non-Mycenean sites, in Anatolia, Cyprus, and the Levant, and even in pre-destruction contexts, any association with putative barbarian hordes has been abandoned. All signs point to the "squatters" on the former palace sites being Mycenaeans themselves, who in some places attempted to restore their old way of life. Parts of Mycenae were reoccupied, while the circuit wall at Tiryns was repaired, the settlement reorganized and even expanded. Several other sites show evidence of a recovery in the following decades, but not to the levels attained before the destructions. Population movements, large but not necessarily massive, would have hampered the re-establishment of an ordered society, as many left their homes to seek safety or opportunity in the new centers. Warfare may have been endemic, since extensive fire damage has been found at important post-destruction sites and implements of war become more prominent as grave goods in this period. Eventually, this recovery proved too delicate and shallowly rooted to survive; as it faded, the last elements of Mycenaean culture disappeared. Cult sites that had survived the destruction of the palaces were abandoned, including the Amyclaeum. Cremation gradually replaced burial as the norm in most areas of the Greek world, with single burials predominating. Elaborate painted pottery ceased to be produced and metal fasteners (*fibulae*) began to be used on clothing. Most importantly, large swaths of Greece, particularly Laconia, underwent drastic depopulation.

These cultural and demographic changes are at the heart of the Dorian problem. Does the appearance of these and other new cultural traits indicate the arrival of a new ethnic group or groups in the regions the Dorians inhabited during the Archaic and Classical periods? In other words, did new groups bring new styles of artifacts and customs with them, effectively replacing or forcing out the Bronze Age inhabitants, or did the population of Greece adopt a different style of life?

On the one hand, pottery evidence for a "barbarian" presence after the destruction of the palaces at the beginning of this period has been shown to be illusory. Also, pottery shape and, at several sites, design show a continuous development from the late Bronze to the Early Iron Age. Knowledge of how to produce surprisingly complex equipment such as chariots also seems to have survived into the Early Iron Age, perhaps along with the practice of chariot racing. The adoption of new skills, techniques, images, and consequently ways of envisioning the world seem to have occurred at different times in different places. The experience of people may have differed profoundly from one place to another as the old world finally faded into obscurity. For instance, the sanctuary site of Kalapodi in Phocis shows a continuous sequence of usage levels from the late Bronze Age until the Roman period, striking evidence that no abandonment occurred, whereas the Amyclaeum in Laconia was deserted for over a century.

On the other hand, breaks in the depositional record like those at the Amyclaeum cannot be ignored, though their interpretation can

2.1 Remains of the Amyclaeum

be ambiguous. The Amyclaeum itself is an important case in point. Pottery found by a retaining wall of this sanctuary seems to show a break in its sequence between the very end of the Bronze Age in the twelfth century B.C.E. and the beginning of Early Iron Age Laconian pottery, which is usually dated no earlier than 950. Because the Amyclaeum was not a settlement, however, it has no clearly defined levels of occupation debris to provide a framework for precise dating. The crucial pottery fragments were found in a single layer of clay, one meter deep, with Geometric pottery at the top, Mycenaean ware at the bottom, and Protogeometric (Early Iron Age) sherds in between, along with a very few fragments of Mycenaean artifacts and later bronzes. The association of Mycenaean and Protogeometric fragments is intriguing, but in the absence of dependable stratigraphy we cannot assume that they are the remains of dedications on display at the same time. Based on the stylistic differences, a gap of over a century has been posited between the two types of pottery.

But even this is not clear cut. The painted decoration on the two sets of sherds is quite different: the Mycenaean fragments are painted in characteristically fluid lines on mostly unglazed surfaces, whereas the Iron Age sherds have cross-hatched full- and half-diamond designs on surfaces glazed mostly black, often with incised horizontal grooves and an unmistakable metallic sheen. Then again, the shapes of some vessels may derive from Mycenaean prototypes, implying continuity in pottery production. Unfortunately, there are too few examples of Early Iron Age pottery from other Laconian sites to bridge the gap, and so the evidence remains double-edged: either the gap signifies replacement of the original population by a new group with new ways of producing pottery, or the signs of continuity indicate that the inhabitants remained essentially the same.

Apart from the equivocal archaeological record, another sort of evidence has been brought to bear – the Greek language itself. Through historical linguistics, it is possible to trace how languages changed over time, to reconstruct their prehistory, and to determine how certain ones were originally connected into "families" by uncovering layers of linguistic development and examining remnants of earlier ways of speaking embedded in later language. Linguists studying the relationship between the language of the Linear B tablets and later Greek dialects have determined that the Mycenaeans spoke a form of the language that most resembled the "East Greek" dialects spoken in the historical period. More precisely, it has recently been argued that the dialects of

Arcadia and Cyprus (Arcado-Cyprian) – which though geographically distant were closely related linguistically – were the original forms of Greek spoken in the Mycenaean states of central and southern Greece. Arcado-Cyprian was later replaced by the Doric dialect in most of the Peloponnese except for Arcadia, while Boeotian replaced it in central Greece apart from Attica. Since Doric, Boeotian, and northwest Greek have demonstrably more in common with one another than with the other Greek dialects, which display more complex and closer relations with Arcado-Cyprian, Doric appears to be an instrusive element into the Greek "dialect continuum." The association with the northwest of Greece has encouraged some scholars to see the Dorians as coming originally from Epirus. But, as we have seen, the traditions about the Dorians, scanty as they are, never mention Epirus, but locate the Dorian homeland in a region of indisputably Mycenaean culture. Although the linguistic evidence does indicate the arrival of speakers of a new form of Greek who may have displaced Arcado-Cyprian speakers, this influx is, therefore, not part of the mythic tradition as it survives today.

The debate over the historicity of the Dorian invasion and its relationship with stories of the return of the Heraclids seems at a stalemate. Strong but not conclusive arguments can be marshaled on both sides. At present, all that can be stated with any degree of confidence is that if the ancestors of the Spartans did migrate into the Peloponnese around the end of the Bronze Age, they did not identify themselves as Dorians until well after their arrival, when they constructed a history to associate themselves with one of the most prominent figures in Greek mythology. As the passage from Tyrtaeus' *Eunomia* quoted at the beginning of the chapter shows, this all-important link was in place by the middle of the seventh century B.C.E. Tyrtaeus located the Dorian homeland in the region of the Erineus and referred to the Dorians coming to the Peloponnese with the Heraclids, to whom Zeus granted (*dedôke*) the city of Sparta. Tyrtaeus implied that the Dorian occupation of Sparta was due to the favor shown by Zeus to the Heraclids, from whom the two royal Spartan houses, the Agiads and Eurypontids, claimed descent (Plut. *Lys.* 24.3). Divine descent must have constituted a major element in the kings' claims to legitimacy. Moreover, if the poem was composed during the period of unrest that gave rise to the Great Rhetra, as most think, Tyrtaeus' deployment of this information shows that the function of the Heraclid myth at Sparta, as with all such "origin stories," was not only to construct a viable past but to reinforce contemporary social and political relationships. Tyrtaeus is also the earliest source to mention the three Dorian tribes, Hylleis, Pamphyleis, and Dymanes (F19 West²), which implies that the story of Hyllus' adoption was circulating in his time.

As the oral tradition cannot be pressed any further on this point, it is time to turn to archaeology again. Among the districts that comprised the ancient city of Sparta, Limnae has proved archaeologically rich. The area east of the acropolis down to the banks of the Eurotas where this obe was located has yielded the greatest concentrations of Protogeometric and Archaic pottery in Sparta. In addition to ordinary and not-so-ordinary burials (one seems to have been the object of cult), a possible heroon and several shrines have been found, including the important sanctuary of Artemis Orthia. All testify to the great antiquity of settlement in the area, confirmed by the discovery in Limnae of burials from the tenth century B.C.E. under rich layers of Protogeometric pottery. They are simple. Grave goods, when any exist, are scarce, mostly small objects of bronze or iron. The graves' value as evidence comes not from the presence or absence of artifacts but from their being dug into virgin soil, which strongly suggests the settlement was newly founded. Unfortunately, in the present state of the evidence we cannot as yet determine without doubt whether the people buried here belonged to a new group arriving in Laconia from outside or were descendants of the people buried in the early Mycenaean graves at Psychiko. Other slightly later burials in large clay vessels (*pithoi*) found in various spots spread all over the ancient city have, however, been identified as typical of burials in Messenia and throughout southwestern Greece and considered corroborating evidence for the Dorian invasion.

The settlement at Sparta in the Early Iron Age was evidently one of few in all Laconia. Survey results suggest that the Laconian population was concentrated in a small number of highly nucleated settlements situated some distance from one another, indicating a large decrease in population after the Bronze Age. This is nothing unusual. The same settlement pattern can be found all over Greece at this time. But when settlements in the rest of Greece began to expand after the middle of the eighth century as population began to increase significantly, Laconian villages remained static. In fact, the total lack of evidence for any expansion within Laconia until the early sixth century seems to indicate that people lived almost exclusively in the Eurotas valley during this long period, probably only at Sparta and Amyclae. If this interpretation is correct, it has implications for our understanding of how Sparta came to dominate the region politically and culturally.

Pausanias provides the only account of this process, casting it as an expansion of Dorian military power over the native Achaeans (3.2.5–7). Thus, Agis' son Echestratus led the first campaign to assert Spartan control over the Cynuria region on the Argive marches, while the centuries-long feud with Argos began under Prytanis, son of Eurypon. On the other hand, the Eurypontids were active almost exclusively against the Argives and Tegea, the leading city in Arcadia (3.7.1–6). Later, the Spartans under kings Archelaus and Charillus first conquered the town of Aigys in northern Laconia before turning south under Archelaus' son Teleclus to crush Amyclae, which had long resisted its larger neighbor.

In Classical times, the Hyacinthia, a major Spartan festival, was held at the Amyclaeum sanctuary in honor of the hero Hyacinthus, Apollo's doomed lover according to later tradition; Pausanias tells us his grave was located there (3.19.3). Words with the suffix -nth- are considered remnants of a pre-Greek linguistic substratum dating back as far as the early Bronze Age which has recently and convincingly been identified as coming from Anatolia. The worship of Hyacinthus at Amyclae has therefore been thought to have been a survival of an original Bronze Age cult that in turn allowed the people of early Amyclae to be identified as pre-Dorian. This thesis can be attacked on two fronts. First, the festival of the Hyacinthia and the month of the same name are both found widely and almost exclusively in Dorian cities. Apollo Hyacinthius was in fact a typically Dorian god. Second, the archaeological evidence for the existence of a Bronze Age cult is more consistent with a female than a male deity. Attempts have been made, unsuccessfully, to explain the "Dorians'" adoption of a divinity with a pre-Greek name before their invasion of the Peloponnese. In the absence of any widely accepted location for post-Mycenaean Amyclae, let alone any material evidence for it from the Early Iron Age, we can only draw conclusions based on the pottery found at the Amyclaeum, which, as noted above, is typical of Early Iron Age pottery found at other sites in Laconia. In other words, if the Amyclaeans were Mycenaean hold-outs, they were completely at home with "Dorian" material culture. After Amyclae fell by force or was peacefully taken over by the Spartans sometime in the eighth century, most scholars hold that it was incorporated into the Spartan state as the fifth constituent community (ôba).

In addition to his conquest of Amyclae, Teleclus had successes against the Achaean cities of Pharis and Geronthrae, but was murdered by sacrilegious Messenians at a sanctuary of Artemis on the border between the two regions, thus providing the *casus belli* for the first Messenian War. The remaining hold-out, Helos on the Laconian gulf coast, was destroyed in the reign of Teleclus' son Alcamenes. The inhabitants of the conquered towns, it is implied, then become the *perioikoi* ("dwellers around"), free citizens of their cities but unequal to the Spartans.

The sparse archaeological record in Laconia cannot reasonably be expected to furnish evidence directly related to Pausanias' narrative. For example, finds from Geronthrae, the single perioecic urban site being excavated, indicate that it was reoccupied in the Early Iron Age after a period of abandonment, but no traces of any structures have yet come to light, let alone any signs of violent destruction. Nevertheless, the pottery that has been found, mostly in sanctuary sites throughout Laconia, is of a similar style and manufacture, implying that its users shared a single culture. Pausanias' Dorian–Achaean opposition is thus shown to be false (Paus. 3.2.6) or at least invisible in the archaeological record. Indeed, the fourth-century historian Ephorus, our earliest source for the conquest of Helos (*FGrH* 70 F117), considered that city to be Dorian at the time of its destruction, since the original Achaean inhabitants had left under a truce some time before.

It is tempting to link this Achaean abandonment of Laconia with the massive depopulation of the Early Iron Age, but such an association cannot be substantiated at present. In any case, parallels can be found within the narrative framework of Sparta's legendary history, when on several occasions groups which for various reasons cannot or will not be accommodated within the larger Spartan community either leave of their own free will or are expelled. First the so-called Minyans, whose story will be told below, left to colonize Triphylia in the western Peloponnese and the island of Thera. Then the Lemnian and Imbrian settlers of Amyclae were shipped off after a failed revolt to colonize Melos and Gortyn on Crete (*FGrH* 26 F1.xxxvi). Finally, the Partheniai founded Taras in south Italy after another rebellion failed. The legends of these withdrawals reinforced an exclusionist ideology consonant with the Spartiate concept of uniformity, which saw its most dramatic manifestation in the policy of periodically expelling foreigners (*xenêlasia*). However accomplished, the consolidation of Spartan power in Laconia was probably a more protracted and significantly less dramatic process than the later Spartans would have liked to believe.

As seems to have happened in the sixth century, some (perhaps a very few) of the perioecic towns may have started out as foundations sponsored by the Spartan state, in a form of internal colonization. Others could have been autonomous new foundations or Bronze Age survivals. Their common denominator was probably land, or rather, insufficient land on which to draw to support the sort of vigorously independent, aggressive city-state that was the Greek norm. The coastal plains and upland valleys in which the perioecic cities were located were perhaps large and fertile enough to produce sufficient food for their inhabitants to survive, but not to enable the development of large regional centers. Only the Eurotas valley possessed such resources. Thus, Sparta was naturally suited to become the dominant regional power.

Spartan aloofness from the so-called colonization movement of the later Iron Age and Archaic periods is well known. But our sources do credit the city with two expeditions sent out to found independent cities outside the Greek mainland. The earlier story, involving the mysterious Minyans, is set quite soon after the Heraclid invasion, in the first generation or so following the foundation of Sparta (Hdt. 4.145–8). Land was still available to be distributed to the newcomers and the Heraclid Aristodemus' sons, Eurysthenes and Procles, were still children. The Minyans, grandsons of the Argonauts and the women of Lemnos, arrived in Laconia as refugees from their home island. Making their way to Taygetus they built fires that caught the attention of the Spartans in the plain, who sent a herald to inquire who they were and what their intentions were. The Minyans convinced the Spartans of their ancestral claim to Laconia through the Argonauts Castor and Pollux, sons of Tyndareus. The Spartans consequently provided land and distributed the Minyans into their tribes, presumably Dymanes, Pamphyloi, and Hylleis. The Minyans then married Spartan women after finding other husbands for their original Lemnian wives. But the ungrateful Minyans began to act arrogantly, making unseemly demands to a share in the kingship. The Spartans came up with an effective if drastic solution – kill them all. After arresting the Minyans and putting them into a stockade, the Spartans waited to execute their prisoners at night according to custom. The Minyans' new wives, from prominent Spartiate families, entered the stockade, however, and exchanged clothing with their menfolk. Escaping from their captivity in this way, the Minyans again camped on the slopes of Taygetus. Meanwhile, Theras from Thebes, maternal uncle of Eurysthenes and Procles, who had been acting as regent during the boys' minority, had been unable to bear being a subject after tasting royal power and so decided to leave Laconia to dwell with his kin, the descendants of Membliarus the Phoenician. Theras now proposed that the Spartans let him take the Minyans with him to colonize the island subsequently known as Thera. The Spartans agreed and Theras set out with three large ships filled with his colonists, among whom were only a few Minyans; the majority preferred to move to Triphylia, on the border between Elis and Messenia, where they founded several cities.

The detail that Eurysthenes and Procles needed a regent during the early years of their reign guarantees an authentic Spartan origin for the narrative, since Spartans alone believed that Aristodemus survived the invasion of the Peloponnese and fathered his sons in Sparta (Hdt. 6.52.1–2). Also specifically Spartan is its setting around the time of the effective establishment of the dual kingship, when Aristodemus' two sons reached maturity and Theras stepped down as regent. Both the Minyans and Theras desired a share in the new form of kingship, but both were excluded. Despite this parallel, the two stories are independent of each other, overlapping only when Theras offers to take the discontented Minyans with him. The artificiality of this link is clear when Herodotus recounts that Theras took only a few with him, showing that the Minyan story probably started out as the charter myth for the Triphylian cities. Details such as the Minyans' two stints camping on Taygetus, lighting a fire both times as Herodotus carefully informs us, and their transvestite escape from the stockade in Sparta would not be out of place in a aetiological myth for a religious festival, while the unions of the Minyans' Lemnian wives with Spartan men may have figured in several old Heraclid family trees.

Outside Sparta, Theras' foundation of a colony among his Phoenician kinsmen was intended, we are told, to be a peaceful enterprise in which the colonists were (unusually) to coexist with the aboriginal population (Hdt. 1.148.1). Although the legend places the foundation of Thera very early in Spartan history, the bulk of the earliest ceramic material excavated on the island comes from the first part of the eighth century, and is not Laconian in origin, but local with some imports from other Aegean islands. The case for the historicity of a Laconian/Cadmean/Minyan foundation of the Dorian state of Thera may appear somewhat tenuous, but to later Spartans and Therans it represented a real tie and probably influenced policy decisions. Ties of kinship also linked Sparta with the city of Cyrene in Libya, which claimed to have been founded by colonists from Thera under the leadership of one Battus (Hdt. 1.150–8). The lengthy story of its foundation and the fourth-century inscription that purports to contain a faithful copy of the original colonists' oath need not detain us (*ML* 5). The significant amount of Laconian pottery found there, including some of the most famous of Laconian-style pieces, however, attests again to a perceived reality whose historicity is beyond doubt.

The story of the Minyans foreshadows that of another discontented group, this time associated with the founding of Sparta's other famous colony, Taras. This latter group, supposedly sent out from Sparta in the wake of turmoil after the end of the First Messenian War, is connected to the founding of Taras (Tarentum, now Taranto) in southern Italy, dated by Eusebius to 706 B.C.E. The accounts that have come down to us attribute the city's foundation to a group of Spartans called the Partheniai ("Maidens' Sons") who were expelled from Laconia after they were discovered to be plotting against the citizens. Two main versions survive, both preserved by Strabo, who includes them in his description of Taras. According to Antiochus of Syracuse (*c.* 430–410), the Partheniai were the sons of early Spartan "draft-dodgers" who had not taken part in the war against Messenia and were consequently degraded to helot status. Led by a man called Phalanthus ("Baldy") who was sent as a spy by "those of the *damos*," the Partheniai planned an attack at the Hyacinthia, which an informant (perhaps Phalanthus himself) revealed to the authorities. With his followers in custody, Phalanthus was sent off to Delphi, where the god revealed to him that Satyrion and the rich land of Taras had been granted them to dwell in and oppress the local aboriginal population. The Partheniai left Sparta and, after helping Achaeans in their wars, founded the city (*FGrH* 555 F13). Ephorus on the other hand identifies the Partheniai as the offspring of irregular unions between unmarried Spartan girls and young men who had been sent back from the front at the request of Spartan women in order to prevent a shortage in warriors during the war, since the Spartans had nine years before sworn an oath not to return until the total defeat of Messenia. At the war's end the Partheniai did not enjoy equal rights because they were born out of wedlock. The Partheniai thus planned an attack in the agora in company with helots, some of whom betrayed the plot. Their conspiracy discovered, the Partheniai were persuaded by their fathers to set out to found a city elsewhere. But if they were not satisfied with the place they received, they could all return and be assigned one-fifth of Messenia. The Partheniai left, met some Achaeans fighting the locals, and founded the city of Taras (*FGrH* 70 F216).

Even at first glance, it is obvious that neither of these accounts can be taken at face value. Both are riddled with inconsistencies and irregularities. The conspiracy fizzles out suspiciously easily in both versions. The references to helots in a late eighth-century context are probably anachronisms, as we shall see. The women who complain in Ephorus' version that they have no men conveniently forget that the youngest and oldest men were left behind to guard the city. Further- more, the idea that Spartan warriors would carry out a multi-year military campaign without ever returning to the city is ludicrous. Phalanthus, who was both the leader and betrayer of his movement according to Antiochus, still led the Partheniai on their colonial venture. Can any sense be made of this?

If the stories are situated in their proper historical contexts it becomes easier to understand why they took the shape they did. At the time Antiochus was writing, Tarentines lived under a moderate democracy which had come to power after a terrible defeat in 473 by an alliance of aboriginal peoples which broke the power of the aristocrats ruling the city. Among the leading clans of the city had been the Phalanthidae, whose claim to ascendency was clearly rooted in their descent (fictive or not) from the city's legendary founder, depicted on Taras' earliest coins. Some have also seen a negative attitude in Antiochus' account towards the Partheniai in general, who are described as slaves with cowards for fathers, and towards Phalanthus in particular, who may have betrayed his own people. Perhaps, therefore, Antiochus or his source had reason to dislike the Tarentines. On the other hand, Ephorus' Partheniai are not degraded to the status of helots because of their fathers' misdeeds, but receive unequal treatment because social rules were inconsistently applied to their situation. Interestingly, Phalanthus does not appear at all, perhaps reflecting a diminution in his status as a founder in favor of the eponymous hero Taras, who, unlike Phalanthus, was not connected with any particular group in the city. Relations between Taras and Sparta were moreover quite close in the fourth century, when the Italian city made use of Spartan military expertise in its quarrels with its neighbors, thus providing a context for a retelling of the foundation legend which showed both sides in a good light.

We can say that at least as early as the late sixth century, when the coins bearing Phalanthus' image appear, the Tarentines themselves believed their city had been founded by a group led by this man. At least from the early fifth century onwards, they believed Phalanthus had led a group from Sparta, since they felt themselves bound in friendship at that time with Cnidus, reputedly another Spartan colony. Definite traces of their Laconian origin existed on the ground at Taras. They worshipped at sanctuaries of Apollo Carneus, Apollo Hyacinthius, and the Dioscuri. A tomb of Hyacinthus even stood outside the city. Their eponymous magistrate was an ephor. Some toponyms were also shared, most strikingly Eurotas, the alternate name for the local river Galaesus (Polyb. 8.33.8–9). Some of these correspondences may be late, self-conscious introductions, however. Such would be the case with the name Eurotas, as well as the ephorate, since earlier texts name a king (*basileus*) as head of government.

Although the site had served as an emporium for Greek traders since the Mycenaean period, archaeological evidence is very scanty for a Laconian presence at the traditional date of the city's foundation, the decades following the first Messenian War. Excavations in the church of S. Domenico in modern Taranto have revealed only a very few Laconian Geometric sherds mixed in with Protocorinthian pottery and local Geometric ware. From another site, Scoglio del Tonno, come two other contemporary sherds, also associated with Protocorinthian. The earliest signs of Greek occupation in the city are three tombs dated to between the late eighth and early seventh centuries on the basis of the Corinthian pottery left there as grave offerings. The appearance of Corinthian pottery is not surprising, given its market dominance at the time. Not until the last decades of the seventh century do we find significant amounts of Laconian pottery, while from then on Tarentines imported large quantities. In fact, more sixth-century Laconian pottery has been found at Taranto that at any other site in South Italy. But does this mean, as has been proposed, that Spartan settlers arrived at the end of the seventh, not the eighth, century? Probably not, because Laconian pottery seems not to have been exported commercially until the last quarter of the seventh century, when it is found in quantity at sites as diverse as Samos, Taranto, and Taucheira in North Africa. The few Laconian sherds found which date to the later eighth century might consequently constitute strong evidence for the arrival of settlers bringing their own household effects with them, since pottery specialists assert that Laconian pottery found outside Laconia before large-scale exports began indicates the presence of travellers from Sparta or Laconia.

The site of Taras thus most likely received some Laconian settlers around the traditional date of 706 B.C.E. They may not have been alone, since pottery imported from other areas of the Peloponnese has also been found. Under what circumstances the settlers left Laconia we cannot discover, given subsequent overlays and distortions, since the later foundation legends justified the city's contemporary relationship with the city Tarentines regarded as their mother city but did not constitute an accurate historical record of events leading to the city's establishment. Perhaps the large quantities of imported Laconian pottery at the end of the seventh century indicate Tarentines' growing awareness and appreciation of their ties to Sparta. If this result seems disappointing, we should remember the legends that grew in a largely literate society over the past several centuries surrounding the American "pilgrim fathers" sometimes have only a tenuous connection to historical reality.

The archaeological record for the later eighth century, then, shows Sparta engaging hesitantly with the colonial project which other cities energetically pursued. In Laconia, Sparta had already long been dominant among the few highly nucleated settlements, if the evidence for cultural homogeneity can bear such an interpretation. During the following century, Spartans at last began to make their mark on the land by developing the extra-urban sanctuaries that constitute our earliest physical evidence for the Spartan state. Politically, Sparta was not immune from the currents that were buffeting other states, as the sources and legitimacy of power became controversial topics in the wake of an expansionist war into neighboring Messenia. The seventh century marked another watershed, for it is during this time that we catch our first glimpses of a Spartan history that is not wholly legendary.

3

Conquest, Crisis, and Consolidation

After worshipping at the sanctuaries of Artemis Orthia in Limnae and Athena Chalcioecus on the acropolis for over a hundred years, the Spartans expanded their cultic horizons towards the end of the eighth century B.C.E. In an Eleusinion near the modern village of Kalyvia Sochas right below Taygetus, Demeter and Kore received their first dedications; at Tsakona northeast of Sparta, the initiation-related worship of Zeus Messapeus began; and on the eastern side of the valley, the prominent bluff towering over the Eurotas where the Bronze Age mansions had once stood now accommodated an altar dedicated to Menelaus and Helen. In the course of the seventh century all these sanctuaries, both in and outside Sparta, were adorned with temples: the most impressive was the Menelaeum site, where the latest findings reveal that the original temple (built 650–625 B.C.E.) possessed a monumental terrace and ramp.

The Menelaeum and the other extra-urban sanctuaries were almost certainly projects initiated by Spartans collectively, as all were established in areas devoid of settlement. Their function was probably to mark the extent of the territory controlled directly by Spartans, as opposed to land under the jurisdiction of the perioeci. By the end of the eighth century, we may reasonably assume, Sparta's dominance was acknowledged by the other Laconian communities. Sparta itself was an unwalled cluster of villages, as it would remain until the Hellenistic period. Despite this, Spartans were also embarking on a remarkably ambitious military project that would test them to the limit and transform their community into a fully fledged and powerful state.

Around the end of the eighth century, the Spartans began to conquer the vast territory of Messenia. Lying west of Laconia on the other side of the Taygetus mountain range and consisting of the broad Pamisus

3.1   The temple and terrace of the Menelaeum

river valley on the east with hilly yet fertile lands stretching westwards to the sea, Messenia was a prize acquisition. Its agricultural wealth, worked by an enslaved population for their absentee overlords, provided Sparta at the fifth-century apogee of its power and influence with the means to maintain the nearest thing to a standing army in Greece by freeing all its adult male citizens from the need for manual labor. Messenians would remain under Spartan rule for centuries, until the Theban general Epaminondas liberated them in 369 B.C.E., two years after the disaster at Leuctra.

The conquest of Messenia must have been a formidable challenge for the Spartans, scattered as they were among their villages and apparently barely exploiting what the Eurotas valley had to offer, let alone controlling the Mount Parnon hinterland further east. It certainly seems to have taken a long time. Our only indicator for the chronology of the struggle is the poet Tyrtaeus, whose activity at Sparta is usually dated to the later seventh century B.C.E. If this chronology is accurate, references in surviving fragments of his works to the capture of Messenia ("a good thing to plough, a good thing to sow," F5 West[2]) become of great interest. Specifically, Tyrtaeus refers to a nineteen-year war for Messenia waged under king Theopompus by "the spearmen fathers of our fathers" that ended only when the inhabitants, who had already fled their farms, abandoned a stronghold on Mount Ithome. Tyrtaeus may be using the expression "fathers of our fathers" conventionally to express the distant past, but students of Spartan history usually take him literally and date the capture of Sparta's neighbor two generations before Tyrtaeus was composing. Working with the conventional ancient span of about thirty years per generation, scholars generally place the war Tyrtaeus mentions here to the end of the eighth or the beginning of the seventh century B.C.E.

Some corroboration of this date has been seen in Pausanias' story (4.8.3, 14.3) of the founding of the perioecic city of Asine near the site of modern Korone in southern Messenia. Exiled from the original Asine on the Argolid one generation before the war when the Argives destroyed their city, the Asinaeans were compelled to fight alongside the Spartans against the Messenians. Once the Spartans won, they were settled on the Messenian Gulf in a city named after their lost home. Since excavations at Argolic Asine have shown that the city was abandoned just before 700 B.C.E., Pausanias' narrative seems in this instance to be confirmed. But reexamination of the archaeological evidence for the abandonment of Asine and its relations with Argos, as well as that of Argos with Sparta, has thrown the likelihood of a conflict involving the three cities in the eighth century into considerable uncertainty. It is also debatable whether Asine suffered deliberate abandonment and destruction or gradually became deserted as its population shifted to another site. If so, one piece of archaeological evidence for the chronology of the Messenian wars must be removed.

All is not lost, however, for excavations at Messene have revealed indications of a late Iron Age or early Archaic period settlement under the impressive remains of the Hellenistic city. Proto-Geometric and Geometric pottery has been found in some quantities at several places in the city center, and there is even some evidence for human activity in the area during the late Bronze Age. The excavator's dating of the pottery to between the eighth and seventh centuries B.C.E. fits remarkably well into the narratives of the wars as we are beginning to understand them, while the lack of any pottery from the intervening centuries before the re-foundation of Messene shows, at the very least, that the site was deserted during that period.

After the first Spartan victory, another war with the Messenians followed, according to late sources, during which Tyrtaeus wrote verses to embolden Sparta's warrior youth. Victorious again, the Spartans divided up Messenia into allotments for themselves and reduced the Messenian population to the status of agricultural slaves called helots. Doubts have been expressed about the historicity of a second war, since Herodotus and Thucydides, our earliest authorities, consistently refer to a single war for Messenia, and Tyrtaeus did not name the current foe in any of the extant fragments. These doubts were somewhat allayed in 1990 when a new papyrus fragment was published in which Tyrtaeus described, in the present tense, a military engagement with the Messenians and their allies, the Argives and (probably) the Arcadians (*P Oxy.* 3316, lines 11–22). The Spartans seem to have needed at least two wars to subjugate Messenia completely; the second probably took place in the later seventh century B.C.E. Archaeological evidence for a military conquest is naturally altogether nonexistent; in its place, the finds from sanctuaries of the Late Iron Age and Archaic periods show that Messenian material culture was gradually becoming more and more Laconian in style. In other words, Messenia was being laconized, likely as a result of being absorbed politically into the Lacedaemonian state.

What led the Spartans to embark on this long struggle with their western neighbors? "Land" has been the most popular answer. Messenia contains some of the most fertile land in the Peloponnese; this agricultural wealth was to constitute the basis of Sparta's way of life. By acquiring that real estate Sparta controlled two-fifths of the Peloponnese (Thuc. 1.10.2) or approximately 8,500 km², by far the largest territory of any *polis* in Greece. With such a large expanse of land at their disposal, it is unsurprising that Spartans participated so little in the great wave of colonization in the later Iron Age and Archaic periods, when many cities relieved the pressure of swelling populations by founding new communities overseas. The Spartans, it was thought, conquered adjacent territory directly instead of sending colonists overseas. But data from the Laconia Survey throw this explanation into doubt, for the surveyors found no traces of extensive occupation in their survey area before the sixth century, even in the Eurotas valley section. Unlike other parts of Greece, Laconia shows no spreading of settlement out from nucleated centers in the eighth or seventh centuries, which implies that population size remained static during this period. The population seems in fact to have increased significantly only after the pacification of Messenia was well underway, and Messenia's great fertility may actually have slowed the exploitation of Laconian land. Although overpopulation was not the driving force behind Sparta's expansion over Taygetus, desire for the Messenians' land may still have been a powerful motive to invade, since Messenia possessed a ready-made dependent labor force. Such an explanation, however, depends on assuming that what the Spartans did after their victory (divide the land up, turn the remaining Messenians into helots) was what they had intended to do when hostilities began. In the sixth century, Spartan warriors carried fetters and measuring rods with them in their unsuccessful invasion of Tegea (Hdt. 1.66.3). Their intention was clear; we cannot be so sure what their ancestors intended when Spartans first clashed with the Messenians.

The lengthy struggle for Messenia was remembered as a time of great disruption. As we have already seen, the rebellion of the Partheniai was set in this period, and Aristotle referred to Spartan demands for the redistribution of land during the Messenian war as an example of the unrest that could arise when too much wealth was concentrated in the hands of too few, particularly during times of conflict (Arist. *Pol.* 5.6.1–2 [1306b–1307a]). As evidence, he cited Tyrtaeus' *Eunomia*, whose name, "Good Government," recalls one of the Classical Spartans' best-known attributes – that they lived under good government and were obedient to the laws. Herodotus called the Spartans "worst governed (*kakonomôtatoi*) of almost all the Greeks" until they changed to "good government" (*eunomiê*), which he attributed to the influence of the legendary lawgiver Lycurgus (Hdt. 1.65). Pausanias added the detail that the crisis was provoked by a decision to keep large tracts of Laconian land uncultivated during the war to prevent the Messenians from profiting from cross-border raids. A famine resulted that almost led to civil strife, which Tyrtaeus averted (Paus. 4.18.2–3). Unfortunately, we have no idea of the source of Pausanias' information and consequently no way of determining its accuracy. In light of his and Aristotle's comments, however, we can safely assume that the *Eunomia* contained some reference to the main reason behind the political crisis – inequality in land ownership.

There was certainly wealth in Sparta during Tyrtaeus' lifetime, whether as a result of the conquest of Messenia or not is impossible to say. Laconian bronzes of increasingly high quality – figurines, mirrors, wine-mixing bowls, etc. – began to be produced then, and the Laconian school of ivory work – by its very nature an index of prosperity – was the most important in the Peloponnese from the earlier seventh century to the first quarter of the sixth. The beauty of Hegesichora, the chorus leader in Alcman's *Partheneion*, surpasses the allure of lavish purple clothing, of an entwined gold snake bracelet, and even of a fashionable headgear from Lydia (*PMGF* F1, lines 64–8). "Wealth makes the man" was a well-known Spartan saying in the later seventh century (Alcaeus F25 Campbell). But, unsurprisingly, Spartan riches were unevenly distributed, which probably resulted in the disorder Tyrtaeus composed his poem to address.

In the popular imagination, Tyrtaeus became a figure similar to the Athenian Solon. But, although they both used poetry to address political problems that arose from the concentration of land ownership, the parallels cease there. Solon received official powers to resolve the problem at Athens and, despite his natural tendencies, attempted to be even-handed in his treatment of the haves and have-nots. Tyrtaeus, as far as we know, held no state position when he composed the *Eunomia*, nor did he conceal his conservative opinions. The preserved fragments emphasize the positive role of the kings from the time of the Heraclid invasion (F2 West^2) to the first conquest of Messenia under king Theopompus (F5 West^2). The most discussed part of the poem concerns the major public institutions of early Archaic Sparta – the kingship, the council of elders, and the popular assembly (F4 West^2). Casting his call to order in the form of a Delphic oracle, Tyrtaeus outlined how Sparta should function in order to attain military supremacy:

> After listening to Phoebus, they brought homewards from Pytho
> the god's prophecies and words of command:
> that in council the god-honored kings rule,
> who care for the lovely city of Sparta,
> and the ancient-born elders; then the men of the people
> replying in exchange with (to?) straight *rhêtrai*
> both speak good things and do everything justly,
> and do not counsel crookedly (?) for the city;
> and that victory and power follows the mass of the people.
> For thus Phoebus made his revelation about these things to the city.

Tyrtaeus' hierarchy is clear. The kings prevail in matters of law because of the favor they received from the gods; subordinate to them are the elders; at the bottom are the "men of the people" (*dêmotas andras*). Tyrtaeus was concerned enough about the men of the people to spend three lines describing their correct behavior. First, in an ambiguous line, they are either to pass proper laws after listening to the elders and kings or to pass laws framed according to correct proposals put before them by the same bodies. Tyrtaeus uses the Spartan word *rhêtra* ("that which is spoken") here, which can mean either the result of the legislative process or a proposal from one body to another that will result in a legal decision. The men of the people are then exhorted to speak and act "justly" (*dikaia*) and (perhaps) not to reach decisions that would be detrimental to the city. Since this particular line is corrupt, scholars have proposed several different readings, from a prohibition against conspiring against the city to an explicit denial of the ability to debate issues put before them. Whatever the line's precise meaning, Tyrtaeus obviously felt that the assembly's proper role was to be obedient. The dividend for complying with the will of the kings and elders was to be military victory and power.

From antiquity onwards, Tyrtaeus' *Eunomia* has been seen as closely related to the earliest and most significant surviving Spartan legal document, the so-called Great Rhetra. Perhaps first drawn by the exiled Spartan king Pausanias for political purposes at the beginning the fourth century, the connection almost certainly existed by the time of the Aristotelian *Constitution of the Lacedaemonians*, preserved for us by Plutarch in his *Lycurgus*, who called the Rhetra itself an oracle. Scholars have regarded the similarity in wording between the two as proof that Tyrtaeus wrote his poem as a sort of commentary on the Rhetra in an effort to win its approval by the Spartan people. Doubts have recently been expressed that Tyrtaeus actually composed the *Eunomia* with the Rhetra in mind. Instead, it has been proposed that the *Eunomia* represents the last known example of an older method of civic reconciliation which used oracles, rituals, and songs, and the Rhetra a new procedure employing explicitly legal measures. Alternatively, Tyrtaeus' poem may have been the poetic equivalent of a political pamphlet articulating the views of the aristocracy against the claims of the *damos*, and the Rhetra the legal solution resulting from that debate. This would account both for the common terminology and the important differences between the two.

The Great Rhetra appears in Plutarch's *Lycurgus*, 6.1–2, where the biographer presents it as an oracle Lycurgus himself conveyed back from Delphi. Despite its contentious first appearance, in Pausanias' polemical pamphlet against the imperialist policy of Lysander, the victor of Aegospotami, almost all historians agree on the Rhetra's authenticity, but concord ceases there. Everything else about the document – its date, significance, grammar, syntax, unity, even the reading of the text itself

– has been subject to intense debate. In fact, it has been claimed, not unjustifiably, that more ink has been spilt over the Rhetra's few lines than over any other comparable text from antiquity. Plutarch presents the text as follows:

> Lycurgus attached so much importance to this institution [i.e. the Gerousia] that he brought back from Delphi an oracle about it, which they call a *rhêtra*. It goes like this:

> after setting up a sanctuary to Zeus Syllanius and Athena Syllania,
> having tribed the tribes and obed the obes,
> having established thirty men as a Gerousia along with *archagetai* (kings)
> to hold the Apellai from month to month (?) between Babyka and
>   Knakion,
> in this way to bring in and stand aside from [legislation?],
> †that for the Damos there be validity and power†

Plutarch then states that the kings Polydorus and Theopompus later on made an addition to the Rhetra, because the many (*hoi polloi*) were "twisting and contravening the intent of proposals by their additions and deletions." Despite Plutarch, however, virtually all historians regard this addition, known as the Rider, as an integral part of the original Rhetra, mainly on grounds of syntax and terminology. Thus, as the seventh and last line of the Rhetra, it gives the final say in legislation firmly to the Gerousia and kings, who jointly comprise a chamber of sober second thought:

> If the Damos should speak (or "choose") crookedly, that the elders and *archagetai* be standers aside.

In translating the Rhetra, I have tried to follow scholarly consensus, but without smoothing out the text's oddities of phraseology and structure. The sixth line, for instance, presents a particularly knotty textual problem: since the manuscript reading is mostly gibberish, historians have had to reconstruct it completely, resulting in several different possible understandings of this obviously vital line, ranging from the *damos* being assigned "validity and power" (*kurian . . . kai kratos*) to the *damos* having the right to make counter-proposals (*antagorian*) along with their "power" over the final say in legislation.

Textual problems are but a small part of the interpretative challenges the Rhetra presents for us today. Even by the second century C.E., much of its meaning was obscure, so Plutarch provided his readership with explanations of the difficult terms that have stood the test of time remarkably well. He wrote that "tribes" (*phulai*) and "obes" (*ôbai*) referred to the divisions of the civic body, the *archagetai* were the kings, that *apellazein* meant "to meet in assembly." He also noted that Aristotle said that Knakion was a river and Babyka a bridge (Plut. *Lyc.* 6.3–4). Plutarch blundered, however, in claiming that the Spartans called the prophecy (*manteia*) which Lycurgus brought back with him from Delphi a *rhêtra*. We know from other sources that *rhêtra*, which was etymologically related to the verb *erô* ("I shall speak"), denoted either a legislative act of the Spartan assembly or a proposal in the process of passage. Also, oracles were nearly always in verse, often riddling and allusive, while the *rhêtra* in its original form, however obscure it now is, made (we hope) perfect sense to its intended audience.

Before examining the Rhetra itself, we should carefully consider the exact nature of the text that has come down to us. Even in translation, certain features stand out – the lack of any expressed subject or main verb, as well as the use of participles in place of finite verbs. In Greek, the peculiarities are even more pronounced, but explainable. The appearance of participles in the accusative case and infinitives in the main clauses show that the text is in indirect discourse, which, together with the absence of any explicit subject, indicates it is an extract from a longer text. We may assume that the extant passages likely come from the section of a law or decree outlining the decisions of a certain body or official. Which official or body – a special committee, the assembled warriors of Sparta, or an official – passed the act unfortunately cannot be discovered. Also, given that the Rhetra was taken from a larger text, nothing guarantees that it is a unitary extract rather than a series of quotations taken from different places in the original. Plutarch used the Rhetra in its present form to highlight the Gerousia's importance. Whether the original described the powers and activities of the assembly and other bodies in greater detail cannot be determined, though most historians would probably deny that it did.

For clarity's sake, I present a line-by-line explanation of the Rhetra's content.

1 A *hieron* (shrine) to Zeus Syllanius and Athena Syllania must be founded (i.e. cults to these deities must be established). Since the Rhetra's provisions entailed a significant shift away from control of institutions by aristocratic families and individuals, new, more

polis-centered cults were needed to give the reforms legitimacy. The old cults, dominated by and identified with kinship groups headed by the elite, may have proved inadequate for the task. Zeus and Athena were often associated with legislative assemblies and councils elsewhere in Greece.

2   Plutarch's explanation still commands near-universal agreement. The population is to be divided up by their tribal affiliation and by their membership in an *ôba* (village/obe), one of the constituent communities of Sparta. Since Tyrtaeus mentions the three Dorian tribes Pamphyloi, Hylleis, and Dymanes (F19 West[2]), and no other tribal names appear until the Roman period, we are not dealing here with a wholesale reorganization of the community. Even so, citizens must now arrange themselves according to tribe and *ôba* before either the Gerousia can be constituted or assemblies meet. Membership in both a tribe and an *ôba* is thus the prerequisite for participation in the festival of the Apellai and in the Gerousia. If the *ôbai* in the Rhetra were territorial and should most likely be identified with Sparta's constituent communities, this procedure may perhaps signal that the city's inhabitants were beginning to distinguish themselves constitutionally from the other inhabitants of Laconia, who could not have claimed membership in a Spartan *ôba* even if they did identify themselves as Dorians.

3   This and the following line represent severe checks on the constitutional powers of the kings. Here, the Rhetra abolishes the royal power to determine the size of the advisory council. From now on, the council must consist of twenty-eight members in addition to the kings themselves, who are styled by their military titles, *archagetai*.

4   Festivals in honor of Apollo, at which the popular assembly meets, are to be fixed in time and place and are no longer at the whim of the kings – an important advance from Homeric practice. Most scholars would identify the Gerousia as the subject of the infinitive *apellazein* ("to hold assemblies"), which implies that the elders and kings preside jointly over meetings of the popular assembly at the Apellai. We should note that nowhere in the text of the Rhetra as it stands can the kings take action by themselves, another sign of their diminished power.

5   If the Gerousia is the subject of the infinitive in line 4, the same should be true of the infinitives in line 5. The power of introducing and rejecting legislation is thus vested solely in the kings and their council, as Plutarch indeed explained. This would confirm the

joint presidency of kings and elders over the Assembly during the Apellai.

6 The only ungarbled words in this line are *kai kratos*, "and power." In the immediate context, this should be the power of effective decision-making. According to the current restoration of the rest of the line, the Damos should hold this particular power, along with the quality of *kuria* ("validity"), in other words, be a body whose decisions have legal force. This provision may not be quite so "progressive" as it initially seems, for, as has been suggested, it would effectively limit the sphere of constitutionally valid action on the part of non-aristocrats solely to the Assembly, a body effectively under the thumb of the aristocratic council and kings.

7 The real power of the kings and elders emerges nakedly in the final line, the Rider of Plutarch. Should the Assembly officially express its legal opinion in a "crooked" way, its members will act as *apostatêres* ("standers aside"). The intent of this provision seems quite clear even if the precise connotations of the Greek elude us. Should the Assembly's decisions displease the kings and Gerousia, they could invalidate them, perhaps by actually walking out, which would cause the Assembly's dissolution.

The Rhetra has the flavor of a compromise, albeit a lopsided one. The Damos gained by having regular meetings of the Assembly and by having a council of elders of a fixed size. The elite gained by ensuring that its control of legal decision-making remained unbroken at the cost of some reduction in its freedom of action. Despite its apparent inequity, the Rhetra's solution was remarkably successful: Sparta avoided the political upheavals that transformed other Greek cities and the procedural framework the Rhetra introduced still functioned even in the Hellenistic period.

If the Rhetra and Tyrtaeus' *Eunomia* were products of a crisis over land during the Messenian Wars, it is noteworthy that nowhere in the preserved parts of either document is land ever mentioned. The reason may lie in King Pausanias' motives for including the Great Rhetra in his pamphlet; since he wanted to prove that the office of ephor was not part of Lycurgus' constitution, Pausanias had no reason to cite passages that he deemed irrelevant. Others in their turn would have preserved only those lines of the *Eunomia* that seemed directly related to the Rhetra, since Aristotle tells us that Tyrtaeus did mention the problem of land (Arist. *Pol.* 5.6.2 [1307a]). Unfortunately, the absence of any reference to land means that we do not know how, or indeed if, the issue was eventually settled. Some doubt that any substantial land distribution ever took place, though as we shall see the Classical Spartan system depended upon each Spartiate owning sufficient land to enable him to make his monthly mess contributions. Later authors credited the legendary Lycurgus with establishing an absolutely equal distribution of land among Spartan citizens. The state assigned lots (*klêroi*) to citizens at birth which they were forbidden to alienate while they lived and which at their deaths either reverted to the state or could be bequeathed intact only to their eldest sons (Polyb. 6.48.3; Plut. *Lyc.* 8; *Agis* 5.1–2). In reality, Spartans had a certain amount of freedom in acquiring and disposing of their landholdings, although by the later fourth century ([Arist.] F611.13 Rose), and perhaps even before, outright sale was considered shameful. Inheritance rules were also much looser than has been imagined: land passed from one generation to the next either intact or divided between heirs both male *and* female – a Spartan peculiarity.

After the conclusion of the Messenian wars, we next hear about Spartans in the middle of the sixth century B.C.E. Perhaps emboldened by their success against their western neighbors, they turned their sights north to Arcadia (Hdt. 1.66–8). A pretext for war was ready, for the Arcadians, along with the Argives, had probably gone to the aid of the Messenians in the last war (Tyrtaeus *P Oxy.* 3316, line 15 [restored]). Armed with an oracle which, despite denying them mastery over all Arcadia, granted them "to dance in foot-pounded Tegea / and to measure out the fine plain with a rope" (Hdt. 1.66.2), the Spartans marched out carrying fetters and measuring sticks. The Arcadian plain was to be surveyed and divided up into allotments for Spartiates, while the Tegeans would become helots like the Messenians before them. This was not to be. The Tegeans inflicted a major defeat, clapped their Spartan prisoners into irons and set them to work in chain gangs in their fields, thus fulfilling the oracle.

Faced with their continuing failure to subdue Tegea, the Spartans changed tactics in the reign of Kings Anaxandridas and Ariston in the mid-sixth century. The symbolic cornerstone of their new policy was the acquisition of the bones of the Achaean Orestes, who according to a lesser-known tradition had been a Lacedaemonian. Spirited out of Tegea where they had lain unrecognized under a blacksmith's yard, the bones were installed in the agora of Sparta (Paus. 3.11.10). From now on, Herodotus assures us, Spartans always prevailed in war, so that most of the Peloponnese was subjugated to them (Hdt. 1.67–8). Modern historians have seen in the "bones of Orestes" incident the beginning of a policy of aggressive diplomacy, by means of which Spartans promulgated a "natural" claim to be masters of the Peloponnese through their Heraclid aristocracy's ties to the pre-Dorian aristocracy. The worship of Agamemnon at Amyclae quite likely also began around this time.

The most durable result of the new Spartan policy was the Peloponnesian League, to use its modern name. In the heady positivist days of the early to mid-twentieth century, general scholarly agreement prevailed about the Peloponnesian League: it was a defensive/offensive alliance of states that met regularly in assembly, where a majority vote was binding except in cases of religious prohibitions, and required all new members to swear a binding oath to have the same friends and enemies as the Spartans and to follow wherever they might lead. But in the last decades, a rather different picture has emerged, that the League was more a collection of states loosely connected to Sparta, perhaps by individual oaths, which met in assembly only when a major offensive was being planned, and whose members had considerable freedom of action, to the point where powerful states such as Corinth and Thebes might chastise or pressure their hegemon (Thuc. 1.69.4, 3.67.1–7). Corinth first appears as an ally when the city aided Sparta in a naval expedition to reinstate an oligarchical government on Samos around 525 (Hdt. 3.46–48.1, 54–56.1). But in 506 Corinthians withdrew from an invasion of Attica, the first recorded joint action by Sparta and multiple allies, causing its collapse, apparently without suffering any negative repercussions (Hdt. 5.75). Lately, it has even been suggested that the requirements that allies have the same friends and enemies and follow the Spartans anywhere, once considered the essential elements of the "Oath of the Peloponnesian League," actually date from as late as the final decades of the fifth century and were imposed by Spartans on recently defeated cities, such as Athens, to turn them effectively into client states. However the League was organized, the power of individual members to influence its policy was significant, as at the first recorded League meeting, when the allies, led by the Corinthians, scuttled King Cleomenes' plans to invade Attica yet again (Hdt. 5.91–3).

Sparta's domination did not extend over the entire sixth-century Peloponnese, however. The hold-out was Argos. According to tradition, rivalry between the two states began in the early years of the Dorian occupation with a conflict over the border territory of Cynuria (Paus.

3.7.2). Raids and retaliations ensued. The battle of Hysiae, usually dated to 669 B.C.E. (Paus. 2.24.7), is slightly better attested, when the Argives defeated the Spartans and perhaps consolidated their grip on the Thyreatis. Their next recorded clash was the famous Battle of the Champions (*c.* 545 B.C.E.), a pitched battle in which the Spartan army prevailed after an inconclusive Homeric-style combat between two sets of picked warriors (Hdt. 1.81.1–2). Survey data indicate that the area of the Thyreatis and Cynuria was already coming under Spartan control in the early sixth century, a process finalized at the Battle of the Champions, corroborating Herodotus' statement that Spartans "held" the Thyreatis for some time before the battle. It is tempting to associate this Spartan victory with the extraordinary spike in settlement activity in the north and central Parnon region beginning around the middle of the sixth century. The internal colonization of this area resulted in the creation of no fewer than eighty-seven settlements in the area of the Laconia Survey, including one new town, Sellasia. Such a burst of activity could be expected in the aftermath of the failed conquest of Tegea, which prevented settlers from moving north, if Spartan success at the Battle of the Champions had removed the Argive threat to eastern Laconia. Herodotus' claims that Argos had previously controlled all of the Parnon range down to and including Cape Malea and the island of Cythera may be a trifle extreme (Hdt. 1.82.2), but the Argives' ability to harass settlers may partly explain why this area of Laconia remained more or less empty until the mid-sixth century.

By the later sixth century, Spartans controlled all the territory of Laconia and Messenia, while most of the other cities in the peninsula regarded Sparta as their hegemon, a leader not reluctant to exercise power. The terms of the treaty with the Tegeans as reported by Aristotle (Arist. F592 Rose) illustrate this well. The Spartans required the Arcadians to expel any Messenians still in their territory and, in a passage whose precise meaning is open to dispute, required them not to make them "useful" (*chrêstoi*) which is usually taken to mean that the Tegeans should not make the Messenians citizens. Whatever "useful" actually meant, the degree to which Spartans felt justified in intervening in Tegean internal affairs is noteworthy.

Sparta's prominence attracted international attention, particularly that of Croesus, ruler of Lydia. He had already conquered the Greek cities clustered along the west coast of Asia Minor and by the early 540s was looking for a Greek ally, probably to secure his rear while he prepared to attack the Persian Empire to the east (Hdt. 1.69–70). Earlier on,

Croesus had cultivated good relations with Sparta by making a gift of the gold that a Spartan delegation had come to his capital at Sardis to buy for the statue of Apollo at Thornax. Once the treaty of friendship and alliance had been concluded, Sparta returned the favor by sending a magnificent wine mixing bowl, the product of Laconia's justly famous bronze-workers, off to Sardis. The bowl never arrived, somehow ending up as a dedication at the sanctuary of Hera on Samos. The Samians, whom the Spartans accused of hijacking their gift, claimed that Sardis had fallen to the Persians while the bowl was still en route (Hdt. 1.69–70). Croesus' defeat prompted the now rather nervous Ionian and Aeolian Greeks to send an embassy to ask the Spartans for help. Unfortunately, their representative chose to appear in a dazzling purple robe, laboring under the misapprehension that this was how to draw a crowd at Sparta and compounding his folly by launching into a lengthy speech. Needless to say, the Spartans rejected his call for military assistance. Herodotus tells us that they did, however, send a team to the area in a fifty-oared ship on an information-gathering expedition; one Spartiate even confronted Cyrus, the Great King, in Sardis, warning him against making hostile moves against any Greek city (Hdt. 1.152). Brave words, perhaps, but when the Persian offensive did come a few years later, Spartans were conspicuously absent.

The decision not to commit troops against the Persian Empire was a sound one. In 525, Sparta attempted to project its power outside the Peloponnese to restore aristocratic rule on the island of Samos, then under the rule of the dictator Polycrates (Hdt. 3.46–56), a project ultimately motivated by longstanding personal ties between leading families of the two states. This early attempt at regime change became bogged down in a lengthy siege which the Spartans abandoned. They were later accused – not for the last time – of having been bought off. Regardless of its outcome, however, the Samian operation was, like the brief alliance with Croesus and the embassy to Cyrus, indicative of Sparta's high standing on the eve of the reign of the king who would firmly establish his city as the leading power in Greece.

4

From Cleomenes to Pausanias

Cleomenes son of Anaxandridas, king of Sparta from about 525 to 480 B.C.E., dominates Herodotus' Greek narrative of the decades before the Persian Wars, when Sparta's prestige was at its peak. The Cleomenes of the *Histories* is in turn principled and underhanded, devout and cynical, a brilliant tactician and what today would be termed a war criminal. He was responsible for some of Sparta's most resounding victories as well as the city's most humiliating reversals. Herodotus describes Cleomenes at his first appearance as "the most just of men" (Hdt. 3.148.2) only to characterize him later as "out of control and virtually insane" (Hdt. 5.42.1). One unifying thread, however, runs through his account of Cleomenes' actions – a single-minded ruthlessness in the pursuit of what Cleomenes deemed to be Sparta's best interests. Not seldom he identified these with his own, a phenomenon familiar today in the cases of members of long-ruling governments.

Fittingly for such a controversial figure, even the circumstances of Cleomenes' birth were unusual. His father King Anaxandridas had come under repeated pressure from the ephors and Gerousia to repudiate his wife, to whom he was reputedly devoted, on the grounds that she could not produce an heir (Hdt. 5.39–40). This Anaxandridas steadfastly refused to do, until a compromise was reached whereby he would take a second wife but not divorce his first, living with both "hardly in the Spartan way," as Herodotus puts it. Anaxandridas' new wife soon gave birth to Cleomenes, her only child, while his first wife finally proved surprisingly fertile, bearing him three male offspring, including Cleomenes' successor, Leonidas. The king's bigamy may not have been entirely motivated by uxoriousness, since his first wife was also his niece and so likely had a sizeable portion of the family estates in her possession. Divorce would have lost Anaxandridas that land, and his eventual production of sons by his first wife ensured it would stay in the family after his death.

Though the son of his father's second wife, Cleomenes was destined to be king because he was the firstborn. Of his three half-brothers, one, Dorieus, was particularly incensed at not ruling himself and so attempted twice to found colonies overseas, perhaps taking other malcontents with him (Hdt. 5.41–8). Both attempts, one to Libya, the other to Sicily, were failures, although Dorieus was careful to plant his colonies in areas with Spartan and, in the case of Sicily, Heraclid ties. Dorieus' death in Sicily after becoming involved in hostilities between local powers, along with the failure of the Samos expedition in 525, may well explain Cleomenes' reluctance to commit forces far from home.

We first meet Cleomenes as king in about 517 B.C.E. when the deposed tyrant of the island of Samos, Maeandrius, who was living in Sparta at the time, attempted to win the king over with offers of gold cups and other precious luxuries (Hdt. 3.148). Seeing that Maeandrius was trying to gain influence in order to induce the Spartans to support him in his return to Samos, Cleomenes wisely advised the ephors to expel the Samian from the Peloponnese. Next, chronologically speaking, comes Cleomenes' expulsion from Athens in 510 of the tyrant Hippias (Hdt. 5.64.1–65.2), the son of the persistent faction-leader Pisistratus whose three attempts to seize power Herodotus has already described in some detail (Hdt. 1.59–64). Cleomenes, unfortunately, went on to back the wrong horse in the ensuing political struggle. His guest-friend Isagoras, bested by Cleisthenes, whose groundbreaking democratic reform program mobilized the people of Athens to his side, induced Cleomenes in 508/7 to order the exile of Cleisthenes, his family, and sympathizers, then the dismantling of his new popular institutions, in particular the advisory council called the *boule*. The Athenian people refused the Spartan orders, whereupon Cleomenes, with the support of a small force of Spartan troops as well as of Isagoras and his supporters, made the mistake of seizing the Acropolis. Uncowed, the Athenians simply shut them up there as they had Hippias several years before. On the third day of the siege, the Spartans under Cleomenes were given safe passage out of Attica, while Isagoras abandoned his three hundred followers to their fate, a sentence of death (Hdt. 5.69–72).

Deeply insulted, Cleomenes then decided to teach the Athenians a lesson. Gathering a huge army from all over the Peloponnese, but without informing the allies that his motive was to punish the Athenians and install Isagoras as tyrant, Cleomenes marched into Attica, where Athenian forces met them on the Thriasian plain near Eleusis. The "Coalition of the Unwitting" very soon turned into a "Coalition of the Unwilling," as word of the Spartan king's true intentions must have leaked out just as battle was about to be joined. First, the Corinthians, Sparta's most powerful allies, abandoned the expedition on the grounds that Cleomenes' objectives were unjust; then, disastrously for Cleomenes, his fellow king, Demaratus, with whom he had had no quarrel in the past, raised objections. With a major part of the force returning home and the two Spartan kings at odds, the other allies extricated themselves and marched back to their various cities. Because of this incident, Herodotus reports, the Spartans decided that only one king should henceforth lead troops on campaign outside Spartan territory (Hdt. 5.74–5).

The embarrassing failure of this mission and his inability to bring the newly installed popular government of Athens to heel seems to have driven Cleomenes to propose even more extreme remedies and to risk further loss of face. It had apparently become known that the Alcmeonids, Cleisthenes' own family, had during their exile from Pisistratid Athens softened up the Delphic authorities by funding the upgrade of the east facade of the temple of Apollo from poros limestone to marble imported from the island of Naxos, "persuading" the Pythia to tell every Spartan inquirer, private or official, to free Athens. Shocked and disappointed, as they no doubt were, by this blatant manipulation of one of Greece's most august religious institutions, the Spartans claimed also to have become aware they themselves had committed a grave injustice by turning on their guest-friend Hippias, son of Pisistratus, for which the Athenians now were not even appropriately grateful. The Spartans thereupon called a general assembly of their allies to discuss regime change in Athens – specifically, although Herodotus does not ascribe the proposal to Cleomenes, the re-installation of Hippias as tyrant of Athens. This was an inauspicious way to start what modern scholars have identified as the first known meeting of the Peloponnesian League. The Spartan proposal was met with perplexity. As the Corinthian representative put it, had the world turned topsy-turvy? Was Sparta, steadfast opponent of tyranny and supporter of liberation movements, now seriously suggesting the League, many of whose members had suffered under tyrannical rule themselves, actually reinstate a notorious ruler like Hippias? Despite a speech from the man in question, the other allies called out in support of the Corinthian position, and the meeting broke up with Sparta's (and Hippias') ambitions frustrated. The ex-tyrant withdrew to his stronghold of Sigeum in the Troad (Hdt. 5.90–4), for the moment.

Shortly after this disappointment, Cleomenes again resisted bribery and the committal of troops far from the usual Spartan sphere of activity. In 499/8, the dubious Aristagoras, former tyrant of Miletus and now ostensibly a democrat, arrived in Sparta canvassing for support for the Ionian Greeks' revolt from the Persian Empire. He tried to win over Cleomenes by using a bronze map to illustrate the wealth of Asia Minor and the ease with which the Spartans could conquer it. After a two-day break, he slipped up by giving a truthful answer to Cleomenes' question of how far the Great King's capital was from the sea. A two months' march was much farther than Cleomenes was willing to go, and he ordered Aristagoras out of Sparta by sundown. Nothing daunted, Aristagoras returned as a suppliant and attempted openly to bribe the king with ever-increasing amounts of money, until he reached the astonishing sum of 50 talents. At this point, Cleomenes' young daughter Gorgo, perspicacious beyond her eight or nine years, said "Father, if you don't get out of here, this stranger will corrupt you." Taking her advice, Cleomenes left the room, and Aristagoras, seeing he was getting nowhere, immediately left Sparta. He had better luck with the Athenian Assembly, since, as Herodotus points out, it was easier to persuade 30,000 men than a single king of Sparta (Hdt. 5.49–51, 97.2).

Cleomenes' most resounding military victory came in 494 with a battle against the Argives at Sepeia in the territory of Tiryns, a few miles east of Argos itself. As we have seen, Argos and Sparta were longstanding rivals; control of the territory on the eastern seaboard of the Peloponnese was among the many bones of contention. But this time the fighting took on a more serious dimension, for Cleomenes, conveniently armed with a favorable Delphic oracle, set out to capture Argos itself. After an unsuccessful attempt to lead his troops over land, Cleomenes transported the Spartan army by boat from their outpost in the Thyreatis, landing on the eastern part of the Argive plain between Tiryns and Nauplia. The Argives drew up not very far from the Spartan lines and, nervous about Lacedaemonian trickery, decided to copy every maneuver their enemy made. Cleomenes soon became aware of this, so he commanded the army to take up arms and attack when the signal for mealtime was made. Caught completely off-guard, the Argive lines were cut to pieces, while the survivors fled to a nearby sacred grove as suppliants. Again, Cleomenes' subsequent behavior tarnished the glory of this victory. He treacherously enticed fifty Argives out of the woods to their deaths, misinforming them that their ransoms had been paid, then ordered the helots accompanying the army to pile up wood around the grove and burn everything and everyone in it alive. Crushing though this victory was, Cleomenes did not follow through with the capture of the city itself, because he learned the name of the sacred wood's tutelary divinity, Argos, from deserters. He had captured "Argos," just not the city. Even so, Argos' power was broken and the city remained riven with internal strife for several decades after the disaster at Sepeia robbed the city of most of its military manpower. Before returning to his own lands, however, Cleomenes committed yet another outrage. Forbidden by the priest of Hera to sacrifice at her temple nestled in the hills overlooking the plain because he was a foreigner, Cleomenes once more got helots to do his dirty work, ordering them to whip the obdurate priest while he himself carried out the requisite rituals (Hdt. 6.76–81).

Back in Sparta, Cleomenes came under suspicion for failing to achieve his mission objective and soon found himself accused of corruption. In the trial before the Spartan Assembly, Cleomenes made a convincing case, to the Spartans at least, that the Delphic prophecy that he would take "Argos" had been fulfilled with his capture of the grove of Argos. For good measure he added a description of a dramatic omen that was revealed to him while sacrificing at the Heraeum, a bolt of lightning that issued from the cult statue's breasts. This, he explained, meant that the divinity's will had been accomplished, since only if it had come from the statue's head would the omen signify the Spartans' capture of the city from the heights of the acropolis down (Hdt. 6.82).

Outside Sparta, the international situation was worsening. Provoked by the Athenians' support for the failed insurgency in Ionia on their western borders, the Persians after 494 had begun preparations to deal with the serious security menace posed by an independent Greece. The last years of Cleomenes' long reign thus lay under the looming shadow of the threat from the east. Before embarking on the military option, the Persians made one more attempt at a peaceful solution to their Greek crisis. Sending heralds to all major Greek cities, probably in 491 B.C.E., they requested a token tribute of earth and water to signify each city's recognition of Persia's leading role in international affairs. The responses of Athens and Sparta were uncompromising. The Athenians threw their herald into a pit, the Spartans into a nearby well (Hdt. 7.133.1). They could thus expect no quarter. Behind their brave facade, however, the Athenians were alarmed by the prospect that their near neighbors on the strategically located island of Aegina, just beyond Piraeus, Athens' new main commercial and military harbor, might succumb to Persian pressure, so, despite the actions of Cleomenes over a decade earlier, they approached Sparta for help. As a result of the Athenian request, Cleomenes himself went to Aegina to demand a number of prominent men as hostages to guarantee the Aeginetans' good behavior. He encountered unexpectedly stiff opposition led by a man named Crius, who accused Cleomenes of having been bribed by the Athenians and, more worryingly, claimed that he did not have the support of the Spartan public, for otherwise he would have come with his co-king, Demaratus. Crius' suspiciously accurate knowledge of Spartan internal politics came, Herodotus tells us, from a letter that Demaratus had written to the Aeginetans. His bluff effectively called, Cleomenes returned to Sparta to deal with his most serious internal threat to date (Hdt. 6.50–51, 61.1).

Faced with Demaratus' second open challenge to his effectiveness as a king of Sparta, made worse this time by his rival's providing aid to potential allies of the Persians as well as orchestrating a slander campaign during his absence on Aegina, Cleomenes turned to a drastic solution – the removal of Demaratus from the throne. To accomplish this, he resurrected an old rumor, that king Ariston, Demaratus' father, had expressed doubt that the child was his when his wife gave birth apparently before her full term. Although Ariston later acknowledged Demaratus as his own son, Cleomenes was able to enlist the support of Leotychidas, another Eurypontid, who held a grudge against Demaratus for stealing his betrothed. Leotychidas swore out a formal complaint that Demaratus was not qualified by birth to hold the kingship in return for gaining the throne himself, then prosecuted Demaratus in what must have been a sensational trial, going so far as to call the former ephors who had been with Ariston when he heard the news of his son's birth as witnesses. Unable to reach a decision, the Spartan court sent a delegation to Delphi, in the hopes that Apollo might provide them with the answer to the question of Demaratus' paternity. Cleomenes swung into action. Using his powerful connections at Delphi, he induced the Pythia to give the answers he wanted. So, when the Spartan ambassadors put their question to the god, they were told in no uncertain terms that Demaratus was not Ariston's child (Hdt. 6.61.1, 63–6).

Once Demaratus had been deposed, Cleomenes and the newly ascended Leotychidas both went to Aegina, where they met with no serious opposition, gathered up the ringleaders of the pro-Persian camp and placed them in the safe, if not exactly friendly, hands of the Athenians (Hdt. 6.73). Cleomenes, however, had little opportunity to bask in the success of his coup, since the sordid details of his suborning of the Pythia soon became public and he was forced into exile. Fleeing first to Thessaly, he then established himself in Arcadia, where he began to foment unrest, playing on the traditional local hostility to Sparta and getting Arcadians to swear fearsome oaths committing them to follow him wherever he led (Hdt. 6.74).

Understandably concerned by his destabilizing activities, the Spartans caught up with Cleomenes and brought him back, evidently agreeing to his conditions that he be restored to all the power he had previously enjoyed. He seems to have spent little if any time as king in Sparta, however, perhaps because it soon became distressingly evident to all and sundry that the great liberator of Athens and victor of Argos was no longer fit to govern and actually posed a physical threat to the public (Hdt. 6.75.1). For, as he wandered the streets of Sparta, the old king would suddenly raise his stick and strike any Spartiate he met in the face. Alarmed by his antisocial behavior and clearly afraid he would do others or himself serious harm, his relatives – surely Cleomenes' half-brothers Leonidas and Cleombrotus – took the precaution of locking him in wooden stocks, with a helot posted to guard him. Bound like a common criminal, humiliated and shamed, Cleomenes resorted to a horrific form of self-injury. Seeing that there was only one helot on guard duty, Cleomenes prevailed on him to give him his knife. Starting at his thighs and moving upwards, Cleomenes sliced great gashes into his flesh until he inflicted the wounds in his stomach which led to his death, probably in 489–488 B.C.E. (Hdt. 6.75).

Greeks tried to account for the shocking end of a man who had once so dominated the political landscape. Herodotus reports the various explanations. Most people, he says, believed that Cleomenes' death was punishment for his sacrilege in corrupting the Pythia in the Demaratus case; the Athenians claimed that he paid the price for burning down the sacred grove at Eleusis; the Argives, for burning the suppliants at the shrine of Argos. But the Spartans themselves, according to Herodotus, had a more down-to-earth explanation. Cleomenes' self-mutilation was a consequence of chronic alcoholism, exhibited in his consumption of unmixed wine, a habit he picked up from a delegation of hard-drinking Scythians who had come to Sparta to negotiate a joint assault on the Persians at the time of Darius' into Scythia (Hdt. 6.84).

Cleomenes' successor was his half-brother/son-in-law Leonidas, undoubtedly the most famous of all Spartan kings. Unfortunately, very little is known of him beyond his actions at Thermopylae. We can safely surmise that he supported Cleomenes' anti-Persia policy, since there is no evidence of any change in the years between his accession and Xerxes' invasion. Steady hands were certainly needed. Outside Sparta, the international situation had unraveled even more during the period of Cleomenes' exile and suicide. Athens' participation in the revolt of the Ionian Greeks and the burning of the provincial capital Sardis in 498 had made it a target for Persian retribution. The blow fell in 490. A Persian fleet sailed across the Aegean, subjugating Greek island states along the way, then attacked and burnt Eretria, a major city on Euboea and ally of Athens. Next, guided by the aged ex-dictator Hippias, the Persians landed at Marathon on the east coast of Attica. The Athenians sent a desperate plea for help by courier to Sparta, only to be informed that the Spartans would come as soon as they could, when the moon was full in a few days time (Hdt. 6.105–6). This is the truest knowable reason for their absence, despite Plato's allegation over a century later, based on an unknown source, that the Spartans were at war with the Messenians at the time (*Leg.* 698d–e). Anyway, as everyone knows, Spartan help was in the event unnecessary, for the Athenians and their Plataean allies won a famous victory on the plain of Marathon and bought crucial time for Greece to prepare for the coming onslaught. Three days after the full moon, a detachment of 2,000 men finally arrived from Laconia, were shown the battlefield, and departed after praising the Athenians for a job well done (Hdt. 6.120). It would be interesting to know what thoughts went through the mind of their commander upon realizing that the Athenians could defeat such a superior force virtually unaided.

During the 480s, a stream of defeatist prophecies issued from the oracle at Delphi. One urged Athenians to flee to the ends of the earth (Hdt. 7.140), another advised Argos to see to its own protection as it was surrounded by enemies (Hdt. 7.148.3). Sparta's predicted that either a king would be slain in battle or the city be destroyed by the Persians (Hdt. 7.220.4). Since no king had ever been killed in combat, this oracle has been properly seen as intended to discourage resistance. Its advice jibed with what could at this time legitimately be regarded as the isolationist streak in Spartan foreign policy. Peloponnesians and many Spartans evidently believed, wrongly in Herodotus' opinion, that they could hold out against an invader from behind a defensive wall across the Isthmus of Corinth. Athens, on the other hand, took the positive step of beefing up her navy, the first step towards the dominance the city would exert later in the century (Hdt. 7.139). At the end of the decade, the Persian danger had become too pressing to ignore, and so the independentist Greek states formed an alliance, the Hellenic Coalition, to organize resistance. Past differences were set aside, oaths were sworn to impose tithes on those Greeks who had willingly gone over to the Persians ("medized") upon the successful conclusion of the war (Hdt. 7.132.2), and Sparta was chosen as head of the Coalition (Hdt. 7.149.2, 161.2).

The Persian forces crossed the Hellespont in early 480 and by the summer were making their way south to the Malian Gulf, meeting little resistance as they went (Hdt. 7.41–131, 179–200). Advising Xerxes was Demaratus, the bitter ex-king who had fled unbearable ridicule at Sparta about ten years earlier to take up a privileged position at the Persian court (Hdt. 6.67–70). Herodotus claims that Demaratus had sent a secret message from Susa to Sparta several years before the invasion to reveal the Great King's plans (Hdt. 7.239.2). It is difficult to assess the veracity of this account, given Herodotus' generally favorable attitude towards Demaratus – who could legitimately be accused of treason – perhaps due to the historian's possible personal contacts with Demaratus' descendants in the Troad. But Demaratus' motives in accompanying Xerxes are crystal clear – reinstatement as king in Sparta under any conditions and at any cost.

The Hellenic Coalition sent out two contingents to meet the Persians. The first stationed itself in the pass of Tempe between Macedonia and Thessaly before the Persians had even crossed into Europe, but was withdrawn for strategic reasons at the cost of Thessaly's allegiance to the independentist cause (Hdt. 7.172–4). The second, under the overall command of King Leonidas (Hdt. 7.204), was ordered to meet the Persians at the narrow seaside pass of Thermopylae, named for the hot mineral springs issuing from the foot of the mountains separating Thessaly from southern Greece. The mission was small – just an advance guard – comprising only 3,100 Peloponnesians, including 300 Spartans, with other contingents from Thespiae, an unwilling Thebes, as well as two local states, the Opuntian Locrians and Phocians (Hdt. 7.202–203.1), for a total of rather more than 5,100 according to

Herodotus. Full mobilization at Sparta would occur after the Carnea festival, and in other cities after the Olympics, which were being celebrated at the time, as nobody expected the Thermopylae campaign to be concluded very rapidly (Hdt. 7.206).

Once at the wider, middle part of the pass, the Greeks reconstructed an old wall, originally built by the Phocians as a barrier against their northern enemies, the Thessalians, and arranged themselves behind it (Hdt. 7.176–7). Leonidas had hardly taken up his position when the Persian army's approach caused serious qualms among his Peloponnesian allies, who called for a tactical retreat to the Isthmus. In order to avoid a serious split with the Phocians and Locrians, who were incensed at any talk of withdrawal, Leonidas called a meeting and put his weight behind staying where they were. To mollify the malcontents, he sent messages calling for reinforcements – an odd move, if Herodotus is correct in characterizing this contingent as only an advance guard (Hdt. 7.207).

For four days each side waited. Then the Persians attacked. The next three days saw what is surely the most famous battle in western history, as the Spartans and their allies repulsed wave after wave of Persian attacks. Herodotus' account of the Greeks' early success leaves the impression that it was due to the superior discipline and battle tactics of the Spartans alone, omitting the contribution of the allies, who were over ten times as many (Hdt. 7.210–12). This stage of the battle is also often represented as a triumph of the heavily armed Greek hoplite soldier, but the Spartans' habit of feigning retreat only to turn on their pursuers actually owed more to the fluid style of fighting seen in Homeric narrative than to the tactics of the massed phalanx popular later in the century.

Xerxes' luck turned when a local man, Ephialtes son of Eurydemus, offered to show the Persians a path that went through the mountains to outflank the Greeks. Winning the Great King's assent, he guided Persian troops along the path in the evening of the second day. The track was not secret, for Leonidas had stationed the thousand Phocian troops high on the mountain to watch over it. But he clearly did not expect a major enemy operation in the area or he would have chosen more, and more reliable, troops for the task. The Persians came upon the detachment suddenly and, after the Phocians had withdrawn to higher ground to prepare to defend themselves, simply passed them by (Hdt. 7.213–18). The Greeks had already learned from incoming deserters of the Persian flanking movement; now their sentries saw the enemy approaching at dawn. With defeat certain, the non-Peloponnesian allies withdrew, either at their own or Leonidas' initiative. Herodotus presents Leonidas as dismissing them when he realized they had no will to fight, but this is surely too harsh a judgement (Hdt. 7.220.1–2). The allied troops' manpower and experience in fighting Persians were too valuable to squander on a heroic gesture. Only the Thespians, who refused to abandon Leonidas, and the Thebans, supposedly under compulsion, remained with the Peloponnesians.

The Spartans at Thermopylae have represented the epitome of valor in the western world for millennia, but we cannot be sure of what actually happened in their final hours. With all the major participants dead, Herodotus' only possible sources may have been descendants of the Thebans who surrendered, or some of the Greek sightseers from the fleet lying off Cape Artemisium on Euboea whom Xerxes invited over after his victory (Hdt. 7.233.1, 8.25.1). Still, his story is plausible and internally consistent. First, the Greeks moved down from the wall and took up a position further out into the wider part of the pass than before. Driven on by whips, the Persian army fell upon the Greeks to great slaughter, during which Leonidas fell. In a scene that could have come from Homeric epic, Herodotus describes the Greeks driving the enemy off four times from his body before they rescued it. At this point the detachment of elite Persians guided by Ephialtes appeared, and so the Greeks withdrew behind the wall to a hillock to take their last stand. The turncoat Thebans made a show of resistance but soon surrendered. The other Greeks on the hill fought with spears. When these broke, they fought with swords. If they lost their swords, they fought on with hands and teeth until all were killed (Hdt. 7.225).

After the battle, Xerxes sought out Leonidas' body and had his head displayed on a stake (Hdt. 7.238). A little later, in a staged propaganda exercise designed to boost morale among his Persian subjects and obedience, if not loyalty, among his Greeks, Xerxes opened up the battlefield to visitors from the Persian ships (Hdt. 8.24–5). Among the Greek corpses were a number of helots, whom people thought were either Spartans or Thespians. If the corpses of the Spartan slaves were indistinguishable from those of their masters, then they were not merely batmen, but were equipped as soldiers and consequently must have fought in the battle line. Sparta would have increasing need of such helot soldiers as the century wore on.

At about the same time, the allied Greek fleet under Spartan command was fighting the Persians in the straits between Malia on the Greek mainland and Artemisium at the northern end of the island of Euboea. The drawn-out engagement ended inconclusively with severe losses on both sides. Finally the Greeks, their position untenable, withdrew southwards (Hdt. 8.1–21), leaving central Greece in Persian hands. Back in Athens, a general evacuation of women and children to Troezen on the southern side of the Saronic Gulf now occurred, while the Artemisium fleet, bolstered by reserves anchored at Troezen's harbor, put in at the island of Salamis just off the Piraeus (Hdt. 8.41). The Persians entered Athens in September 480 and sacked the city. On Salamis, consternation reigned, and much talk of flight to defend individual cities. The Peloponnesian army, their various festivals now over, rushed to fortify the Isthmus of Corinth as a last barrier against Persian attack. Many Peloponnesians on Salamis evidently wished to trust their chances to this wall rather than to their skill in naval combat. After much heated discussion, a few threats, and a mysterious message from Themistocles, the Athenian commander, to the Persians that may or may not have been the trick he later claimed it was, the two sides joined battle in the narrow straits between Salamis and the mainland (Hdt. 8.74–98). The location suited the smaller and heavier Greek fleet, which could outmaneuver the larger Persian fleet and inflict serious damage. Upon witnessing the rout from his vantage point on Mt. Aegalees, Xerxes retired back to Persia and the remnants of his fleet over the Aegean to Asia Minor. But the Great King had not abandoned the Greek project completely, for the Persian land army under his general Mardonius wintered in Greece after withdrawing from Athens to quarters in friendly Thessaly (Hdt. 8.113.1).

The 480 B.C.E. campaigning season ended with the Athenians returning to their battered city and the victorious Greek fleet returning to Salamis after a failed attempt to capture Andros and a successful raid against Carystus at the south end of Euboea (Hdt. 8.121.1). In the autumn, Themistocles, the hero of the hour, visited Sparta to great acclaim. His standing among his fellow commanders was such that, in a vote held earlier at the Isthmus, he was almost everyone's second choice as the most deserving of recognition for his contribution to the war effort, after themselves, naturally (Hdt. 8.123.2). The Spartans awarded him a special olive crown, just like the one they had given Eurybiades, their commander at Artemisium. They also presented him with the finest chariot in Sparta – a sign of their love of horse racing. On his departure, Themistocles was given the unique honor of being escorted to the Arcadian border by the crack three hundred "knights" (*hippeis*), who normally accompanied only the kings to battle (Hdt. 8.124) – perhaps a temporary and symbolic elevation to royal status. Over the winter of 480/79, events at Sparta and elsewhere in Greece moved rapidly.

Upon the death of Leonidas at Thermopylae, the Agiad throne had passed to Pleistarchus, the young son of Leonidas and Gorgo, for whom Leonidas' brother Cleombrotus acted as regent, commanding the Spartan and Peloponnesian land forces at the time of Salamis. Within a few months after returning home with his troops once the trans-Isthmian wall was built, Cleombrotus too was dead (Hdt. 8.71, 9.10.2). He left behind an adult son, Pausanias, who took up his father's post as regent for the young king. The new regent had little time to settle into his position. Worried that the Athenians even at this late stage might succumb to the blandishments of Mardonius and switch sides, the ephors sent envoys to Athens in early 479 to counter the arguments of the Persian mouthpiece Alexander of Macedon (Hdt. 8.140–3). Their success in persuading the Assembly to keep the Hellenic Coalition united put the endgame into play, as Mardonius moved his forces down from Thessaly (Hdt. 9.1–3). The Athenians, who had once more withdrawn to Salamis, and the other allies sent to Sparta for help; the envoys were understandably upset when they came upon the Spartans celebrating yet another festival, the Hyacinthia (Hdt. 9.3.2, 6–7.1). To their impassioned plea for military assistance, the ephors prevaricated, delaying the decision for ten days – a tactic that even Herodotus found difficult to justify. The inclination to stay close to home, combined with the knowledge that the wall across the Isthmus had reached completion, may have been battling with the Spartans' more panhellenic sensibilities (Hdt. 9.7.2–8.2). Finally, however, the ephors reached a decision which, true to Spartan form, they did not impart to the Athenians until after the fact. Under cover of darkness, they mobilized the Spartan army, appointing Pausanias as commander (Hdt. 9.10.1): a massive levy of 5,000 Spartiates, representing perhaps two-thirds of their available manpower, set out secretly from Laconia accompanied by helots. When the still-livid envoys upbraided the ephors the next day for their inaction, they were confronted with the ephors' sworn statement that the army had already left and immediately hurried after the Spartan force together with another 5,000 elite soldiers from the perioecic cities (Hdt. 9.11.2–3). Behind this tale of the Spartans' astonishingly swift mobilization of most of their manpower may lie a reality of careful preparation, kept secret from their allies of course, over the ten days the ephors stalled.

When Mardonius learned of the Spartan movements he withdrew from Athens after putting the city to the torch (Hdt. 9.12.2–13.2) and led the bulk of his army into Boeotia, dominated by the pro-Persian city of Thebes (Hdt. 9.14.1–15.1). Stationing his forces near Plataea, the Persian general had his soldiers construct a massive wooden stockade enclosing approximately 4 km^2 (Hdt. 9.15.2–3). When Pausanias entered Boeotia he encamped the Coalition forces on the slopes of Mount Cithaeron to the south of the Persian position (Hdt. 9.19). The Persians opened hostilities with a series of skirmishes in which their cavalry commander was unhorsed and killed (Hdt. 9.22.2–3). After moving his forces downhill, closer to water sources and repositioning units to adapt to the hilly landscape, Pausanias settled a dispute between the Tegeans and Athenians over their disposition in the line and bided his time (Hdt. 9.25.1–28.1). For over a week, he and Mardonius waited each other out, neither willing to take a decisive step. Pausanias may have been expecting reinforcements (Hdt. 9.38.2), while Mardonius was perhaps attempting to avoid a pitched battle by cutting the Greek supplies coming through Cithaeron's passes and preventing his enemy from drawing water easily (Hdt. 9.37–41).

Battle was finally joined, in a way, at dawn on the twelfth day. The Persian cavalry attacked, sending a hail of missiles against the Greeks and making their only water supply, the Gargaphia spring, unusable (Hdt. 9.49.2). This setback prompted a meeting of the various Greek commanders where it was decided to move the whole army some 600 m to an area called "the island" where the river (or rivers) enclosed an area large enough to accommodate all their men and water was available safe from Persian attack. In addition, half of the army would withdraw to the Cithaeron passes to rendezvous with the supply trains (Hdt. 9.51). The rest of the day was spent in warding off repeated cavalry assaults. With nightfall came the time for redeployment, and discipline broke down almost completely. Rather than an orderly withdrawal, most of the Coalition forces simply made for the protection of Plataea's walls; when they reached a sanctuary of Hera about 4 km distant in front of the town, they took up position (Hdt. 9.52). Isolated as he was, Pausanias believed that the planned maneuver was underway and ordered his men to follow the rest of the army. Everyone obeyed except the leader of one unit named Amompharetus, an officer who had not been privy to the commanders' discussion and now refused to sully his Spartan honor by, as he saw it, fleeing in the face of the enemy (Hdt. 9.52). A herald sent by the Athenians to discover why the Spartans were not deploying to their new position came upon the unseemly scene of Pausanias and Amompharetus in the midst of a blazing row (Hdt. 9.54.1–55.1). At one point, Amompharetus even picked up a large rock and placed it at his commander's feet, saying that this was his vote for staying put (Hdt. 9.55.2). The play on words between "vote" and "rock/pebble," both of which were *psêphos* in Greek, has led to the suggestion that the story, which hardly shows Spartan military discipline in the best light, was told to Herodotus by Athenians, who usually voted with pebbles, whereas the Spartans normally voted by shouting. But the usual word for "vote" in Greek was *psêphos* (pebble), and so the anecdote about Amompharetus' dramatic gesture may well be genuine.

Turning to the herald, Pausanias essentially said, "See what I have to put up with?", then instructed the Athenians to join up with his forces and follow their lead (Hdt. 9.55.2). At daylight, exasperated at a whole night's worth of Amompharetus' intransigence, Pausanias called his bluff and began to move off with his own detachments, accompanied by the Tegean troops. As the Spartans and Athenians moved off, Pausanias kept to the hillocks and spurs of Mount Cithaeron, supposedly to avoid the Persians, while the Athenians stayed on the plain. When Amompharetus finally realized that Pausanias was in earnest, he began to move his own forces slowly to close the gap that had opened up between them (Hdt. 9.56.1–57.2). Mardonius and the Persian cavalry then galloped against the original Spartan position. Finding it deserted, they hurried after the Spartans, catching up with them just as Amompharetus and Pausanias were joining forces near a sanctuary of Demeter. Other Persian units joined in to press the cavalry's attack (Hdt. 9.57.3–59.2). Pausanias sent an urgent message to the Athenians on the other side of the hills that now was the time to fight for freedom, but they had their hands full dealing with the Greek units in the Persian army, who chose that moment to attack (Hdt. 9.60.1).

The Lacedaemonians and their Tegean allies were on their own. Spartan religious scruples, which required the proper omens before undertaking vigorous self-defense, created another surreal scene, as Pausanias and the Tegeans frantically slaughtered victim after victim to obtain the right signs while Persian arrows rained down from behind a barricade formed by their wicker shields, killing and wounding many allied soldiers. Driven to desperation, Pausanias called on Hera for aid just as the Tegeans could restrain themselves no longer and began to counterattack. Luckily, Pausanias at this moment finally received the omens he wanted, and the Lacedaemonians joined the onslaught (Hdt. 9.61.1–62.1). The fighting reached a crescendo as the Persians abandoned their bows for desperate hand-to-hand combat. They fought bravely even after their wicker barricade fell and the battle moved to the temple of Demeter itself. Herodotus acknowledges the Persians' bravery, but their disorganization and flimsier armor put them at a distinct disadvantage compared to the Spartans (Hdt. 9.62.2–3). At this juncture, Mardonius himself entered the battle, rallying his troops. The effect was short lived. Mardonius was soon cut down by a Spartan appropriately named Aeimnestos ("Forever Remembered"), and the Persian troops, their spirit broken, fled in disorder back to their stockade (Hdt. 9.64.1–65.1).

Greek victory was now just a matter of time, especially since the Persian general Artabazus, seeing defeat unfolding before him, led his own detachment of reinforcements in tight formation away to Phocis and safety (Hdt. 9.66). Even with triumph certain, the other Greek troops again showed their lack of discipline, rushing out after the fleeing Persians only to be slashed to ribbons by the Theban cavalry, who killed 600 of them and pursued the routed survivors up into Cithaeron (Hdt. 9.69). For their part, the remnants of Mardonius' army holed up in the wooden stockade they had built and strengthened their defenses in anticipation of a siege. The Spartans called on the Athenians for help, supposedly because they had superior knowledge of siege tactics, although there is no evidence for previous Athenian involvement in sieges. The Athenians duly breached the wooden wall, but the Tegeans were the first through and succeeded in plundering Mardonius' tent. The stockade built to protect the Persians now became their slaughterhouse, with the Greeks killing most of their 300,000-man army, according to Herodotus (Hdt. 9.70).

Pausanias was noble in victory. He graciously freed a woman from Cos who had been the concubine of a high-ranking Persian official (Hdt. 9.76). He angrily rejected as unhellenic a suggestion by an Aeginetan that he behead Mardonius' corpse as payback for Persian mistreatment of Leonidas' cadaver at Thermopylae – the battle's carnage had settled that debt (Hdt. 9.78.2–79.2). He attempted to enforce a fair (to his lights) distribution of the spoils by ordering the helots to gather up whatever the Persians had abandoned, rather than letting the Coalition troops engage in unseemly plunder. Not everything went as planned, however, as rumors spread that helots stole a good deal of the valuables and were then cheated by the Aeginetan fences they sold it to (Hdt. 9.80).

On the other hand, the regent did not shrink from extra-judicial killing
when he thought it necessary: he executed several prominent Theban
medizers on his own authority rather than risk their acquittal at a trial
(Hdt. 9.88).

Success crowned Hellenic arms in the eastern theater as well. Allied
forces under King Leotychidas defeated the Persians at Mycale on the
Asia Minor coast opposite the island of Samos (Hdt. 9.96–105). The
combined effect of the two victories was to nullify the Persian threat
to Greece and the Aegean for the foreseeable future. All that remained
were mopping-up operations to remove the remnants of Persian power
from the cities of Asia Minor. Despite a dispute over the future of the
Ionian cities provoked by an unsuccessful Spartan proposal to evacuate
the Ionians to Greece and settle them on the land of medizing cities, the
Greeks and Spartans, including Pausanias himself, had good reason
to consider this their finest hour. He and Themistocles were "the most
renowned of all Greeks of our time," in the words of Thucydides
(Thuc. 1.138.6). A celebratory elegy by Simonides put the battle
within an epic framework, describing Pausanias' departing Sparta for
Plataea in the company of the Dioscuri and Menelaus (F11 West², lines
24–34). No one could have foreseen that, in a little over a decade,
Pausanias would be disgraced and dead, starved to death by his own
countrymen, while Sparta's place as leader of the Hellenic Coalition
would be taken by Athens.

On the face of it, Pausanias' later career is the story of a weak-willed
man so corrupted by power and wealth that he was prepared to
betray the very cause for which he had fought. There was later even
a widespread fear that he aimed at establishing a Persian-backed
tyranny over all of Greece (Hdt. 5.32). But Herodotus was not so
sure of his guilt, since for him Pausanias remained the author of "the
most beautiful victory of all we have ever seen" (9.64.1). In contrast,
Thucydides uncharacteristically followed popular opinion in his account
of Pausanias' decline, which is replete with telling details and dramatic
incidents (Thuc. 1.94–95, 128.2–135.1). Historians reconstruct the
regent's actions in the years following Plataea based on Thucydides'
narrative but condemn his conclusions regarding Pausanias' culp-
ability, and even several narrative details, as distortions or outright
falsehoods.

Things began to go wrong after Pausanias was appointed commander of the naval forces in 478/7. He started putting on airs, treating
his allies with disdain – even violence – and making access to himself

extremely difficult (Thuc. 1.94.2–95.1). Worse followed after the capture of Byzantium (winter 478/7 or spring 477). Pausanias adopted Persian dress, started eating off luxurious Persian tableware – an ironic turnaround from his dismissive attitude towards the luxury of Mardonius' plate at Plataea – and in an expedition through Thrace employed Median and Egyptian bodyguards rather than Greeks (Thuc. 1.130). During this period, he also erected two notorious dedications. One was an immense bronze krater beside the mouth of the Hellespont (Hdt. 4.81.3). The other was the tripod dedicated at Delphi as a thank-offering from the booty seized at Plataea (Thuc. 1.132.2). This monument consisted of a gold tripod resting on the heads of three entwined snakes set upon a round stone base, the top block of which is now lost. Although the dedication had nominally been made by all the allies together, the base originally carried the following inscription:

> When as leader of the Greeks he annihilated the Medes' army,
> Pausanias dedicated this to Apollo as a monument.

After news spread of this egotistical epigram which accorded Pausanias sole credit for the victory, the allies were beside themselves. The Spartans were called to account before the Amphictyonic Council that administered the sanctuary at Delphi and fined an astronomical 1,000 talents ([Dem.] 59.96–8); the inscription was erased and a new, simpler one engraved onto the coils of the serpents listing the 31 states that fought the war, headed by Sparta, Athens, and Corinth.

Discontent in the armed forces had become so rampant, especially among the newly liberated Ionian Greeks, that all the allies, apart from the Spartans and the other Peloponnesians, approached the Athenians to request that they take over the leadership of the Coalition themselves, as Pausanias' behavior had become intolerable – more like a dictatorship than a normal Greek military command. By this time, word of the situation had finally reached Sparta and Pausanias was recalled (perhaps late summer 477) to face an investigative committee. He was convicted of some wrongdoing involving private individuals but acquitted of the more serious charge of treating with the Persians, although Thucydides avers there was considerable proof. The ephors did not attempt to inflict Pausanias on the allies again, but sent out a replacement called Dorcis. He, however, was not allowed to take up his generalship and returned home after abandoning hegemony of the Greek forces to the Athenians (Thuc. 1.95).

Pausanias meanwhile sailed out from the port of Hermione, ostensibly without official authorization, to prosecute what he called "the Greek war," though Thucydides was convinced he was simply continuing the quest for dominance that he had already started (Thuc. 1.128.3). More plausibly, Pausanias may have left Sparta, driven on the one hand by a perceived obligation to complete the unfinished business of avenging Heraclid honor by waging his own private war with the Persian Empire and on the other by anger at the stain on his personal honor caused by his forced removal from the Coalition's command. Such motives were hardly unknown in Spartan history before Pausanias. A few decades before, Pausanias' uncle Dorieus left his homeland on a quixotic quest to found a colony after being passed over for the throne by his half-brother Cleomenes, while the founding myth of Thera has Theras leaving Laconia because he could not bear being ruled by others after tasting power himself (Hdt. 4.147.3). Pausanias made his way back to Byzantium and established himself in power there for the next seven years (Just. *Epit.* 9.1.3). During this period, Pausanias perhaps began a correspondence with the local Persian satrap as part of his efforts to buttress his position, although the letters that were produced after his death purporting to be from an exchange with the Great King himself were undoubted forgeries.

The Hellespontine region around Byzantium was traditionally fertile ground for adventurers and malcontents. Miltiades of Athens had ruled on the Thracian Chersonese and the Pisistratids had a *pied-à-terre* at Sigeum in the Troad, while at the end of the Peloponnesian War, another time of flux, the bloodthirsty Spartan Clearchus became tyrant of Byzantium in 403 (Diod. Sic. 14.12). The unsettled circumstances surrounding the campaigns of Athens and her allies to bring all the Greek cities in the area under the umbrella of the Delian League, as the Hellenic Coalition was now called, would have allowed Pausanias a free hand for a few years. His freedom ended in 471/0, however, when the Athenians and their allies drove him out after a siege (Thuc. 1.131.1). With the pro-Spartan Cimon dominant at Athens, Athens and Sparta possibly came to an agreement to rid themselves of the mutual embarrassment that Pausanias represented. Removed from Byzantium, Pausanias then went to Colonae in the Troad where, after perhaps two years, a herald from Sparta brought him an official order from the ephors to return home or face being declared an enemy of the state (Thuc. 1.131.1).

Despite everything, Pausanias came back to Sparta convinced that he could prevail in any court case through the tried-and-true method of bribery. When he was in fact imprisoned directly upon his arrival, he soon succeeded in getting himself released (Thuc. 1.131.2). Then the ephors learned that Pausanias was intriguing with the helots by offering them freedom and citizenship if they joined in his revolution. Even at that point, the ephors chose not to take any action due to lack of direct evidence as well as to Pausanias' still-excellent reputation and his status as regent for Pleistarchus, though how he still managed to retain that title after abandoning his royal obligations so many years before is unclear (Thuc. 1.132.4–5). At last, one of Pausanias' supporters, a man from Argilos in Thrace who had become suspicious when asked to take a letter to Persia – a journey from which no one ever returned – turned on him and produced the letter before the ephors; it purported to be Pausanias' last to the Great King and contained the customary request that the bearer be executed (Thuc. 1.132.5). A plan was devised to entrap the regent into revealing his designs: the Thracian went as a suppliant to the shrine of Poseidon Taenarius in Sparta town and sat in a hut divided by a partition. When Pausanias spoke to his friend, the ephors sitting behind the partition heard everything: the Thracian's complaints about his treatment despite always having worked for Pausanias' interests in his dealings with the King, and Pausanias' apologies and requests that he continue the negotiations with Persia on his behalf (Thuc. 1.133.1–134.1).

Things then moved quickly. The ephors now had the hard evidence they needed and so decided to arrest Pausanias then and there, right in the street, after he had left the shrine. But he noticed from their expressions and from a signal by one of their number that he was in danger. He fled to the temple of Athena of the Bronze House on the acropolis and went into a small room in the temple.

After ascertaining his whereabouts, the ephors had Pausanias walled up and posted guards to ensure he would starve to death. Just before the fallen hero expired, he was removed from the sacred precinct, so that he would not pollute the temple, and died immediately. Spared the final ignominy of having his corpse hurled into the Caeadas chasm where Spartans threw criminals and rebels, Pausanias was buried near the sanctuary, only to be reburied later at the orders of the Delphic oracle exactly where he died in order to remove the curse his death had brought on Sparta (Thuc. 1.134.2–4).

4.1   The foundations of the temple of Athena Chalcioecus

Pausanias is a conundrum. Herodotus presents him as a valiant and courageous leader, cool in the face of extreme danger, as when he persisted in trying to take the omens under a hail of Persian arrows, and a gracious, humble victor not at all dazzled by the glamor of the Persian lifestyle. To Thucydides, he was a megalomaniac who took to oriental ways like a duck to water and was prepared to sacrifice Greece's freedom for his own aggrandizement. Despite Thucydides' conviction that Pausanias was guilty of the most heinous crimes and planned to rule all of Greece as a Persian client, it is more likely he was gradually trapped into certain self-defeating courses of action by a combination of his own character, shaped by the competitive and honor-obsessed society in which he lived and in whose values he was inculcated during his years as a citizen-in-training, the unprecedented status he won as victor over the Persians, and his failure (shared by many other Spartans) to understand that other Greeks were neither Spartiates nor helots. His wearing of Persian clothing and use of Persian tableware during his first stay at Byzantium can be justified in Homeric terms as display of the tangible signs of honor (*geras*) due him as conqueror of the Persians, as can his Egyptian and Median bodyguards in Thrace. After all, they were booty too. His medism, if genuine, is less excusable, but may be understood as the result of what he perceived as personal betrayal by his former allies and even his city, which declined to support him when his leadership came under attack. Like other Heraclids before him, he had decided to leave Laconia and carve out a state for himself that would accord him the honors he was due. Since the Athenians were likely hostile to this project and the Spartans clearly unwilling to help, Pausanias' only recourse, as he perhaps saw it, was to approach Persia. Did he dream of returning to Sparta as ruler, with the help of his old enemy? We cannot tell, but the personal tragedy of Pausanias may lie in the fact that the qualities that had made him a good war leader – courage, decisiveness, and self-assurance – engendered pride and jealousy of his entitlements when dealing with people who were supposed to be on his side. He has much in common with the notorious American traitor Benedict Arnold, a brilliant general and tactician but also tactless and thin-skinned, who eventually turned on his compatriots because of slights to his standing as an officer and a gentleman.

5

Helots and Perioeci

In 465/4, only few years after Pausanias' death, an earthquake struck Sparta (Thuc. 1.101.1–2). How much damage the city suffered can never be accurately assessed, despite accounts in later authors such as Diodorus Siculus, who claimed almost all its buildings were destroyed in the quake and a long series of aftershocks (11.63.1–3; cf. Plut. *Cim.* 16.5–7). The long-term effects of this earthquake and its sequel have been much debated; some historians see it as a veritable watershed in the development of Spartan society. In any case, the quake had an immediate and frightening consequence, at least to the Spartans: their helots actually revolted. The threads of two main historical traditions are visible in the few surviving accounts. One, traceable back to Ephorus in the fourth century (Diod. Sic. 11.63.4–64.1; Plut. *Cim.* 16.6–7), involves both Laconian helots, described as mounting an unsuccessful attack on the city, and those in Messenia, who either planned the operation with their Laconian comrades or joined in the revolt after the attack was repulsed. The other, represented by Thucydides, concentrates on the rebellion in Messenia and justly dominates modern studies, for whatever unrest broke out in Laconia after the news of the disaster at Sparta spread was swiftly crushed.

The revolt in Messenia was another matter. As it dragged on, with the rebels stubbornly dug in at their mountain stronghold of Ithome, the Spartans were obliged to call upon their allies for help, even approaching the Athenians, with whom relations had cooled appreciably since the heady days of Salamis and Plataea. Now that Cimon was wielding the greatest influence in Athens, the city sent a contingent under his command to help put down the insurgency. But the Spartans became so suspicious of the Athenian soldiers' ideological orientation that they sent them back, alone of all the cities that had sent troops, claiming (with transparent falsity) that their help was not actually needed after all (Thuc. 1.102). The fallout from this particular incident was decisive for Athens, as Cimon fell from favor and the radical democrats Ephialtes and Pericles could begin their reform program. By the war's tenth year (or fourth, if we accept an emendation to Thucydides' text), the Spartans and Messenians came to terms (Thuc. 1.103.1–3). The rebels and their families were given safe passage out of the Peloponnese, with immediate enslavement reserved for any who dared to return, and were settled by the Athenians near the town of Naupactus on the north coast of the Corinthian Gulf.

Thus ended the most serious threat to the territorial integrity of the Laconian lands since the Spartan expansion into Messenia in the eighth and seventh centuries B.C.E. In 465/4 the Spartans had faced not simply a slave revolt but, west of Taygetus, what might today be recognized as a nationalist uprising fed by a sense of identity that enabled the rebels to withstand the combined might of Sparta and her allies for several years. To Thucydides, the rebellion was the most serious internal crisis in Laconia between the Persian and Peloponnesian Wars. He twice mentions that Sparta resettled Aeginetan exiles on the east coast of Laconia in return for their help against the rebels (2.27.2, 4.56.2) and in 427 has a Plataean spokesman remind the Spartan judges sent to decide the fate of their former ally after its surrender that fully one-third of Plataea's manpower went to Sparta's aid during the revolt (3.54.5). Fear of another revolt is also among the motives he attributes to the Spartans for concluding the Peace of Nicias in 421 (5.14.3). Thucydides may have regarded the revolt as an inevitable consequence of what he presents as the intensely hostile and inherently violent relationship between the helots and their masters. His picture is a pessimistic one: every incident described or comment made concerning helots outside a purely military context is marked by violence and distrust. As he puts it in a celebrated passage, "The greater portion of Spartan policy towards the helots is particularly concerned with security" (4.80.3).

We have already seen that Pausanias was accused of conspiring with helots after his return from Asia Minor; on another occasion, helot suppliants were seized from the sanctuary of Poseidon Taenarius, contravening all Greek norms of behavior (Thuc. 1.128.1). Even more shocking is the "disappearing" of 2,000 helots, which Thucydides offers as an example of the extremes which Spartan precautionary measures might reach (4.80.3). The Spartans called on the helots to select those who claimed to have served with distinction in war, leaving the impression that they would be given their freedom. In fact, the Spartans wanted potential subversives identified on the grounds that men who put themselves forward in this way and were ready to claim freedom might turn against Sparta in the future. The Spartans garlanded the 2,000, paraded them around the city's temples as if to emancipate them, and then eliminated them so secretly that no one knew how they had been killed. This cold-blooded parody of a sacrificial ritual foreshadows for us today the procedures of the death camps, though the Spartans' motive was not genocide, but rule by fear. Dating this horrific event is difficult, for although Thucydides places it in his narrative of events for 425/4, he provides no chronological indicators to link it with the surrounding passage. In fact, there are reasons for doubting it could have happened at the time when Sparta was recruiting the first detachment of helots to serve as hoplites. But Thucydides also describes the Spartans as being quite apprehensive of unrest among helots and eager to despatch 700 helot soldiers off to Thrace with Brasidas (4.80.5). Whatever the date, Thucydides surely meant to highlight the unusually overt hostility Spartans showed toward their slave population.

Herodotus, who must also have known about the helot revolt, shows the helots in a completely different light. Helots posed no security threat to Herodotus' Spartans. They served in the army, fighting and falling beside Leonidas at Thermopylae (8.25.1); their dead were buried in one of the three mounds raised at Plataea after the battle (9.85.2); and during the Argive campaign Cleomenes I employed helots to avoid direct involvement in the sacrilegious burning of the sacred grove at Sepeia and the flogging of the priest of Hera (6.80.1, 81.1). Herodotus mentions helots only twice in non-military roles – when they participated in the ritual mourning at the funerals of kings (6.58.2–3) and when the helot guarding Cleomenes foolishly let himself be persuaded to give the insane king a knife (6.75.2). But these two passages are enough to show that Herodotus viewed the helots as integrated into Spartan society to the same extent as slaves in any other city. Unlike Thucydides, Herodotus' helots even have rudimentary personalities and act as individuals. In addition to Cleomenes' guard, he mentions another helot who was batman to Eurytus, one of two Spartiates sent away from Thermopylae by Leonidas because they suffered from ophthalmia (7.229.1). Learning of the Persian advance behind the Spartan lines,

Eurytus ordered his helot to take him back to the battlefield. He rushed into the fray; the helot fled. After the victory at Plataea, helots stole much of the booty Pausanias had ordered them to collect, but sold their loot to Aeginetan middlemen at knock-down prices (9.80.1–3). These helots are far from the faceless mass of simmering resentment presented by Thucydides. As individuals, they could be cowardly, dishonest, and gullible – in other words, similar to the stereotypical slaves found in Aristophanes and other comic writers.

What was it about helotage that brought two intelligent contemporary authors to reach such radically different conclusions? In other words, who, or what, were the helots? The question is easier to ask than to answer, since almost all aspects of helotage continue to be subjects of wide-ranging debate. One thing is certain: the helots were the foundation upon which Sparta's economy and society rested. But beyond this bald statement, our inability to comprehend the true face of Spartan life is compounded in the case of the helots, who lived in total obscurity on the margins of a society little interested in recording its own history, let alone that of the slaves whose labor supported it.

Even the origins of helotage are uncertain. The earliest writer to touch on this subject is Antiochus of Syracuse (c. 430–410), in his account of the Partheniai revolt and the foundation of Tarentum. Antiochus describes how the Partheniai came to have their name: "when the Messenian War had begun, those Lacedaemonians who did not take part in the campaign were judged slaves and called helots. And all the children born during the campaign they called Partheniai, and they judged them to be without rights" (*FGrH* 555 F13). For Antiochus, the fathers of the Partheniai were the first helots. They had originally been full Spartan citizens, but were degraded to slave status because they evaded conscription. Thus, the institution of helotage came about quite late as a consequence of the Messenian Wars and was effectively an internal Spartan affair, not even Laconia-wide.

Ephorus' account is quite different, at least superficially, and was much more influential, since all later writers seem to have followed it to a greater or lesser extent. Ephorus placed the origin of helotage much earlier than Antiochus, crediting the first Agiad king, Agis, son of Eurysthenes, with its foundation (*FGrH* 70 F117). According to Ephorus, after the conquest of Laconia, the aboriginal Achaeans left under truce with their king for Ionia, their lands then being divided into six parts to be ruled by "kings" sent out from Sparta. Since Laconia was short of manpower after the migration of the Achaeans, these kings were enjoined to accept as citizens any foreigner who wished to settle. At first these *perioikoi* possessed equal rights with Spartans, sharing in citizenship and eligibility to office. But Agis removed those rights and made them tributary to Sparta. All the Laconian communities submitted except for the city of Helos in the south, whose inhabitants were called Helots. The Spartans reduced the city by force and enslaved the Helots under certain conditions. The war was called "the war against the helots."

Ephorus provided the canonical ancient account of the helots' name and origin. That the helots came from Helos was the most widely accepted explanation in antiquity, although historians today give it little credence; many prefer to see the helots as a conquered people descended from the original non-Dorian inhabitants of Laconia. Interestingly, though, neither Antiochus nor Ephorus identified the helots in this way. Instead, they present the original helots, first, as either Spartans by birth or at any rate non-Achaeans, and, second, as degraded from an earlier position of equality with other Spartans. The major structural difference between the two accounts results from chronology: for Antiochus, the invention of helotage was contemporaneous in Laconia and Messenia, while for Ephorus the Messenians were simply assimilated into a long pre-existing category of servitude. Unfortunately, both accounts have fatal flaws. Antiochus may well have been motivated by contemporary concerns, as we have seen, to attribute helot parentage to the Partheniai. Likewise, despite the best efforts of Ephorus and other ancient scholars, the Greek word for helot, *heilôs*, cannot be made to derive from Helos. The two words are etymologically distinct.

Although Antiochus and Ephorus are of little use for explicating the origin of helotage in Laconia, a reference in a poem by Tyrtaeus to the defeated Messenians being compelled to pay tribute in kind to their new masters, "just like donkeys, worn down by heavy burdens" (F6 West[2]), is almost universally considered to be an allusion to the helotization of Messenia. Unfortunately, the process by which the Spartans reduced their neighbors to the status of helots is still unknown, as is the time it took to achieve. Literary sources, except for those few lines of Tyrtaeus, are completely lacking, while the archaeological evidence is tantalizing but inconclusive. Archaic pottery and bronze artifacts found at Messenian sites identified as sanctuaries are indistinguishable from their counterparts east of Taygetus, possibly indicating the increasing dominance of Sparta. Some of these sites – the famous Iron Age settlement at Nichoria, a Poseidon sanctuary near the mouth of the Pamisus, and a possible shrine situated on a hill to the west of the Pamisus valley – show signs of violent destruction. But the probable dates assigned these events vary widely, and, considering the difficulty in pinning the Messenian wars down chronologically, we should not rush to link any of them with Spartan military activity.

On the other hand, surface surveys conducted out in the region of Pylos in southwest Messenia have revealed a distinctive pattern of habitation for the Archaic and Classical periods, characterized by a few sizeable settlements relatively isolated in the landscape rather than a scattering of small farmsteads. A similar pattern has been proposed for the Soulima valley running northwest from the Stenyclarus plain in the upper Pamisus valley. Substantial Archaic complexes at Vasiliko and Kopanaki, two other neighboring Messenian sites, have been tentatively identified as the dwellings of Spartiates overseeing the workforce on their estates, suggesting that helots lived together under surveillance, not spread out in small family groups over the cultivable land. The same pattern may exist in Laconia as well, which shows a remarkable absence of seventh-century evidence for habitation in the Eurotas valley, surely the heartland of Spartiate-owned estates, that would indicate the presence of a few centralized communities of helots to work the land. In the Parnon hinterland east of Sparta, developed only in the course of the sixth century, an alternative pattern predominated, containing many small single-family farmstead and hamlet sites which the surveyors surmised were inhabited for the most part by *perioikoi* and helots. After the mid-fifth century, however, the number of sites diminished dramatically while their size increased, perhaps as a result of Spartan security concerns following 465/4. Given these differences, variation in helot settlement patterns throughout the Laconian lands was most likely the norm, conditioned by factors such as geography, agricultural fertility, political conditions, and of course Spartan tradition.

While the vast majority of both Messenian and Laconian helots worked the land for their Spartiate masters, certain helots performed a variety of other functions. Helots were domestic servants, wet nurses, grooms, personal attendants to Spartiates on campaign, light-armed troops, and even hoplites between 424 and 369 B.C.E. Although most of these occupations might be filled by servile labor in other cities, several factors distinguished a helot from the slave normally found in Archaic and Classical Greece, the so-called "chattel slave" who was the absolute property of his or her owner, to be used, sold, or traded at will. Unlike these slaves, who might have had wildly disparate origins, helots were born and bred in either Laconia or Messenia and were not legally permitted to be freed on individual initiative nor sold beyond the borders of the Laconian lands (*FGrH* 70 F117).

Such restrictions on what might be called property rights point to another distinguishing characteristic of helotage, the question of ownership. In a famous passage in Strabo's *Geography*, helots are described as "sort of public slaves" for whom the Spartans established places of residence and particular tasks (Strabo 8.5.4). This fits in nicely with the idea of equal parcels of land for all Spartiates, since the so-called *klêroi*, like the helots who worked them, were ultimately the property of the state which effectively lent them out to individual Spartiates. Strabo's statement is, however, inapplicable to the Classical period, and the idea that Spartans held equal lots of land then has come into serious doubt. Helots were probably individually owned, albeit with certain restrictions on their use. Xenophon wrote (*Lac.* 6.3) that Lycurgus allowed anyone in need to use another's hunting dogs, horses, or helots, here called "servants" (*oiketai*). Thus, Xenophon classes helots with horses and hunting dogs, which were indisputably private property (Xen. *Hell.* 6.4.11; Isoc. 6.55). Private property helots might have been, but the ban on manumission and foreign sale represented two significant restrictions on their owners' ability to dispose of such property. No securely attested instance of helots being sold outside Laconia and Messenia is known. The Laconian cook reputedly bought by Dionysius of Syracuse (Plut. *Mor.* 236f) could just as easily have been a chattel slave, and a small series of prehellenistic inscriptions recording individual manumissions at the sanctuary of Poseidon on Cape Taenarum resist interpretation (*IG* V.1 1228–33). On the other hand, some positive evidence exists for state involvement in the manumission of helots: during the Sphacteria crisis in 425/4, the authorities offered helots their freedom in exchange for helping to supply the Spartiates trapped on the island with food. The same prize was dangled before Laconian helots on the eve of the Theban invasion in 369, drawing so many volunteers that the Spartans swiftly retracted their offer (Xen. *Hell.* 6.5.28–9). In 424, the general Brasidas was accompanied on his Thracian campaign by 700 helot soldiers (Thuc. 4.80.5), who were voted their freedom after their return three years later (Thuc. 5.34.1). Finally, from the opening years of the Peloponnesian war onwards there was a class of non-Spartiate soldiers called *Neodamôdeis*, who, according to the most plausible theory, were helots who had served as hoplites and, after proving their worth and loyalty to the Spartan system, gained their freedom to serve several more years in the army (cf. Thuc. 5.34.1).

The repeated involvement of the Spartan state in the liberation of helots might appear to support the idea that the state in fact owned all the helots, since only an owner usually had the right of manumission. But in other cities even chattel slaves could be freed by a decree of the assembly. Slaves who had been conscripted to take part in the naval battle at Arginusae in 408 B.C.E. were manumitted and given Athenian citizenship (Xen. *Hell.* 1.6.24; *FGrH* 323a F25). Towards the end of the fourth century, the Rhodians manumitted and gave citizenship to the slaves who had fought against Demetrius Poliorcetes after buying them from their masters (Diod. Sic. 20.84.3). Despite some similarities, however, helots and chattel slaves were not interchangeable. Helots probably lived together in communities, perhaps even with some sort of vestigial social hierarchy, if the mysterious term *mnoionomos*, as has been tentatively proposed, denoted a customary chief of the helots. They apparently had some right to own property, since Thucydides implies that helots sailed in their own boats when called on to provision the Spartiates trapped on Sphacteria (4.26.5–6). In the third century, 6,000 helots answered Cleomenes III's call to enroll in the army and gain freedom for the not inconsiderable fee of five Attic minae per person (Plut. *Cleom.* 23.1). Helot (or perhaps more accurately Messenian) religious practice has been recognized in the reuse of several Mycenaean tholos tombs as cult places in Messenia during the Classical period.

Other, less positive distinctions tend to support Thucydides' negative view of the relationship between Spartans and helots. In fact, Spartans engaged in systematic and even ritualized degradation of helots: Theopompus in the fourth century characterized the situation of "the nation of helots" as "cruel and bitter in every way" (*FGrH* 115 F13). Myron of Priene stated that helots wore a sort of uniform consisting of a soft leather hat and a coat of animal skin (*FGrH* 106 F2). He also claimed that helots were flogged annually for no reason just so they would not forget they were slaves, and that any Spartiate who allowed a helot to become more physically developed than was suitable for a slave would be fined and the unlucky helot executed. Unfortunately, it is difficult to assess the validity of Myron's statements, since even the travel writer Pausanias, not usually known for his perspicacity in source criticism, castigates Myron for "not caring whether his statements appear to be false or improbable, especially in his history of the Messenians" – the source of these particular pieces of information (4.6.4).

Plutarch, a generally more dependable source, states that during festivals helots were compelled to consume unmixed wine – a drink beyond the pale for civilized Greeks – and then paraded into the public messes (*sussitia*) to make fools of themselves. The motive, we are assured, was to teach Spartan youths the evils of drunkenness, but a more likely reason was to humiliate the helots as representatives of their class (Plut. *Lyc.* 28.1; *Dem.* 1.5). Theopompus relates an anecdote about king Agesilaus during his campaign in Thrace that, even if not historically accurate in every detail, betrays a similar attitude towards helots (*FGrH* 115 F22). When the people of the island of Thasos sent gifts of well-fattened cattle and many other sorts of edible animal, along with cakes and sweetmeats of all kinds, Agesilaus kept the meat animals for himself and the Spartiates, while handing the confections to his helots because "they would be much less corrupted by eating them than he and the Spartans present would." His contemptuous sentiment rings true, at least: helots were deemed to be gluttonous and lacking in self-respect.

Violence marked helots' interactions with Spartans. Violence on an individual level came in the form of physical punishment by the master or, more unusually, at the hands of other Spartiates, who were empowered to punish any helot they caught misbehaving. On the state level was the mass murder of 2,000 helots. But there was more. Every year, the incoming ephors declared war on the helots (Arist. F543 Gigon), which Plutarch interpreted as a precaution against ritual pollution should anyone kill a helot in the course of the year (*Lyc.* 28.4). Random state-sanctioned killing probably took place on a more or less continuous basis, since Sparta regularly sent young elite soldiers out into the countryside as armed death squads to murder any helot they found on the roads after dark or any working in the fields they thought too robust (*Lyc.* 28.3). This policing function has often been identified with a traditional withdrawal from the city of all young Spartiates training for citizenship called the Crypteia.

Plutarch dismissed the declaration of war and murder of helots as post-Lycurgan institutions, introduced after the shock of 465/4 and motivated largely by fear of another revolt. Many modern historians follow him, but there is no evidence proving or disproving Plutarch's reconstruction: they may just as easily be as old as the institution of helotage itself. Indeed, the whole complex of practices designed to humiliate and cow the helots is not completely without parallel, for such ritualized degradation can be found in other slave societies in which lengthy cohabitation gave rise to a common cultural heritage. Harsh, even brutal, the Spartans may have been towards helots, but stupid they were not, as they realized (or circumstances forced them to realize) that repression alone cannot keep an inferior population down permanently. The repressed must be persuaded that they have a stake in the dominant society. Aristotle saw this as the crucial problem of Spartan helotage: if given too much licence, helots would forget their subservient place; but if treated too strictly, they would tend to become actively hostile (*Pol.* 2.6.4 [1269b]). Thinking perhaps of the newly resurgent Messenia, Aristotle felt that the Spartans had not found a solution, but the institution of helotage, in which a remarkably small minority wielded absolute power over a servile population that vastly outnumbered them, lasted for about a century and a half after Aristotle formulated his criticism. Hostility certainly existed: the subversive Cinadon at the beginning of the fourth century thought he could capitalize on the discontent of Sparta's lower classes – helots among them – who hated the Spartiates so much they could eat them raw (Xen. *Hell.* 3.3.5–6). But no uprising broke out when Cinadon was arrested and publicly executed.

Sparta's strategy for co-opting the helots was twofold. One involved the state's interaction with helots, the other took place on an individual and domestic level. After 424, when the first helots to serve as hoplites were sent off with Brasidas to Thrace, receiving their freedom and the title *Brasideioi* upon their return, military service became a prime avenue of advancement for ambitious helot males. In 421 the *Neodamôdeis* appear (Thuc. 5.34.1). Their situation was different from other helot hoplites in that they had apparently already been manumitted, as their name "New Citizens" implies. They were probably ex-helots who had served as light-armed troops or in some other ancillary capacity before being freed to serve as hoplites. From a force of only 500 in 421, the Neodamodeis grew to about 2,000 by 397, another sign of the decline in the Spartiate population (Xen. *Hell.* 3.4.7; *Ages.* 1.7). For the Spartans, who had to face the consequences of an increasingly critical drop in citizen numbers, they constituted a useful pool of manpower for less-than-crucial duties such as guarding supplies, garrisoning, and for missions in which they did not want to risk precious Spartiate lives. In 413, for example, 600 of the best helots and Neodamodeis were sent with other allied hoplites to reinforce the troops under Gylippus at Syracuse (Thuc. 7.19.3). The recruitment process is completely unknown, but it has plausibly been suggested that helots must have volunteered.

On an individual level, co-optation involved creating ties of loyalty that would bind helots to the households of their masters. Most simply, helots would be taken from agricultural work to serve as household servants. The helots so chosen would probably have been members of helot families already with some privileges and perhaps even a tradition of "service." Spartan households needed an unusually large number of domestic attendants, both male and female, since tasks such as wool working, which was usually carried out by the unmarried free girls in a Greek house, were slaves' work at Sparta (Xen. *Lac.* 1.3–4). Servile attendants are mentioned several times in the sources without being explicitly identified, but these servants were most likely helots. The relationship between some of these helots and their owners could, it has been argued, be quite close and lasting. The most visible relationship was that between a Spartiate and his personal attendant. Herodotus famously stated that each Spartiate at the battle of Plataea was accompanied by seven helots, and Eurytus was led back to the battle of Thermopylae by his helot servant (9.28.2, 7.229.1). Plato stressed that the youths undergoing the Crypteia had to fend for themselves, thereby implying that at other times they would have had valets to cater to their needs (*Leg.* 633b). Several ancient sources name these attendants as *mothônes*; one observes that they were slaves reared alongside the free children to be their companions and attendants (Harpocration s.v. *mothôn* 336; schol. ad Ar. *Plut.* 279; schol. ad Ar. *Eq.* 634; Hesychius s.v. *mothônas*).

Sexual relations between masters and slaves must have been commonplace. Among the troops king Agesipolis led in the Olynthus campaign of 381 were men Xenophon calls "bastard sons (*nothoi*) of Spartiates, very good to look at and not unacquainted with the city's ideals" (*Hell.* 5.3.9). The *nothoi* were almost certainly offspring fathered on helot women by Spartiate men. We have no way of knowing how many, if any, of these sexual relationships were fully voluntary on the helot women's part; sexual domination is, after all, another way to express social domination. But the Spartans seem to have accepted the half-helot products of these unions as closer to their own status than their mothers' and to have included them in the life of the city to some extent. Xenophon's reference to the *nothoi* being familiar with the city's ideals may mean they could even participate in citizen training and the common messes. Traditions such as the communal feasts on the second day of the annual festival of the Hyacinthia, at which Spartiates dined with their acquaintances and slaves (*FGrH* 588), would also have contributed to the formation of bonds between Spartiate households and their house helots, though we can assume that field helots enjoyed no such ties. That must have been doubly true of the helots working Spartiate land in Messenia; few if any would have been thought trust-worthy enough to be allowed into a Spartan house.

How effective this carrot-and-stick approach was can best be judged by helotage's long survival into the early years of the second century. Spartan brutality was balanced to a certain extent by the promise of a degree of social advancement and the ability to share in the Spartan mystique. But we should not glamorize the Spartan treatment of domestic helots; their attitude evidently shocked even their Greek con-temporaries, who did not share our aversion to buying and selling human beings. A new insight into the topography of the city of Sparta brings this point home. For many years, the sanctuary of Poseidon Taenarius, where Pausanias was entrapped into revealing his seditious plans and from which Spartans sacrilegiously extracted, then executed a group of helot suppliants (Thuc. 1.128.1), has been confidently identified as the temple of Poseidon on Cape Taenarum, about 80 km south of Sparta. The helots were consequently thought to be escapees from Spartan estates who made their way there. But it has recently been established that the sanctuary Thucydides describes was a satellite cult precinct located in the city itself, so that the helots more likely ran away from domestic service than from the fields. Life as a helot, even in a household set-ting, was to live as the least free of men (DK 88 F37).

What were the helots, after all? Although the name "helot" was unique to the Laconian lands, similar dependent populations could be found in several other areas of the Greek world, for example the Penestai in Thessaly, the Mariandynians in the territory of Heraclea Pontica on the Black Sea (Plat. *Leg.* 6.776d), and the Kyllikyrians at Syracuse (Hdt. 7.155; [Arist.] *Const. Syr.* F586). Little beyond their names is known to us, however. Recently, parallels have been drawn from other soci-eties in which systems of unfree labor operated to provide models to explain the exiguous Spartan evidence; they have been especially fruitful for understanding the methods Spartans may have used to exploit the potential of their landholdings. The question of their status remains unclear. To the Spartans they were simply slaves (Thuc. 5.23.3) but, as we have seen, helotage was different from the chattel slavery pre-dominant elsewhere in the Greek world. Perhaps the best answer to the question of what the helots were is that they were just that, helots. This is not as frivolous a solution as it may seem, for the word itself and its associated verb *heilôteuein* ("to make into a helot") are found almost always associated with Sparta in all of the surviving texts from antiquity. In the very, very few cases when they were used metaphorically – by Isocrates and by Theopompus – the power of their imagery depended upon awareness of the Spartan institution. Helotage was characteristic of and unique to Sparta.

The other major non-Spartiate element in the Laconian population were the perioeci ("dwellers around"), who lived in communities scattered throughout Laconia and in Messenia. They were freeborn Lacedaemonians, as we have seen, but lacking the rights (and obligations) of Spartiates, namely access to the common messes, attendance in the Assembly, and election to any Spartan office. The perioecic cities were dependent *poleis* allowed a measure of internal autonomy but with foreign policy controlled by Sparta. Nonetheless, this apparently did not stop the Argives from attempting in the 470s to curry favor among the perioeci of northeastern Laconia by appointing a man from Oinous as their diplomatic representative (*proxenos*) (*SEG* 13 239). It has been suggested that Sparta had bilateral treaties with the perioecic cities that required them to follow the Spartans wherever they might lead, but the extant sources give no hint of this. The relationship was unlikely to have been so formalized; rather, it developed over the long term as Sparta's influence grew and the other Laconian communities looked to it for protection as well as a market for their goods. A clue to this relationship may be that some perioecic cities were thought of as "colonies" of Sparta, probably because no formal treaties existed. Instead, the perioeci were tied to Sparta by a complex web of cultic, social, and economic bonds similar to those binding true colonies (*apoikoi*) to their mother cities.

The origins of the perioeci are a matter for speculation. Ephorus (*FGrH* 70 F117) maintained that they were foreigners invited in to repopulate Laconia after the departure of the aboriginal inhabitants, later stripped of their equal status with Spartiates under King Agis I. Replacement of the Achaean inhabitants is also a motif in Pausanias' accounts (3.2.6) of the "Dorianization" of Amyclae, Geronthrae, and Pharis. Also, elements of the settler population who were dissatisfied with their lot might find themselves expelled from Laconia. Both motifs stress the ethnic and social homogeneity of the free Laconian population in the Classical period, as well as the commanding role of Sparta. Stories such as the founding of perioecic Asine in Messenia for refugees from the Argolid (Paus. 4.8.3, 14.3) reinforce the impression that perioecic cities were essentially expressions of Spartan power, while the resettling of Aeginetans at Thyrea in 431 (Thuc. 2.27.2) shows that the Spartans continued the practice well into historical times. Archaeological evidence exists, too. Most strikingly, it was recently discovered that the site of the perioecic city of Sellasia, northeast of Sparta, was first settled only in the mid-sixth century. Although the evidence presently available is insufficient to state categorically that Sellasia was founded by an act of the Spartan state, it remains a distinct possibility.

Culturally and linguistically, perioeci were indistinguishable from Spartiates by the Classical period. Their hoplites formed part of the Lacedaemonian army and by the later fifth century marched alongside Spartiates to war. Unlike the helots, perioeci were, with only a few (Messenian-based) exceptions, remarkably loyal until Sparta faltered in the fourth century B.C.E. Perioeci could be trusted with sensitive intelligence missions (Thuc. 8.6.4) or to command large naval forces (Thuc. 8.22.1). Their festivals attracted Spartan visitors, like the magnificent Damonon and his son, victors in chariot racing and athletics at several Laconian sanctuaries (*IG* V.1 213). Although not bound to the rigid Spartan social system, they, or at least their elite, identified themselves wholeheartedly with the dominant culture, for example volunteering *en masse* for an expedition to Asia Minor in 381 (Xen. *Hell.* 3.5.8–9). This phenomenon is expressed visually through Laconian art, usually thought to have been produced mostly if not exclusively by perioeci.

It is well known that a Spartan's only trade was war. Herodotus (2.167.2) and Aristotle (*Pol.* 8.1.1–2.2 [1337b]) noted that Spartans disdained manual labor even more than other Greeks. In Xenophon (*Lac.* 7.2) and Plutarch (*Lyc.* 24.2) this hostile attitude became a law, backed up by the authority of Sparta's lawgiver Lycurgus. Perioeci are thus imagined to have supplied nearly all of the Spartans' material needs, from drinking cups to spears and shields. But the reality may have been more complex. For instance, pottery, as we have seen, was produced in Laconia well before a rigid distinction between Spartiates and perioeci was drawn. Also, several sixth-century Laconian sculptors may well have been Spartan citizens, and there is some archaeological evidence for pottery production within the city during the Archaic and Classical periods. Moreover, the immense number of small lead votives – wreaths, branches, warriors, fantastic beings, and the like – found at the sanctuary of Artemis Orthia compared to other Laconian sanctuaries strongly implies they were manufactured at Sparta. Outside Sparta, none of the sites in the area of the Laconia Survey, with the possible exception of Sellasia, was large enough to support specialist artisans, leading the surveyors to conclude that the source of manufactured items even for perioecic use was in fact Sparta itself. Excavations at perioecic Geronthrae, 26 km to the southeast, have produced an iron anvil as evidence for industrial activity in the Archaic period, but this is a slender thread from which to hang a Laconian arms industry.

Distance is another factor weighing against Geronthrae specifically being a major supplier of finished goods for Sparta. A similar objection can be made against the site of Analipsi in northern Laconia as the sole source of Laconian red-figure pottery, a local substitute for the more famous Athenian variety, which began during the Peloponnesian War and ended in the 370s. That cartloads of goods (especially breakable pottery) trundled from specifically designated production centers along rough roads over quite long distances to market in Sparta presupposes a highly developed road network and a centralized, even command, economy that would have been impossible to maintain given the administrative resources available at the time. The majority of objects produced at these and other as-yet-undiscovered places were far more likely normally for local use and trade within a quite restricted area. Notable exceptions to this rule would be luxury objects of bronze like the vast, highly decorated wine-mixing bowl (*kratêr*) commissioned by

5.1   View west from the acropolis of Geronthrae to the Eurotas valley

the Spartan state as a gift for Croesus of Lydia (Hdt. 1.69.1) and the famous krater found in a royal burial at Vix in southern France.

Most perioecic settlements were probably very small, with only 400–600 inhabitants who lived spread out on farms around an "urban" center containing communal cult sites that also functioned as a local market, with their public affairs, such as they were, under the control of a small, landed elite. How perioecic social and governmental institutions functioned we have no idea, though a fragmentary terracotta roof tile from Geronthrae bearing a stamp that can be restored "Of Apollo. The people of Geronthrae" lightens the darkness somewhat, since the stamp indicates the tile came from a publicly funded repair of the temple in the early Hellenistic period. Whether the construction was paid for by a special collection or from a public treasury funded by taxation of some sort is unknown.

Excavation of a rural shrine near ancient Aegiae, a few kilometers north of Gytheum, has also provided some information on perioecic religion. Cult at the site began in the seventh century with the construction of an apsidal building and was directed towards a local hero perhaps named Timagenes. By the sixth century, this building had been transformed into a Doric temple with a female cult statue, probably of Artemis. A few miniature lead votives may indicate visitors from Sparta. These votives also suggest that the Artemis of Aegiae shared some traits with her more famously militant Spartan cousin, since slightly over a quarter of them represent warriors. Three other offerings reinforce this impression: a bronze Corinthian-style helmet, a strigil (athletic body-scraper), and a single inscribed jumping weight (*haltôr*) dedicated to Timagenes by Tachistolaos ("Swiftest of the People"), probably for a victory in a local athletic festival. As at Sparta, Artemis here seems to have functioned as a nurturer of youth (*kourotrophos*) for both boys and girls, though the nature of the votives shows that a majority of her devotees were female. Perhaps the most significant thing about this assemblage is how little it differs from cult assemblages found in or near Sparta itself – a strong indication of Sparta's dominant role in Laconian culture.

As mentioned before, Spartans may have presented themselves as the natural leaders of Laconia by playing on the associations of the ancient designation *Lakedaimonia*. The stories of the early post-conquest years in turn reinforced a sense of ethnic unity between Spartans and perioeci reflected in material culture. But more tangible methods were also in use. The kings held estates in the territories of many perioecic cities, which may have been leased to perioeci (Xen. *Lac.* 15.3). Perioeci also paid regular tribute directly to the kings (Pl. *Alc.* I 122e). Representatives from the perioeci throughout Laconia were required to attend royal funerals (Hdt. 6.58.2–3). All of these practices emphasized the direct relationship between the perioeci, as Lacedaemonians themselves, and the king. Although not Spartiates, the perioeci seem likewise to have been liable to the occasional war tax (*eisphorai*) (Arist. *Pol.* 2.6.23 [1271b]), and the so-called "foster sons" (*trophimoi*) who went through the Spartan citizen training system may well have been sons of rich perioeci. Perhaps the most succinct way of expressing the place of the perioeci relative to the kings and Spartans is to regard them as "Lacedaemonian citizens," with personal freedom but without the full rights (and onerous duties) of Spartiates.

6

Governing Sparta

It is easy to underestimate the kings of Sparta. For Aristotle, a Spartan king was nothing more than a sort of permanent army chief-of-staff (Arist. *Pol.* 3.9.2 [1285a]), while Xenophon made him into a run-of-the-mill *polis* magistrate (Xen. *Lac.* 15.1). The kings' powers seem pale in comparison with those of the ephors. But Lysander, the hero of Aegospotami, schemed to become king, not ephor, and the names of kings are far more prominent than those of any ephor. Spartan kings were not absolute rulers in any sense of the term, but they had the resources to deploy patronage and prestigious (and lucrative) postings, so that in the hands of dynamic, ambitious, and talented incumbents the kingship might gain an abiding, indeed dominant influence over the course of Spartan policy for decades.

Herodotus saw the kingship as one of the institutions marking Sparta as a distinct society. The survival of a Greek monarchy into the Classical period would have been reason enough to attract his attention, but the Spartans had an even stronger claim to uniqueness – a dyarchy, or double kingship, held by two different royal families both claiming Heraclid ancestry. The Spartans characteristically attributed the foundation of their double kingship to an oracle that assigned joint rule to Eurysthenes and Procles, the twin sons of Aristodemus, the great-great-grandson of Heracles. According to Herodotus (Hdt. 6.52), after Aristodemus' death their mother Argeia refused to divulge who was the elder so that both would rule. In answer to a petition sent by the Spartan authorities, the Delphic oracle commanded that the two sons together should become kings but that the elder be accorded greater honor. Curiously, it was a Messenian who advised the Spartans to observe the order in which Argeia washed the twins. If she always followed the same routine they would know which was the elder. Argeia did wash the twins in the same order, so the Spartans took the elder son and raised him at public expense, naming him Eurysthenes and his brother Procles. Their sons, Agis and Eurypon, in turn, became the eponymous ancestors of the two Spartan royal houses. Beyond explaining the origin of the Spartan dyarchy, the story also performs a vital function by grounding the establishment of the double kingship in a divine command and providing a convenient *aition* for the traditional ascendancy of the Agiads over their junior partners, the Eurypontids.

Lists of Spartan kings going all the way back to Heracles circulated widely in antiquity. They must have also varied wildly, as no surviving two are exactly alike. Herodotus' rhetorical fanfare announcing the entrance of Leonidas I, the hero of Thermopylae, into his *Histories* (Hdt. 7.204) presents the earliest list of the members of the Agiad house, while his description of Leotychidas II's command of the Greek fleet in 479 contains one for the Eurypontids (Hdt. 8.131.2). Later versions are provided by Plutarch (*Lyc.* 1–2) and Pausanias (Paus. 3.2.1–7, 3.1–8, 7.1–10). The accuracy of these lists has important implications beyond the merely Spartan, because ancient scholars used them *faute de mieux* as a chronological framework for early Greek history. Luckily, we do not have to deal with such implications here. Suffice it to say that the lists evidently underwent so much scholarly "correction" over the centuries that what historical value they might once have had was lost, at least in the upper reaches. The lists must originally have been orally transmitted from generation to generation, preserved in the same way as ruler lists in other oral societies, eventually taking the form we see in Herodotus.

The lists have certain obvious attributes in common with oral lists: several of the names in the earliest generations of the Eurypontid list are personifications of concepts essential to Spartan self-definition – Soos ("Safety/Stability"), his grandson Prytanis ("Councillor"), and the latter's son Eunomos ("Goodlaw"). Further back, we find the twins Agis and Eurypon, the eponyms of the two ruling houses, another feature of oral lists, which usually "preserve" the names of dynastic founders. The other feature, even more striking, is the regular, unbroken succession from father to son over the first sixteen generations in the Agiad line and the first twenty in the Eurypontid. Scholars have, of course, long realized that this is completely impossible, though attempts have been made to salvage some chronological sense from the lists regardless. However unreliable these lists may be as evidence for the early kings of Sparta, they remain interesting as historical artifacts. For example, it is unlikely to be a coincidence that several of the ancestors of king Theopompus, whom Tyrtaeus mentions in connection with Sparta's victory over the Messenians (F5 West[2]), bear names related to ideas that were surely bandied about in the political debates of the seventh century. Did the Eurypontid king or kings of the time present themselves as the hereditary guarantors of stable government?

Although the Spartans may have been confident that they knew how their kings got their positions, modern historians are less fortunate. Many different scenarios have been proposed for the development of the dyarchy, from the kings as leaders of two bands of Dorian invaders who split up as they advanced into Laconia along both sides of the Eurotas, to the Agiads initially being kings of Achaean Amyclae who entered into a power-sharing agreement with the Dorian Eurypontids. Now that the very historicity of a Dorian invasion has been cast into serious doubt, as we have seen, and given the appalling unreliability of the earlier entries in the king lists, all such theories must be set aside. In their place is something much more modest, yet surprising: the first kings we can be absolutely sure reigned together are Leon and Agasicles, in the earlier sixth century (Hdt. 1.65.1). Theopompus and Polydorus, who reigned in the previous century (*Lyc.* 8.9), are also good candidates as joint kings. In his account of the passage of the Great Rhetra, Plutarch implied that Tyrtaeus referred to them both in a passage from *Eunomia*, "From Pytho where they heard Phoebus, they brought home the god's prophecy and infallible words" (F4 West[2]). However, since their names do not appear in the surviving text, their joint kingship may well be a conjecture of Plutarch or, more likely, of Aristotle before him.

The kings might have enjoyed no outward sign of their position, such as palaces or crowns, but they possessed exalted status. They were not properly "Equals" (*Homoioi*) like the other Spartiates, since heirs apparent did not (as a rule) go through the rigors of Spartan citizen training (Plut. *Ages.* 1). In fact, the kings were not really even members of the *polis* itself. In a monthly ritual that established a kind of contract, oaths were sworn between the ephors on behalf of the *polis* and the kings (Xen. *Lac.* 15.7). As descendants of Heracles, the kings were Achaeans, not Dorians, which also set them apart. Cleomenes I justified his presence in the temple of Athena on the Athenian

Acropolis when he replied to the priestess who forbade him entry as a Dorian, "Woman, I'm no Dorian. I'm an Achaean" (Hdt. 5.72.3). The Spartan letter before the battle of Plataea demanding compensation from Xerxes for the death of Leonidas distinguished explicitly between Spartans and their rulers – "O King of the Medes, the Lacedaemonians and the Heraclids living in Sparta demand justice for murder" (Hdt. 8.114.2).

As a sign of their special status, kings received a whole catalog of honors and privileges. These two dozen *gerea*, as Herodotus called them (6.56–8), spanned the domestic and military spheres and were bestowed in death as well as in life. Although the royal *gerea* included priesthoods and rights to certain parts of sacrificial animals, they were in no way considered to be a "god-given" right; Herodotus is clear when he states that the Spartans themselves "granted" (*dedôkasi*) these privileges to their kings (Hdt. 6.56). Spartans probably thought of them as part of the monthly contractual oaths sworn by the kings and the ephors, in which the kings pledged to reign according to the city's existing laws and the ephors to preserve the kingship unshaken, if they kept their word.

In the religious sphere, the kings held first and foremost the priesthoods of Zeus Lacedaemonius and Zeus Uranius (Hdt. 6.56). In addition, Xenophon tells us that they alone had the right to perform all public sacrifices while at home (*Lac.* 15.2). While on campaign, they were responsible for all military sacrifices, from the initial offerings to Zeus Agetor before the army left home and those to Zeus again and Athena when the army reached the frontier, to those crucial pre-battle rituals when victims' entrails would be professionally consulted to ascertain the favor of the gods (Xen. *Lac.* 13.1–5). As commanders-in-chief of the Spartan army, the kings initially even enjoyed the joint right to wage war whenever and wherever they pleased (Hdt. 6.56). After the split between Cleomenes I and Demaratus stymied the vast allied forces the Spartans had raised to invade Attica in 506, however, the Spartans decided that henceforward only a single king might lead troops on campaign at any one time, and was to be accompanied by two ephors (Hdt. 5.75.2). This nullifed any residual power to declare war the kings might have had, and from then on the Assembly voted on questions of war and peace under the direction of the ephors. In battle, the king usually (but not always) fought on the right wing, in the place of honor usually reserved for commanders, and in the company of an elite guard of 100 men picked from the 300-strong crack corps of *hippeis* (knights), who, despite their title, fought as infantrymen (Xen. *Lac.* 13.6; *Hell.* 6.4.13–14; cf. Thuc. 5.72.4).

Peacetime kingly prerogatives included front-row seats at public festivals and the right to choose two officials called Pythioi, who were sent to consult the Delphic oracle on matters of state and who ate with the king at public expense. Any oracles received were preserved in an archive to which only the kings and the Pythioi had access (Hdt. 6.57.2). The kings also had the right to appoint *proxenoi*, which may mean they had the highly unusual power to designate Spartans as representatives of other cities' interests at Sparta – a power which, except for this instance, was exclusively within the purview of the foreign city being represented. As regards food, Herodotus says that a king received double portions in the communal messes, as well as an allotment of grain and wine should he wish to dine at home, so that he might host private guests (Hdt. 6.57.3). The rules were strictly kept, as Agis II (not the ephors' favorite king) learned after returning from campaign in the early years of the Peloponnesian War, when he ordered his ration sent round so that he might dine with his wife at home. The polemarchs refused and even fined him the next day because, in a fit of pique, he refused to perform the customary sacrifices (Plut. *Lyc.* 12.5).

Kings were charged with keeping the public roads in good repair, probably to facilitate rapid mobilization of the army. They oversaw all adoptions and alone designated the legal guardian of an heiress (*patrouchos*), whose father had died before making arrangements for her. A *patrouchos* literally "held the patrimony" of her family and guidance was thought essential to ensure she married appropriately. The Athenian custom was to marry her off to her nearest male relative so that the property remained under her family's control. If a Spartan *patrouchos* had not been betrothed by her father either before his death or in his will, the king adjudicated between claimants to be her legal guardian, affording the successful candidate the right to marry her himself or to anyone he chose. Adoptions also involved inheritance, since the adoption of males into families without living sons would provide heirs for the family estates. The royal involvement in family matters such as the marriage of heiresses and adoptions shows the level of Spartan state interest in such fundamentally important socioeconomic activities. The final privilege living kings received was to employ proxies in the Gerousia, a right no other Spartan possessed. As laid down in the Great Rhetra, the two kings were members *ex officio* of the Gerousia. Thus, in the event of their absence from meetings, usually on campaign outside Laconia, the Spartans assigned the kings' votes to the two members of the Gerousia most closely related to them (Hdt. 6.57.4–5).

Modest though their state-sanctioned perks may appear to have been in life, in death kings were the focus of rituals and honors unparalleled elsewhere in Greece. Herodotus perceptively found them comparable only to the funerals of the Great King of Persia (Hdt. 6.58.2). When a king died, horsemen took the news to every corner of Laconia. At Sparta, one free adult man and woman from every household was compelled to dress in mourning on pain of a hefty fine; from the rest of Laconia, perioeci were required to attend the funeral. Crowds at royal funerals could reach many thousands, since even helots were included. The dead king was always mourned as the best king of all and worshipped as a semi-divine hero. During the ten-day mourning period after his burial, there was no commercial or political activity. Lastly, upon his accession, the new king declared an amnesty for anyone who was in debt to the public treasury (Hdt. 6.58).

Herodotus was justified in finding nothing comparable in the rather restrained burial practices of his contemporary fellow Greeks, but Spartan funerals in general were probably more elaborate in earlier centuries. Tyrtaeus in the seventh century promised fallen warriors public burial with extensive mourning by both young and old, tombs among those of the renowned, and immortality in the time to come (F12 West[2], lines 27–34). Even dead civilians rated mourning by all their slaves, both male and female (F7 West[2]). While archaeology cannot as yet confirm Tyrtaeus' picture in all its details, some evidence suggests funerals could sometimes be more lavish in the late Geometric and Archaic periods than the fifth-century norm. In and around Sparta, several large clay amphorae that marked graves of aristocratic warriors have been found, elaborately decorated with mythological and martial motifs, together with ivory plaques depicting the laying-out of the corpse.

Impressive as his funeral might have been, the powers of a living king appear less than awe-inspiring apart from his total command of the armed forces in the field. At home, he could be taken more or less for a combination of priest and family court judge. But appearances can be deceiving. We should first make two distinctions: first, between the role of the kings as entrenched in the Spartan constitution – essentially the prerogatives and rights just discussed – and their role in Spartan politics; second, between the kings' economic resources and their deployment of those resources to further their political aims. At Sparta, in other words, the kings were expected to politic as well as to reign. Only they, along with only the ephors and gerontes, had the right to speak in the Spartan assembly; all others needed an invitation. Still more significantly, in the Assembly, the kings spoke first (Thuc. 1.79.1–2).

Outside the Assembly, Spartan kings routinely utilized their private resources to further their political interests. They had the purses to do it, as their riches were reputed to surpass not only those of other Spartans, but even those of all other Greeks (Pl. *Alc.* I 123a). This may be an exaggeration, because king Pleistoanax was forced into exile in 446 B.C.E. when he could not pay a staggering fine of 15 talents (*FGrH* 70 F193). Even so, in the normal run of things, the kings had ample wealth not only from their royal estates, located in the territory of the perioeci, but also from the tribute they received directly from the perioeci, and of course, from any booty that came their way.

Another source of potential influence lay in the very nature of the kingship itself. In Sparta, like other *poleis* either democratic or oligarchic, the vast majority of the offices of state were annual. The Gerousia, whose members had lifelong tenure, was the single exception. Even the powerful board of ephors changed every year. This situation gave a capable king a significant advantage – continuity. With the king's capacity to dispense patronage in the form of gifts and behind-the-scenes influence over several years came the opportunity to shape Spartan policy. The two kings who reigned at the beginning and at the end of Sparta's greatest period of power – Cleomenes I and Agesilaus II – best exemplify the latent power of the kingship. Both dominated their eras at Sparta. Both forged foreign policy according to their will. It is probably no coincidence that their reigns were among the longest of any Spartan kings, giving them the opportunity over the years to create a formidable "king's party" to defend their interests at home against any rivals.

That the power of the kingship depended on the personality of the king is well illustrated by the fate of Cleomenes' fellow king, the unfortunate Demaratus, who vainly struggled to assert his position in the shadow of Cleomenes at the end of the sixth and beginning of the fifth centuries. The conflict between the two first erupted in the disastrous Athenian campaign of 506, when Demaratus caused the Peloponnesian coalition to collapse by returning home, ostensibly because he objected to the invasion on moral grounds. Although Herodotus assures us that he had had no previous quarrel with his senior partner, one cannot help but think that such a drastic step was the culmination of a long period of resentment (Hdt. 5.75.1). Subsequently excluded from even a share of military command, he attempted to win back some prestige with a victory in the four-horse chariot race at the Olympics in 504, a unique feat for a king of Sparta (Hdt. 6.70.3). Although Spartans could, and often did, attain leadership positions solely on the strength of their Olympic victories, Demaratus was still unable to break Cleomenes' iron grip on Spartan foreign policy. His attempt to undermine Cleomenes again, by sabotaging his mission to extract hostages from the Aeginetans in 492, proved to be his undoing, for Cleomenes retaliated by having him deposed on the grounds of illegitimacy, and he deserted to the Persians to become one of Xerxes' advisers (Hdt. 6.67.1).

At the end of the fifth century, Agesilaus II unexpectedly came to power through the political influence of his former lover, Lysander. But their relationship could not withstand the pressures of Spartan public life, and Lysander soon discovered that the new king was a formidable master of the game of status. Throughout his long reign, Agesilaus showed himself particularly adept at the grubby fundamentals of Spartan politics, binding followers to him through gifts and peddling his influence to aid his allies. One event stands out as exemplifying this king's cynically effective deployment of his power. The notorious trial of the commander Sphodrias in 378 allowed Agesilaus to transform a damaging international incident which revealed Sparta's complete lack of a coherent foreign policy into an opportunity to extend his personal influence and reinforce his domination of the domestic political scene (Xen. *Hell.* 5.4.20–33). Sphodrias, commander of Spartan forces in Boeotian Thespiae, had made an unprovoked incursion into Athenian territory one night with the announced intention of capturing the Piraeus by daybreak despite its being almost 100 km distant from his base, over very difficult terrain. Not only were Sparta and Athens officially at peace, but Spartan ambassadors were actually in Athens carrying out negotiations at the time of the raid. Xenophon's explanation that the Thebans bribed Sphodrias, while quite plausible given the sorry record of Spartan commanders outside Laconia, is usually rejected by historians, who mostly prefer to see the hand of Cleombrotus, Agesilaus' co-king and rival, behind Sphodrias' "cowboy" tactics (Diod. Sic. 15.29.5). Perhaps Cleombrotus approved Sphodrias' raid as a way of embarrassing Agesilaus on the international scene and reducing his influence at home; doubts have even been raised as to whether the attack had any purpose beyond stirring up mischief. But if Cleombrotus hoped to take the other king down a peg, he was to be disappointed.

Immediately arrested by the Athenians, the Spartan ambassadors only gained their freedom by vociferously announcing their and their superiors' complete ignorance of Sphodrias' actions and assuring them that his fate was sealed. Consequently, the ephors called Sphodrias to trial, but given the hostile climate and the apparently open-and-shut case against him, he ignored the summons home. The court that tried him in absentia was split into three: the "friends" of Cleombrotus, who would acquit Sphodrias; Agesilaus and his supporters, whose influence was daunting; and the uncommitted, who were thought to be shocked by the severity of Sphodrias' crime. Sphodrias then played his ace – his son, Cleonymus, whose good looks had previously attracted the eye of Agesilaus' own son, Archidamus, with whom he had had an affair. Archidamus, at Cleonymus' request, persuaded his own father to use his influence in Sphodrias' favor in the trial. Once it became clear that Agesilaus was going to vote to acquit, the open-and-shut case became a triumph for Sphodrias and he went free.

Nothing shows the importance of personal influence better than this trial. Agesilaus' own status, attained through decades of (only partly) successful military action combined with deployment of his own personal resources, had attracted to him a formidable set of partisans whose social power was such that even those Spartans not specifically aligned with it would follow his lead in matters of importance. His stated reason for acquitting Sphodrias – that Sparta needed such soldiers – may seem questionable to us, but Agesilaus came out of the affair with his prestige substantially enhanced (Xen. *Hell.* 5.4.32). More than just superbly outfoxing Cleombrotus' attempt to embarrass him, he had effectively stolen the allegiance of an important member of Cleombrotus' own faction, for we can expect that Sphodrias would from then on have become more amenable to Agesilaus' view of foreign policy than he had been. In fact, Xenophon tells us that he died honorably at Leuctra seven years later, along with Cleombrotus, fighting against the Thebans, Agesilaus' bitter personal enemies.

Agesilaus' career also reveals some of the methods a king might use to attract supporters to his side and cement their loyalty. Agesilaus' friends and relatives enjoyed high military command; incoming members of the Gerousia received a newly woven garment, called a *chlaina*, and an ox from the king's household and estates (Plut. *Ages.* 4.5). As we have seen in the case of Sphodrias, Agesilaus proffered his support under certain circumstances even to those attached to his political opponents – a benefit also enjoyed by Phoebidas, instigator of another ostensibly unauthorized Spartan military action, the illegal occupation of Thebes' acropolis in 382. Unable this time to sway the court to acquit Phoebidas of the capital charges, the king persuaded it to inflict a lesser penalty and perhaps paid the fine from his own pocket (Diod. Sic. 15.20.2). Extensive estates allowed a king like Agesilaus to be generous: he also made loans to impoverished Spartiate families, thus binding them to himself through ties of obligation. Though hardly all-powerful despots, Spartan kings could be a predominant force in the city's politics and social life. But a king's power derived from his personal skill in exploiting the potentialities of the resources at his disposal, not directly from the kingship's position in the Spartan governmental hierarchy.

The office that did possess considerable power precisely because of its place in Spartan government was the ephorate. Its earliest known incumbent was also one of the best-known Spartans in antiquity. Chilon's fame as one of the Seven Sages grew through the centuries, so that by the third century C.E. he appears in Diogenes Laertius' collection of potted biographies fully equipped with a corpus of written works, including a 200-line poem, a collection of letters, and a set of appropriately laconic aphorisms (DL 1.3 [68–73]).

For Herodotus, the earliest author to mention him, Chilon's fame arose from his uncanny foresight. His Chilon urged the Athenian Hippocrates (future father of Pisistratus), who had found cauldrons for the sacrificial meat at Olympia mysteriously boiling of their own accord, to avoid producing a son or to disown any son already born (Hdt. 1.59.2). Later, when Demaratus tried to advise Xerxes to seize the island of Cythera off Laconia's southern coast to use as a base for ravaging the mainland, he added that Chilon, one of the wisest Spartans, had once said that it would be better if the island sank into the sea since he recognized its strategic importance to an enemy (Hdt. 7.235.2). Neither of these anecdotes has a strong claim to historicity – Chilon's meeting with Hippocrates is chronologically impossible and his fears about Cythera smack of *post eventum* prophecy, since the Athenian Tolmides occupied the island in 456/5, several decades before Herodotus composed his *Histories*. For modern historians, Chilon is best known as a member of the board of ephors ("supervisors"), and his elevation to the post dated to around 550 B.C.E. Diogenes Laertius in fact reports that one of his predecessors credited

Chilon with instituting the ephors as yoke-mates for the kings, while another attributed the ephorate's foundation to the lawgiver Lycurgus several centuries earlier (DL 1.3 [68]). The great power ephors wielded in Classical Sparta seems to have led to a fierce internal debate over their legitimacy, a debate whose vague outlines can be glimpsed at times from the early fourth to the later third century B.C.E. In the later fifth and early fourth centuries respectively, Herodotus (1.65.5) and Xenophon (*Lac.* 8.1–3, 5) accepted that the ephorate was an integral part of Lycurgus' settlement. But by the later fourth century, Aristotle in his *Politics* (5.11.2 [1313a]) carefully distinguished between the two original pillars of the Spartan constitution – the kingship and the council of elders (Gerousia) – which existed "from the beginning" and the ephorate which was later introduced by king Theopompus in order to enable the kingship to last longer by moderating its power. Plato reflected the same opinion in the *Laws* (692a) when, without naming names, he referred to a "savior" who made the ephors a moderating influence on the Gerousia and kings.

Modern historians have traced the change in attitude toward the foundation of the ephorate back to a mysterious pamphlet that King Pausanias wrote during his exile following the death of the powerful general Lysander in 395. Unsurprisingly, hard evidence about the precise nature of Pausanias' booklet is almost completely non-existent. Only one source refers to it, a fragment of Ephorus preserved in Strabo's *Geography* (8.5.5), which is relevant to another crux of Spartan historiography, the Great Rhetra. This short passage has been so plagued by problematic manuscript readings that it is unclear whether the text says Pausanias wrote his pamphlet "on behalf of" (*huper*) or "against" (*kata*) the laws of Lycurgus. However, his enmity towards Lysander makes it more likely that he was promoting his own vision of the Lycurgan constitution against what he viewed as its recent distortion. Pausanias wanted to abolish the ephorate (Arist. *Pol.* 5.1.5 [1301b]), so it makes sense for him to have denigrated the magistracy as somehow "un-Lycurgan." This new interpretation appears gradually to have been accepted as orthodoxy. Cleomenes III would later use the argument that the ephorate was not a creation of Lycurgus himself to justify his bloody suppression of the magistracy in 225 B.C.E. (Plut. *Cleom.* 8.1–4, 10.2–6).

As with so many Spartan institutions, the ephorate's origins are shrouded in mystery. The list of ephors compiled by Charon of Lampsacus in the fifth century (*FGrH* 262 T1) probably stretched back to the mid-eighth century, given the contemporary association of the ephorate with the work of Lycurgus, but the absence of the ephorate in the remaining text of the Great Rhetra has led most modern historians to conclude either that the magistracy was a later development, or, if it did exist, that it was quite insignificant in the early years of the city's history. According to one modern theory, the ephors began as a college of astrologers, who were charged with observing the passage of a star on a moonless, clear night every eight years in order to determine whether a king had displeased the gods. Unfortunately, the only time the ephors are recorded as doing this is during the extremely unsettled period in the mid-third century B.C.E., when this supposedly ancient ritual became a convenient tool for dethroning king Leonidas, who opposed the young king Agis' popular reform program (Plut. *Agis* 11.4–5). That the origins of the ephors lie in this ritual is at best doubtful, even if it had been practiced for centuries without attracting the notice of any writer including Xenophon.

Interestingly, upon their first appearance in the historical record (Hdt. 5.39.2–40.1), attempting to head off a succession crisis during the reign of Anaxandridas (*c.* 560–520 B.C.E.), the ephors could merely advise the king to divorce his barren wife and remarry. After Anaxandridas ignored this advice, only an insistent threat from the ephors and Gerousia collectively to take the matter before the Assembly, where the Spartans might reach a decision "less than good" for him, forced the king to accede to their counsel that he take a second wife. This may indicate that the ephors had yet to gain the overwhelming influence over all officials which so impressed Xenophon (*Lac.* 8.3) in the fourth century, since Anaxandridas only yielded when confronted with a possible decree from the popular Assembly. Since the ephors' attendance at the birth of Dorieus, Anaxandridas' son by his first wife (Hdt. 5.404.3), indicates their close relationship with the royal families, the office may actually have been a creation of the kings themselves as a voluntary limitation of royal authority under pressure for reform. Scholarly consensus has coalesced around a "revival" or "revalorization" of the ephorate in the mid-sixth century as a result of the development of the network of alliances with Sparta's neighbors that became what is known today as the Peloponnesian League. While this hypothesis may be correct, it is important to note that Herodotus' narratives of sixth-century Sparta – Anaxandridas' singular marital arrangements and Cleomenes' reaction to Maeandirus' attempted bribery (3.148.2) – show the ephors as subordinate to the king.

The later position of the ephors in the fifth and fourth centuries was, to say the least, anomalous. Impressed by their power, Xenophon could liken them only to tyrants or the judges at athletic festivals (*Lac.* 8.3–5). One of their number served as eponymous ephor, which meant that the year was named after him. Aristotle, on the other hand, granted that the ephorate was one of the Spartans' greatest offices but drew attention to the humble and poverty-stricken origins of many incumbents, which made them liable to bribery (*Pol.* 2.6.14 [1270b]). This is probably an exaggeration, as office holders were Spartiates with sufficient land to produce the necessary contributions for their *sussitia*. To political theorists like Aristotle (*Pol.* 2.7.5 [1272a]), the ephorate represented the main democratic element in Sparta's admired mixed constitution, since ephors were elected from the population at large and, despite the often savage infighting that characterized Spartan politics, were actually a force for stability, because they gave the people a stake in the constitution. Ephors were probably elected in the same way as members of the Gerousia, by receiving the loudest shouts, which struck Aristotle as "childish" (*Pol.* 2.6.16 [1270b], 2.6.18 [1271a]). Ephors served one-year terms and, as far as can be determined, re-election was forbidden – a sensible precaution, considering the extensive administrative and executive powers concentrated in these magistrates' hands.

The ephors were the ultimate arbiters of foreign policy and domestic security in Classical Sparta. They received ambassadors and introduced them to the Spartan Assembly. They may have acquired their position in external affairs shortly before the Persian Wars, since at that time heralds from Athens and other cities approached the ephors directly for military assistance, rather than importuning the king, as Maeandrius of Samos and Aristagoras of Miletus had in the sixth century (Hdt. 9.7.1, 9.9.1; cf. 6.106.1). Managing Sparta's complex web of alliances must have taken up a large portion of the ephors' year in office, as it was their responsibility to convene assemblies of the Peloponnesian League (Thuc. 1.67–88, 113–125). As a great portion of Sparta's foreign relations consisted of its armies traipsing uninvited over the territories of other states, two ephors routinely accompanied the king on campaign (Xen. *Lac.* 13.5). This reform was introduced after the crisis caused by the falling-out of kings Demaratus and Cleomenes during the invasion of Attica in 506 B.C.E. (Hdt. 5.75.2, cf. 9.76.3). Even when they stayed home, the ephors kept a close eye on the behavior of Sparta's commanders: faced with complaints from the Ionian allies about the regent Pausanias' increasingly outrageous behavior in

Asia Minor, the ephors promptly recalled him (Thuc. 1.95.3, 128.3). Commanders were keenly aware of the ephors' long-distance supervision of their actions. After their misstep in arbitrarily proposing the destruction of Athens at an allied meeting after Aegospotami in 404 (Paus. 3.8.6), Agis and Lysander were careful to stress, in their dealings with the representatives of Athens and other states, that only the ephors could make substantive decisions on foreign policy.

The military responsibilities of the ephors were prominent at the beginning of hostilities: following a vote by the Spartan Assembly, they were in charge of mobilizing the troops, "to show the guard" (*phrouron phainein*) as Spartans called it (e.g. Xen. *Hell.* 4.2.9) – cavalry, infantry, and engineers – and declaring which age groups were to be called up (Xen. *Lac.* 11.2). The ephors may also have assigned the cavalrymen their horses at this point (Xen. *Hell.* 6.4.11). Whether the ephors alone appointed the commanders for each campaign or were part, albeit an influential part, of a wider decision-making process remains unclear. During the campaign itself, two ephors accompanied the king in command. Their jurisdiction over military and foreign affairs, moreover, meant that the ephors were concerned with state security at all levels. It was the ephors, acting as Sparta's executive power, who expelled the undesirable Maeandrius in the sixth century through a herald's announcement; furthermore, they may have been responsible for the (in)famous periodic deportations of foreigners (*xenêlasiai*) meant to keep Spartan society free of ideological contamination (Thuc. 2.39.1; Xen. *Lac.* 14.4). The ephors were also supposed to have declared war on the entire population of helots every year when they entered office, thus removing the taint of ritual pollution from their murderers (Plut. *Lyc.* 28.6).

Our most vivid glimpse into the ephors' role in suppressing internal subversion comes early in the reign of Agesilaus (397 B.C.E.), when their swift and decisive action headed off a revolt led by a man called Cinadon (Xen. *Hell.* 3.3.5–11). The revolutionary movement was widespread, according to an informant, and Cinadon claimed the sympathy of virtually all people – helots, the newly enfranchised (*Neodamôdeis*), and "inferiors" (*hupomeiones*) – who like him lacked full Spartiate status and who hated their superiors so intensely they could eat them raw. Weapons were plentiful and to hand: sympathizers in the army would provide what was necessary, the central arms warehouse could easily be broken into, and farm implements made good makeshift weapons. Working only on a need-to-know basis with the members of the

Gerousia they could trust, the shocked ephors sent Cinadon on a fake mission to a small perioecic town well away from the city, ensuring that he was accompanied by an small escort of six elite young soldiers who had all been apprised of the real situation, and with a contingent of cavalry arriving as back-up in case of trouble. Cinadon, who had carried out earlier missions for the ephors, suspected nothing until he was arrested far from Sparta and forced to divulge the names of his sympathizers, a list of which was dispatched post-haste by horseman to the ephors. The ephors acted none too soon: Cinadon had given up the names of many prominent subversives, even including the state prophet Tisamenus. The crisis shows how complete the ephors' mastery of the state apparatus was: they questioned the informant and on his evidence consulted members of the Gerousia; they dispatched troops for missions and empowered them to make arrests on their behalf. The ephors must also have conducted undercover operations regularly, since Cinadon is said to have been their agent on other occasions. Most interestingly, the ephors did all this apparently without consulting either king.

Their judicial powers were extensive (Xen. *Lac.* 8.3). Ephors levied fines on whomsoever they wished and could collect them immediately; they had authority to remove from office, imprison, and even bring capital charges against any magistrate. In other cities, such as Athens, legal action against an official for illegal activity had to wait until the end of his year in office, when accounts were rendered. The ephors, however, did not by themselves try kings on capital charges, but sat in judgement with the other king and the members of the Gerousia. Murder trials were usually held before the Gerousia, while single ephors decided cases concerning contract law (Arist. *Pol.* 3.1.7 [1275b]). Certain cases involving what would be called "disturbing the peace" were also under the ephors' purview. They punished offences by underage Spartans only indirectly, by penalizing the boys' adult lovers (Ael. *VH* 3.10), but were empowered to levy large fines directly on young men of the *hêbontes* age grade (aged twenty to thirty years) brought before them by the *paidonomos* (Xen. *Lac.* 4.6). The *hêbontes* were also under the ephors' particular supervision, who examined the new soldiers' clothes and bedding daily and carried out periodic inspection parades (*FGrH* 86 F10). From among the eldest *hêbontes*, they also designated the three *hippagretai*, who chose 300 *hêbontes* to serve as the "cavalrymen" (*hippeis*), the crack royal bodyguard (Xen. *Lac.* 4.3). The *hippeis* also seem to have constituted a special strike force at the ephors' direct disposal, available for such sensitive assignments as the arrest of Cinadon. The ephors' jurisdiction even intruded into personal behavior. One example is the ephors' famous annual exhortation upon taking up their duties, that every Spartan citizen shave his moustache and obey the law (Plut. *Cleom.* 9.3; *Mor.* 550b).

They also played an important legislative role. The ephorate served as the Assembly's probouleutic committee, drafting bills and drawing up the agenda. Headed by the eponymous ephor, they presided over Assembly meetings – a departure from the situation envisaged in the Great Rhetra, where the Damos was to be supervised by the kings and the Gerousia. The ephors executed and enforced decisions taken by the Assembly. Represented by the eponymous ephor, the ephors also had the useful duty of supervising the voting and determining the result. Just how useful can be seen in the Assembly meeting just before the Peloponnesian War, at which the hawkish ephor Sthenelaidas, after putting the question of whether or not Athens had broken the treaty, claimed not to be able to distinguish which side's shouts were louder. In an apparently unprecedented move, he then called for a literal division, in which the "yeas" and "nays" were told to stand in separate places in the meeting area (Thuc. 1.87.1–2). Sthenelaidas thus stripped the last shred of secrecy from the voting procedure, since peer pressure would quite likely have induced less confident assemblymen to join the larger group. This episode gives insight into just how much influence ephors wielded, extending as far as arbitrarily changing the voting procedure. Among the ephors themselves, only a majority vote was needed to make decisions valid and binding on all members of the board; no minority or dissenting decisions were allowed (Xen. *Hell.* 2.3.34).

The ephors' social origins still remain obscure. Aristotle's ideas about the ephors' lower-class status must be modified. Men of distinction certainly served as ephors: not counting Chilon in the mid-sixth century, among the eponymous ephors were Brasidas in 431/0 (Xen. *Hell.* 2.3.10); Leon, Olympic victor and founder of a Spartan colony, in 419/8 (Xen. *Hell.* 2.3.10); Endius, scion of a ancient wealthy family with a century-old guest-friendship with the family of Alcibiades the Athenian, in 413/2 (Thuc. 8.6.3); and Antalcidas, negotiator of the peace treaty that bore his name, in 387/6 (Plut. *Ages.* 32.1). On the other hand, the prohibition on iteration, combined with the relatively small (and steadily decreasing) number of full Spartan citizens would have resulted in many ephors being drawn from families that were far from prominent or wealthy. The small pool of available candidates for office may be the reason why the ephorate could be held at any point in a Spartan's political career; some seem to have held it while relatively young, while others, such as Chilon and Leon, were ephors well into their maturity.

While the ephors changed annually, Sparta's other prominent public body almost matched the kingship in stability of membership. The Gerousia was an ancient institution, rooted in the city's history and descended from the early kings' circle of advisers. The Great Rhetra regularized its composition and frequency of meeting in the seventh century while still reserving for the kings and the Gerousia the ultimate decision-making powers. For many centuries, the Gerousia was endowed with a luster afforded few other institutions in the ancient Greek city. Writers were impressed by the respect afforded the Gerousia: Demosthenes (20.107), Aristotle (*Pol.* 2.6.15 [1270b]), and Plutarch (*Lyc.* 26.2) all called membership in the Gerousia "the prize of excellence," while Polybius (6.45.5) stated that the Gerousia and kings together administered all the affairs of state. This last is an exaggeration. Prestigious the Gerousia was, but its powers and jurisdiction were limited by its nature as a mainly deliberative body and the existence of the ephorate.

For Spartans, the Gerousia was a cornerstone of their ancestral constitution, founded by Lycurgus. Modern scholars believe that the institution probably had its origins in a group of noble councillors like those found in Homeric epic (e.g. *Il.* 2.402–8, 10.194–5). Until the late third century B.C.E., its membership was fixed at twenty-eight, and qualifications were simple: candidates had to be over sixty years of age, that is, to have completed their period of eligibility for military service, and to have led an exemplary life (Plut. *Lyc.* 26.1). Although members of the Gerousia were drawn from the Spartan elite, several of whom could claim Heraclid ancestry, there is no evidence for any explicit legal restriction on eligibility. Spartan tradition was enough. Election was by acclamation, with the successful candidate being the man who, in the judgement of specially sequestered adjudicators, elicited the loudest cheers (Arist. *Pol.* 2.6.18 [1271a]), which was the normal Spartan method for voting on important matters of state.

Members of the Gerousia served for life and, like the kings, provided an element of continuity for the Spartan state. Indeed, they normally sat together with the kings to deliberate on legislation or to judge cases brought before them. The Gerousia and the kings constituted the state's most powerful court, with jurisdiction over capital cases punishable by death or exile – murder, treason, and the like (Xen. *Lac.* 10.2; Plut. *Lyc.* 26.2). That jurisdiction extended even over the kings themselves, as we can see from the account of Pausanias' trial in 403, when, luckily for that beleaguered king, opinion in the Gerousia was so divided that a solid vote for acquittal by the board of ephors was enough to set him free, although his fellow king, Agis, had voted against him (Paus. 3.5.2). The relationship between the two Spartan institutions was close. Already in the sixth century, the ephors and Gerousia jointly cautioned king Anaxandridas to marry a new wife to ensure the survival of his line, while in the fifth century, these two bodies and the kings seem to have constituted "the authorities" (*hoi en telei/ta telê*) (e.g. Thuc. 1.58.1, 4.15.1, 6.88.10; *ID* 87) who made most foreign policy decisions. Even in the late fourth century, the Gerousia retained its legal power over the kingship when it adjudicated between rival claims to the throne, while the ephors endeavored to console the unsuccessful claimant with honors and an appointment as head of Sparta's armed forces (Paus. 3.6.2–3).

Only once is the Gerousia's role in legislative procedure clearly visible. In 243/2, King Agis IV attempted to push a program of reform legislation through the Gerousia and the Assembly. Unable to obtain the Gerousia's necessary unanimous consent, he used his ally Lysander, the eponymous ephor at the time, to introduce the bill directly before the Assembly, which approved his populist measures. Yet the reforms came to nothing, because the Gerousia and the kings later voted the bill down by a single vote (Plut. *Agis* 9, 11). In strictly constitutional terms, this incident reveals how closely the Spartans still followed the strictures of the Great Rhetra centuries after its promulgation. The passage also provides enough information to reconstruct the procedure followed in Hellenistic Sparta to pass a law. First, a proposal was laid before the Gerousia and the kings *ex officio*. For the proposal to proceed to the Assembly, the Gerousia needed to give its unanimous consent. If the Gerousia and kings did not all agree, the right of the eponymous ephor to present legislation directly to the popular Assembly provided a safety valve. There the proposal would be debated and decided, presumably by a majority. If the Assembly gave its approval, the legislation would go back to the Gerousia for reconsideration. This time, only a simple majority sufficed to make the proposal law.

In practice, this process allowed for more flexibility in the Spartan constitution than a strict reading of the Great Rhetra might imply. The "unanimity clause" could have allowed a tiny minority within the

Gerousia and the kings to block legislation favored by the majority. Recourse to the Assembly through the ephor made such a scenario unlikely, since legislative proposals that had won the people's approval there would not then need the unanimous assent of the probouleutic council to become law. Normally, however, ephors would not have dared to alienate the Gerousia by making proposals directly to the Assembly, since the implied insult would almost certainly have resulted in the Gerousia rejecting the bill. (Matters of foreign policy seem to have been the exception.)

Nonetheless, despite being involved in legislation and foreign affairs, the role of the Gerousia itself was circumscribed. Unlike the ephors, who could and did make executive decisions at any time that directly affected Spartans' lives, the Gerousia functioned only if officially summoned to deliberate. We know that the ephors had the power to summon extraordinary meetings of the Gerousia if need arose (Xen. *Hell.* 3.3.8), and it is possible that the eponymous ephor also called the Gerousia to regular meetings. The Gerousia was a quintessentially deliberative body which either accepted or rejected proposals put before it but lacked the power to initiate discussion or action on its own. In the Classical period, the Gerousia dealt with other states only in conjunction with the ephors. The situation had changed by the late Hellenistic period, when, on one occasion in 148, the Gerousia alone dealt directly with Diaeus, general in charge of the powerful Achaean League (Paus. 7.12.6–7). At the time, Sparta was an unwilling member of the League under a constitution forcibly altered to conform to Achaean norms, so the Gerousia's independent action in this case probably had nothing to do with any similar power it may have had earlier. While the Gerousia may not have had an easily discernible independent role, its members wielded significant influence as a group in combination with the kings and ephors. As already mentioned, that skilled Spartan political player king Agesilaus went out of his way to cultivate newly elected gerontes, presenting each with a robe and a bull upon his entry into office (Plut. *Ages.* 3.5).

The fourth main pillar of the Classical Spartan constitution was the popular Assembly, called the *Ekklesia*, not the *Apella* as once thought. Although far from being a cockpit of free-wheeling debate and legislative initiative like the Athenian Assembly, the Spartan model was no mere rubber stamp for decisions of the magistrates. The contrast in our knowledge of the two bodies, however, could not be more stark. Compared to the wealth of detailed evidence about the Athenian *Ekklesia*, very little is indisputably known about the Spartan Assembly. For example, in the present state of our evidence it is impossible to determine conclusively who had the right to speak at meetings. Almost everyone who is recorded as having spoken can be identified, with widely varying degrees of certainty, as an ephor, king, or member of the Gerousia. But who the possessors of various "opinions" mentioned by the historians were and whether they might have expressed them in debates remains unknown.

In contrast, we know that, unlike the Athenian *Ekklesia*, the Spartan Assembly could not initiate or emend legislation nor make counterproposals. Only voting on the proposition before it, handed down from the Gerousia or introduced by the ephors, was permitted. The Great Rhetra (Plut. *Lyc.* 6.1–2) assigned the Assembly power, albeit significantly compromised, to pass legally valid acts and seems (as Aristotle and Plutarch believed) to have provided for regular meetings at a fixed location, but where Babyka and Knakion actually were is a complete mystery to us, while the Greek phrase *ex horas eis horas* used to indicate the frequency of meetings can be translated "from season to season," which implies very few meetings annually, or "from month to month." The second interpretation may be the correct one, as it enjoys the slender support of a late *scholion* to a passage in Thucydides (1.67), which states that the Spartans met at the time of the full moon. Besides regular meetings, the Assembly may also have met at times of crisis, as Xenophon's remark (*Hell.* 3.3.8) that the ephors did not have time to convene "even the Little Assembly" to deal with the Cinadon conspiracy implies they had the power to call the full Assembly together when necessary. The ephors also summoned and presided over regular meetings of the Assembly (Thuc. 1.67.3) in the fifth century. In the early years, meetings would have been at the kings' pleasure; only with the passage of the Great Rhetra were regular meetings legally mandated. By the later sixth century, however, the ephors had acquired this power, which they used to great effect in forcing king Anaxandridas to bend to their will in the matter of his conjugal arrangements (Hdt. 5.40.1).

The Assembly was also involved in settling constitutional disputes relating to the royal houses: the ephors succeeded in convincing Anaxandridas to change his mind only when, along with the Gerousia, they threatened to put the matter before the Assembly (Hdt. 5.40.1). The trial of Cleomenes I's rival king Demaratus in 491 concluded with a vote "by the Spartiates" to consult Delphi about his legitimacy

(Hdt. 6.66.1). And at the end of the fifth century, the struggle for the succession after Agis II's death in 400 was settled by "the city" choosing Agesilaus over Leotychidas (Xen. *Hell.* 3.3.4; *Ages.* 1.5). The Assembly's decision in this particular case may well have been in accordance with those taken by other bodies, but was perhaps also regarded as conferring due legitimacy on such decisions.

Given the bias of our sources, the prominence of the Assembly's involvement in foreign affairs comes as no surprise. Ambassadors from other states regularly addressed the Spartan Assembly. Those from Croesus in the sixth century offered the Spartans gifts and requested an alliance (Hdt. 1.69.1–2). Just before the Peloponnesian War, Athenian ambassadors spoke at a joint session of the Assembly and the Peloponnesian League in an attempt to justify their actions against Spartan allies (Thuc. 1.67.3, 72.1), while several decades before, the wily Themistocles had perplexed Spartans by speaking only to magistrates during his visit in 478, when he was expected to put his case concerning the reconstruction of Athens' city walls directly to "the public" in the Assembly (Thuc. 1.90.5). At a second joint session of allies and Spartans in 382, the Chalcidians requested military aid against the encroachments of the people of Olynthus (Xen. *Hell.* 5.2.11–12), and we know that Theban and Athenian ambassadors addressed another of these sessions during the peace negotiations that led to the badly flawed treaty of 371 (Xen. *Hell.* 6.33.3). In the debate over whether to send aid to Syracuse in the winter of 415/14, Thebans, Syracusans, and the renegade Athenian Alcibiades (acting as a private individual) all addressed the Assembly (Thuc. 6.88.10). We can also assume that the heralds Darius sent in 491 to demand earth and water were hurled to their deaths at the orders of the Spartan Assembly (Hdt. 7.133.1). It was the Assembly that, after several inconclusive meetings some years later, finally managed to find two volunteers to go to Susa to offer their lives in compensation for this flagrant act of Spartan impiety (Hdt. 7.134.2). Matters of war and peace in general were decided by the Assembly. In 432, it voted that Athens had violated the Thirty-Year Peace (Thuc. 1.87.1–2). In 401, the Assembly and the ephors decided to teach the Eleans a lesson after a series of provocative acts directed against Spartan officials and individuals (Xen. *Hell.* 3.2.22–3). The Assembly also officially authorized the army to go on campaign (Hdt. 7.206.1), a technicality that Cleomenes I apparently ignored to his cost in his eagerness to check the Aeginetans' pro-Persian tendencies in the 490s (Hdt. 6.50.2). Sometimes commanders unsure of the public mood might refer to the Assembly on matters of strategy, such as when, on the eve of Leuctra in 371, king Cleombrotus was instructed, against the sensible objections of at least one top Spartan, to keep his army in the field and stay in Phocis (Xen. *Hell.* 6.4.3).

This last incident leads into the role of debate in the Assembly. Differing opinions were certainly expressed there. Hetoimaridas successfully persuaded the majority of the Assembly to abandon their support for a war to regain hegemony of the Hellenic Coalition in 477 (Diod. Sic. 11.50.2–6). In 432, king Archidamus vigorously opposed taking the steps towards war which the ephor Sthenelaidas advocated and an overwhelming majority supported (Thuc. 1.80.1–85.3). In 415/14, Alcibiades persuaded the Spartans to send military aid to the Syracusans in the face of resistance by the ephors and other high magistrates (Thuc. 6.88.10). Finally, in 418/17, the hapless king Agis managed to dissuade the Spartans, livid with him for losing Orchomenos, from destroying his home and fining him 10,000 dr (Thuc. 5.63.2–4). All of these passages attest to differences of opinion at meetings of the Assembly. That meetings were not, as we might have expected, quiet and sedate affairs is apparent from two incidents related by Xenophon, both dated to 371. The first is the Assembly's response to the speech delivered by the Athenian delegation member Autocles, which contained some uncomfortable truths about the lack of autonomy among Sparta's allies and the folly of seizing the Theban Cadmea. Autocles' plain speaking was met with complete silence (Xen. *Hell.* 6.3.10). Later, the Assembly overruled a proposal by one Prothoos that Cleombrotus be instructed to demobilize his army in Phocis and that the framework for a voluntary force to ensure the autonomy of cities be put in place, because "after hearing this, it considered him to be spouting nonsense" (Xen. *Hell.* 6.4.3). The silence that followed Autocles' speech was clearly noteworthy, while we can imagine that Prothoos' ideas provoked noisier expressions of sentiment.

7

Leotychidas to Lysander

Events in Greece had not stood still during Pausanias' quixotic career in Asia Minor. Leotychidas, Cleomenes' replacement for Demaratus and victor against the Persians at the Battle of Mycale in 479, paid for his role in corrupting the Pythia, in Herodotus' eyes at least, when he was caught red-handed with a Persian sleeve stuffed with silver while leading an expedition against the pro-Persian Thessalians in 476 (Hdt. 6.72). Condemned at Sparta, his house demolished, he went into exile in Tegea and died there by 469, perhaps still formally a king. In 475, a vigorous debate broke out over losing the hegemony of the Greek Coalition along with its concomitant opportunities for enrichment and enhancement of Sparta's prestige (Diod. Sic. 11.50.2) – a salutary reminder that Spartan public opinion was far from monolithic.

In the later 470s, Spartans had to deal with problems on several fronts. Twice the Tegeans fought the Spartans, once in alliance with Argos, once with the support of almost all the Arcadians (Hdt. 9.35.2). Themistocles may have been at work here, since, after his enemies had succeeded in ostracizing him from Athens, he took up residence in newly democratic Argos and traveled extensively in the Peloponnese, certainly not on sightseeing trips (Thuc. 1.135.3). Spartan victories brought the region back into the fold. But then, probably at the end of the decade, developments at Elis in the northwest Peloponnese took a worrying turn when all the separate communities within its boundaries amalgamated into a single city-state (Diod. Sic. 11.54.1). The process, known as synoecism (*sunoikismos*), was usually the precursor to converting to a democratic constitution – not the Spartans' favored form of government.

The earthquake and subsequent revolt in 465 had far-reaching political consequences. Because of their desperate situation, the Spartans were unable to carry out their secret pledge of support for Thasos when that northern Aegean island tried to withdraw from the Delian League in protest over an attempted Athenian seizure of valuable trading and resource assets on the Thracian mainland (Thuc. 1.101.1–3). Thasos was besieged by the Athenians, stripped of its mainland possessions, its walls demolished, and a punitive tribute levied. Even so, reconciliation between Sparta and Athens might have been possible if the Spartans had not later rejected the Athenian contingent sent during the Messenian revolt (Thuc. 1.102). Aggrieved by their abrupt dismissal, the Athenians had no compunction in allying themselves to Argos, once anathema because of its enthusiastic medism in the Persian War. Public opinion in Athens turned against the Spartans, and conciliatory voices were silenced, including that of Cimon, who was subsequently ostracized in 461 (Plut. *Cim.* 17.3). One outcome of this hardening of attitude was the Athenians' provocative settling of Messenian refugees from Ithome at the newly acquired city of Naupactus, whose strategic position on the north coast of the Corinthian Gulf controlled the gulf's entrance (Thuc. 1.103.3). The clash became inevitable and resulted in the on-again, off-again conflict known as the First Peloponnesian War that lasted through the 450s and into the early 440s.

The Megarians made the first move. They switched allegiance to Athens because of an unsuccessful border war against the Corinthians (Thuc. 1.103.4). The Athenians then helped fortify Megarian harbor installations, thereby gaining control of the narrow land corridor leading north from the Peloponnese and incurring the Corinthians' bitter enmity. Athenian attacks on the northern Argolid and Aegina in 460 roused the Corinthians and other Peloponnesians to military action, but the Spartans, their traditional approach to Attica through the Isthmus blocked, remained aloof (Thuc. 1.105–6). In 458 or 457, the Spartans finally acted. A large force of Spartan and allied hoplites under the command of the uncle of the underaged king Pleistoanax, son of Pausanias, crossed the Corinthian Gulf, ostensibly to defend the towns of Doris, the Dorian homeland, from Phocian attack (Thuc. 1.107.2). The Phocians were quickly forced into a treaty and out of Doris, but the Spartan force did not withdraw immediately from Boeotia. While Nicomedes may have been unsure of the least dangerous route back home, his thousands of troops, more than needed to liberate Doris, were more likely intended for a more ambitious project – the re-establishment of Theban hegemony in Boeotia (Diod. Sic. 11.81.1–2) and, if opportunity arose, the invasion of Attica from the north. He would have been encouraged by approaches by oligarchically inclined Athenians who wanted the democracy overthrown while there was still time, before the Long Walls connecting the city with Piraeus were completed (Thuc. 1.107.5). The Athenians responded decisively with a general mobilization and marched into Boeotia accompanied by allied forces. The two armies met at Tanagra in a battle marked by bloody slaughter on both sides. The Spartans won the day but quickly withdrew fighting through the Megarid, their inability to capitalize on the victory an early sign of vulnerability to casualties because of the chronic lack of citizen manpower at Sparta (Thuc. 1.107.5–108.2). Just over two months later, the Athenians marched back into Boeotia and with a decisive victory at Oenophyta gained control of central Greece as far west as Phocis and Locris.

Sparta's troubles were compounded by the defeat of Aegina in 457, which was forced into the Delian League, and the completion of the Athenian Long Walls, which rendered the city and its harbor virtually impregnable (Thuc. 1.108.2–4). Worse came the following year when an Athenian naval expedition attacked and burned the Spartan naval yards at Gytheum (Thuc. 1.108.5). But the Athenian resources were being stretched thin. At the beginning of the decade, they had opened another front by sending massive military aid to the Egyptians, who were rebelling against the Persians (Thuc. 1.104). When the Persians finally responded, crushing the rebellion in 454, Athens lost many thousands of fighting men (Thuc. 1.110). Important allies revolted against the Delian League, and Athenians felt the need in 454/3 to centralize League institutions on their own territory (Plut. *Per.* 12.1). A five-year peace between Athens and Sparta was concluded in 451, facilitating Cimon's return from ostracism (Thuc. 1.112.1; Plut. *Cim.* 18.1).

Sparta's position was also secured by a thirty-year truce with Argos (Thuc. 5.14.4). Regaining confidence, the Spartans sent another expedition across the Corinthian Gulf probably in 449, this time to restore to Delphian control the sanctuary of Pythian Apollo, which had been seized by the Phocians. The Phocians were no match for Spartiate arms, but as soon as the Spartans left the Athenians restored control of the Pythian sanctuary to their allies (Thuc. 1.112.5). Athens would not remain the dominant power in central Greece for much longer, however. In 446, a combined army made up of anti-Athenian Boeotian dissidents decisively defeated an Athenian punitive force at Coronea, forcing the Athenians to abandon central Greece (Thuc. 1.113). Megara and Euboea chose this moment to revolt, threatening Athens' strategic interests on land and sea. An army under Pericles was despatched to deal with the more serious threat a hostile Euboea posed to the sea routes linking Athens and her allies (Thuc. 1.114.1). Sparta pounced. Pleistoanax, son of Pausanias, led a army up through the Isthmus and began to ravage Athenian territory (Thuc. 1.114.2). Pericles was forced to abandon the Euboean expedition to defend Attica itself. But instead of engaging the Athenians, Pleistoanax and his adviser, the ephor Cleandridas, took their army back to the Peloponnese. Pericles turned round and dealt with the rebels on Euboea, expelling the inhabitants of Histiaea and confiscating tracts of land from Chalcis (Thuc. 1.114.3). A little later, in the year 446/5, Athens and Sparta negotiated a peace treaty for thirty years that brought their war to a close.

Back in Sparta, Pleistoanax and Cleandridas paid the price for abandoning the invasion. Rumors of bribery naturally abounded. Such a huge fine was imposed that the young king was forced into exile rather than pay it (*FGrH* 70 F193), while Cleandridas went into voluntary exile, the Spartans condemning him to death in absentia (Plut. *Per.* 22). Despite the juicy story that Pericles included an item for the sum of ten talents in his accounts for that year headed only "necessary expenses" (Plut. *Per.* 23.1), Pleistoanax, son of the notorious Pausanias, was surely not so foolish as to accept a bribe on his first major mission outside the Peloponnese. Much more likely is that the Athenian general agreed to abandon any claims to Megara and the northern Argolid in return for Sparta allowing the Athenians a free hand in Euboea. The two Spartan leaders likely fell afoul of Sparta's vicious political infighting upon their return when the "hawks" used the courts to make a point about foreign policy. Calmer heads soon prevailed, however, and the treaty with Athens was signed. Pleistoanax later returned to Sparta and resumed his royal duties at the behest of a Delphic oracle, which naturally he was afterwards accused of obtaining corruptly (Thuc. 5.16.3).

Before the crises of the late 430s, the only serious threat to the peace between Athens and Sparta came in 441/0 when rebellious Samian oligarchs approached the Spartans for Peloponnesian aid. The Corinthians later claimed that it was only their vote at a League congress that prevented war, the other allies being evenly split (Thuc. 1.40.5, 41.2). Since, as evidence suggests, formal meetings of the Peloponnesian League to decide on taking military action usually followed decisions taken at Sparta, this must mean that only a few years after the signing of the treaty with Athens, a majority of Spartans were again prepared to go to war.

The events leading up to the declaration by the Spartans that the Athenians had violated the oaths of the Thirty Years' Peace are well known. In the west, Athens accepted the island of Corcyra as an ally against the wishes of Corinth, from where the island's original Greek settlers had come. Athenian naval support helped the Corcyreans soundly defeat the Corinthian fleet in an engagement off the Sybota islands in 433 (Thuc. 1.24–55). In the northeast, anti-Athenian agitation in the city of Potidaea on the Chalcidic peninsula, which was in the anomalous position of being both an ally of the Athenian Empire and a colony of Corinth, escalated to the point where the city went into full revolt and the Athenians besieged it (Thuc. 1.56–67). Closer to home, the Megarians felt the wrath of the Athenians, whose alliance they had rejected, in the form of a trade embargo that prevented any Megarian goods passing through the Empire's ports (Thuc. 1.67.4). Livid at what they considered Athenian interference in their sphere of interest, the Corinthians led a contingent of like-minded allies to Sparta, where Thucydides presents them as the prime force behind the subsequent declaration of war. But an overwhelming majority of Spartans voted for war in 432 despite King Archidamus' reservations. The Spartans did not merely acquiesce to Corinthian demands; they had their own reasons for going to war.

In the interval between the vote in the Spartan Assembly and the final meeting of the League allies, the Spartans sent several envoys to Athens with a series of ultimatums that the Athenians were unlikely to accept – the exile of Pericles, the raising of the siege of Potidaea, the rescinding of the Megarian decree, and finally the effective dissolution of the Empire (Thuc. 1.139.1, 3). Convinced by Pericles, the Athenians rejected the Spartan demands but kept the door open for further negotiation on all points in accordance with the principles of the Thirty Years' Peace (Thuc. 1.145). The last embassy returned to Sparta, and the Peloponnesian League decided on war.

Thebans, not Spartans, were responsible for the first military action in the conflict, a disastrous attempt at capturing Plataea, which by virtue of its alliance with Athens had avoided incorporation into the Theban-dominated Boeotian League. By the operation's end, Plataeans had killed all of the Theban attackers including 180 prisoners, under murky circumstances (Thuc. 2.2.2–5.7). The Athenians had tried to control the situation at Plataea, probably to exploit the captured Thebans as prisoners, but in the end supported their ally to the hilt, garrisoning the town and removing the civilian population to safety in Attica (Thuc.

2.6.2–4). Sparta's answer came in the form of an allied force under the command of Archidamus which invaded Attica after he attempted one last time to reach an agreement with Athens (Thuc. 2.10, 12). Thus began the so-called Archidamian War (431–421 B.C.E.), during which the Peloponnesians ravaged Attic farms almost annually once the rural population was evacuated to Athens according to Pericles' war policy. For several years, neither side gained significant advantage despite the Spartan incursions and Athenian naval raids on coastal settlements in the Peloponnese as well as actions further afield in the Adriatic and Aegean. Even the arrival of a virulent plague in crowded Athens in 430, which carried off many Athenians including Pericles himself over a two-year period, did not substantially weaken the war effort. Nor did the fall of Plataea in 427 (Thuc. 3.52–68) alter the strategic balance.

In 425, an Athenian fleet on course for Corcyra and Sicily was blown onto the headland of Pylos, at the north end of a large bay largely closed off by an island called Sphacteria (Thuc. 4.3.1). Sailing with the generals in command was a general-elect for the following year, Demosthenes, who saw the strategic importance of this easily fortifiable site on Messenia's west coast. Athens' Messenian allies from Naupactus could form the garrison; since they were familiar with the territory and spoke the same dialect as the Lacedaemonians, they could inflict serious damage (Thuc. 4.3.3). After building a fort, the generals left Demosthenes and a small force behind and went on their way (Thuc. 4.4–5). At Sparta, the news was received with *sang froid* and they continued celebrating their festival; the Athenians would either withdraw or be easily overcome (Thuc. 4.5.1). A message was sent to Agis commanding the army in the field, who immediately broke off ravaging Attica and returned home, no doubt partially because his own estates in the area were threatened (Thuc. 4.6). Upon reaching Pylos and supplementing their forces with perioeci, the Spartans mounted an assault by land and sea, landing several hundred hoplites on Sphacteria in order to keep it out of Athenian hands (Thuc. 4.8.9). This maneuver proved a fatal mistake, as superior Athenian naval forces prevailed in battle the next day (Thuc. 4.14). The men on the island were marooned.

After an official party from Sparta had surveyed the situation at Pylos, a local truce was quickly concluded whereby fixed amounts of food and drink might be transported to the Lacedaemonian hoplites trapped on Sphacteria with their helot attendants (Thuc. 4.15–16.1). An embassy went immediately to Athens to offer peace in order to obtain their return. The terms they offered – a vague promise of peace and alliance allowing the two cities to split the hegemony of Greece between them – were not enough to weaken the opposition of Cleon, one of a new breed of politician, who made rigorous counter-demands (Thuc. 4.17–21). The mission was a failure and hostilities at Pylos resumed.

A stalemate ensued, with the Spartans trapped on Sphacteria but the Athenians unable to dislodge them. The Lacedaemonians offered rewards, including freedom to local helots, to anyone who could smuggle provisions onto the island. In the early days, some even managed to swim over with food in goatskin bags before the Athenians took preventative measures (Thuc. 4.26.5–9). In Athens, Cleon was placed in command of a force to deal with the situation at Pylos (Thuc. 4.28). Just before his arrival, a brush fire on Sphacteria, started accidentally by a Spartan during food preparation and driven by the wind, had consumed most of the island's undergrowth. This enabled the Athenians to see just how many enemy soldiers were stationed there (Thuc. 4.30.2–3). When Cleon arrived with his contingent, he and Demosthenes made a token attempt to come to an agreement with the Spartans before launching a night landing on the island (Thuc. 4.31). Despite overwhelming odds, the Lacedaemonians held out for hours until attacked from behind by archers and light troops (Thuc. 4.36). Of the 292 hoplites who survived at the surrender, 120 were Spartiates (Thuc. 4.38.5).

The capture of so many full Spartan citizens was a severe blow to Sparta, both psychologically and materially. According to the myth of Thermopylae, Spartans were not supposed to surrender (Thuc. 4.36.3). Greek opinion was shocked (Thuc. 4.40). In practical terms, the loss severely depleted Spartan citizen manpower, as the number of Spartiates continued to decline throughout the fifth and early fourth centuries. The continuing existence of an enemy fort at Pylos manned by free Messenians was another seriously destabilizing factor, acting as a magnet for discontented helots and increasing the threat of a revolt, besides serving as a launchpad for regular guerilla raids into the neighboring areas. A sign of the severity of the situation was that Spartans repeatedly sent embassies to Athens over the next few years, vainly attempting to recover their lost compatriots (Thuc. 4.41.3–4). The situation deteriorated as the Athenians pressed their advantage. They conducted a large-scale raiding expedition in 424 down the whole east coast of Laconia, capping it with the occupation of the island of Cythera, thus putting several important coastal communities at risk (Thuc. 4.53–4). Further Athenian successes in the Peloponnese followed (Thuc. 4.56).

But the tide was beginning to turn. In the early winter, the Thebans dealt the Athenians a severe defeat at Delium on the border with Attica (Thuc. 4.89–101). At Megara, the general Brasidas, who had distinguished himself in the early days of the Pylos campaign, faced down an Athenian army and saved the city from capture (Thuc. 4.70–4). Brasidas was on his way to Thrace at the head of a force whose composition was radical for Sparta. Among the hoplites were 700 helots, their inclusion due partly to security concerns and partly to Sparta's chronic lack of manpower (Thuc. 4.80.5). Brasidas' mission was to weaken the Athenians' war effort by destabilizing their allies in northern Greece. In this he was spectacularly successful. In late 424, he captured the important Athenian colony of Amphipolis on the river Strymon (Thuc. 4.103). Other cities soon fell or willingly switched allegiance, won over by his talk of liberation (e.g. Thuc. 4.85.15, 108.2), so that by late 422, following the expiry of a one-year truce, the Athenians sent a relief force under Cleon to re-establish their influence (Thuc. 4.117–19, 5.2.1). After recapturing Torone, he set off to wrest Amphipolis from Brasidas' control (Thuc. 5.3.6). In a pitched battle outside the city gates, the Spartan army triumphed over the Athenian, but both Brasidas and Cleon were killed in action (Thuc. 5.10).

With the principal advocates on both sides for continuing the war out of the picture and both belligerents exhausted by years of conflict, the way was clear for a negotiated settlement. The Peace of Nicias, named after its leading Athenian proponent, came into force in 421. Controversial from the start, since it allowed Athens and Sparta to emend provisions without consulting any of their allies, the Peace provided for the return of captured territory and a prisoner exchange (Thuc. 5.18–19). Several Spartan allies refused to comply, and Athens retained control of both Pylos and Cythera. It was only after Sparta and Athens had concluded their own side agreement to a defensive alliance, one of whose clauses required Athens to aid Sparta in the event of a helot uprising, that Athens sent the Sphacteria hostages home (Thuc. 5.22–4).

The years of the Peace of Nicias were not tranquil for Sparta. The Sphacteria hostages, for whose return Spartans had worked so hard, came to be seen as threats to the state. Even though some now held office, they were temporarily stripped of that right and excluded from economic activity (Thuc. 5.34.2). The helot veterans of Brasidas' Thracian campaign were liberated by an act of the Assembly and, though at first allowed to reside wherever they wished, were shipped off a little later along with another group of newly manumitted helots, the *Neodamôdeis*, to garrison the town of Lepreon on the border with Elis, now at odds with the Spartans (Thuc. 5.34). Outside Laconia, several allies of the Peloponnesian League were drifting out of Spartan influence, induced by their opposition to the Peace of Nicias to draw closer to Argos now that its peace treaty with Sparta had ended and negotiations on another had foundered (Thuc. 5.41). In 420, Athens, Argos, Mantinea, Elis, and their subject cities entered into a long-term defensive alliance, even though the Peace of Nicias was still supposed to be in force (Thuc. 5.47–48.1).

Conflict between the Spartans and the Argive coalition, interspersed with half-hearted attempts at negotiation, sputtered on until 418 (Thuc. 5.52–9). The campaigning season opened with a magnificent army of Spartans and their allies arrayed on the borders of Argos. It advanced no further, however, because its commander, King Agis, agreed to a four-month truce with the Argives after consulting only the ephor accompanying him (Thuc. 5.60.1). After his return to Sparta, news of the fall of Orchomenus to the Argives and their allies so enraged the Assembly that Agis barely escaped a huge fine and the demolition of his house, and had to endure the imposition of an "advisory board" of ten Spartiates with the power to prevent him from commanding an army (Thuc. 5.63). Agis soon redeemed himself at Mantinea in Arcadia, leading a large Peloponnesian army into battle with the Argives, Athenians, and their allies (Thuc. 5.66–74.1). The Spartan victory took the life out of the nascent anti-Spartan movement in the Peloponnese and cured what would now be called the "Sphacteria syndrome" (Thuc. 5.75.3). Argos sued for peace and got a fifty-year truce, on Sparta's terms (Thuc. 5.76–9); Mantinea came to terms (Thuc. 5.81.1); and the Spartans intervened successfully to support oligarchs in Sicyon, Achaea, and Tegea, though they could not dislodge the Argive democracy for long (Thuc. 5.81.2, 82.1–5).

An opportunity to face the Athenians soon came. Full-scale fighting in mainland Greece broke out again in 414 with a truce-breaking Athenian raid on the east coast of Laconia (Thuc. 6.105) which led to the Spartans resuming their invasions of Attica in 413 (Thuc. 7.19.1). The catastrophic end of the Sicilian Expedition in the same year severely weakened Athenian resolve and emboldened discontented allies to revolt (Thuc. 8.21). Political infighting and public hysteria had also, for the time being, robbed Athens of one of its best, though unpredictable, military minds. Alcibiades, nephew of Pericles, the highest-profile proponent of invading Sicily, was now acting as a military consultant at Sparta. On his advice, the Spartans had sent Gylippus over to Sicily to advise the Syracusans and had established a fort at Decelea in northeastern Attica as a Spartan version of the Athenian fort at Pylos. Within sight of the city, the fort prevented Athenians from exploiting some of their arable land and encouraged slaves to defect, especially from the silver mines further down the coast (Thuc. 6.91.4–7, 93.2, 7.19.2). Dissident groups soon appeared asking for Spartan support in rebelling against the Athenians (Thuc. 8.5). Two Persian officials also made competing offers of financial support contingent upon Spartan intervention in cities under Athenian control within their areas of command (Thuc. 8.5.4–6.1). The Peloponnesian League in 412 decided to give priority to the Chians and the Persian Tissaphernes, commander of the western district of Asia Minor (Thuc. 8.8.2). Accompanying Chalcideus, the Spartan general sent in command of the Peloponnesian fleet, was Alcibiades, who had been supporting the Chians' claims (Thuc. 8.6.3). No doubt he found a foreign assignment convenient, since rumors were flying in Sparta about his affair with Agis' wife Timaea (Plut. *Alc.* 7–8). Making their way secretly to Chios, the duo persuaded the Chians to revolt; they were soon joined by Erythrae and Clazomenae (Thuc. 8.14).

The revolts shifted the focus of the war permanently eastwards to Asia Minor. Persian aid and how to secure it now became important in the calculations of both sides. At first, the Spartans were the recipients, at the cost of a series of shameful treaties that gave all the Greek cities of Asia Minor, for whose "liberty" they had claimed to be fighting the Athenians, back to the Great King (Thuc. 8.18, 37, 58). By the end of 412, suspicion at Sparta, coupled with Agis' enmity, had caused Alcibiades to flee the Peloponnesian camp ahead of a Spartan death warrant for the court of Tissaphernes, where he now advised the Persian to be more equitable in his dealings with the opposing sides so that the Greeks might wear themselves out (Thuc. 8.45–6). He also had a hand in the early planning of a coup that brought the short-lived oligarchy of the Four Hundred to power in Athens in 411 (Thuc. 8.47–8), but was lucky (or canny) enough not to be included in its execution (Thuc. 8.63.3–4). He was invited back by the Athenian fleet at Samos and elected its commander (Thuc. 8.81–82.1), easily surviving the regime's fall four months later.

Since Alcibiades' defection to Tissaphernes' court, a bad situation had become worse. Persian financial aid was slow in arriving and insufficient when it did. Unrest over pay broke out within the ranks of Sparta's allies (Thuc. 8.83–84.3), who eventually persuaded the Spartan commander Mindarus to move the fleet north, where Pharnabazus, Persian commander of the Hellespontine region, had long urged them to come (Thuc. 8.99). But Mindarus had no success campaigning there and met his death in the debacle at Cyzicus in 410, where the Athenians under Alcibiades and Thrasybulus thrashed the combined forces of the Peloponnesians and Persians by land and sea (Xen. *Hell.* 1.1.16–18; Diod. Sic. 13.49.5–51). This victory handed Athenians naval supremacy in the region and brought despair to those Spartans who survived. An intercepted message read "Ships gone. Mindarus dead. Men starving. We don't know what to do" (Xen. *Hell.* 1.1.23). The Spartan authorities were shocked into offering peace terms (Diod. Sic. 13.51.2), which were rejected (Diod. Sic. 13.53.2). And so the war continued into its third decade. Over the next few years, the Athenians engaged their disobedient allies or the Persians in the region with varying success, their rule of the waves unhindered by any serious Spartan challenge. It eventually came because of one man.

Lysander is a Spartan who belies the traditional image. Anyone less mindlessly obedient, stolid, or content to be a cog in the state machinery would be difficult to find. Lysander appears abruptly on the historical stage as navarch, supreme commander of the newly commissioned Spartan naval forces, the highest-ranking office he ever attained. With the Peloponnesian War dragging on and despite the serious setback they had suffered in Sicily, the Athenians still fought with renewed vigor under the leadership of Alcibiades, whose previous exploits had been, if not exactly forgiven and forgotten, at least overlooked for the moment. This phase of the war culminated in the famous Athenian victory over the Peloponnesian fleet at Cyzicus in 410 B.C.E. Perhaps spurred by this, the Spartans made the happy decision a couple of years later to appoint Lysander as "commander of the fleet" (*nauarchos*), possibly the first incumbent of the newly minted position (Xen. *Hell.* 1.5.1). Of his earlier career we know nothing. His family, though aristocratic and of Heraclid descent, was poor and the young Lysander entered the Spartan citizen training system not in his own right as the son of a Spartiate in good standing, but as a *mothax*, which probably indicated that he had gone through a form of fictive adoption into another Spartiate family (Plut. *Lys.* 2.1). His straitened economic circumstances did not hinder his social advancement, however; in his youth he became the lover of King Agis' lame second son, Agesilaus. This relationship would have profound consequences for the future of Sparta (Plut. *Lys.* 22.6).

Lysander wasted no time. When the Great King of Persia's son Cyrus arrived in Sardis on orders from his father, Lysander formed a close relationship with the teenager that would have huge historical significance. The Cyrus–Lysander nexus meant that the Persians now decided to get off the fence, stop playing one side against the other, and commit themselves wholly to the Spartan cause. At Lysander's request, Persian money started flowing to the fleet in considerable quantities, enabling Lysander to lure crew away from the Athenians with the promise of higher pay (Xen. *Hell.* 1.5.2–7). At the same time, with the cunning of a Mafia don, he began to build up a network of like-minded oligarchs throughout the Aegean who were bound to him personally through the exchange of favors and who expected to ride to power on his coattails after the Athenian empire's inevitable dissolution (Diod. Sic. 13.70.4; Plut. *Lys.* 5.6). The high point of this phase of Lysander's career came at Notium (406), when he defeated the mercurial Alcibiades' helmsman, who had been left in charge of the entire Athenian fleet. The inevitable result was that Alcibiades was yet again exiled from Athens, this time for good (Xen. *Hell.* 1.5.10–17; Plut. *Alc.* 35.4–6).

When Lysander's one-year term as navarch ended, he grudgingly handed his command over to Callicratidas, himself a *mothax*, but one who had actually internalized all the lessons about Spartan morality he had received during his training to be a citizen (Xen. *Hell.* 1.6.1; Diod. Sic. 13.76.2). Idealistic, unbending, and totally at a loss as to how to deal with "foreigners," Callicratidas suffered humiliation from his predecessor as well as from his supposed ally. On the heels of a whispering campaign waged by his supporters against the new navarch, Lysander sabotaged Callicratidas' ability to pay the fleet by unexpectedly sending all the cash still in hand when he left office back to Sardis (Xen. *Hell.* 1.6.4, 10). Unwilling or unable to use Lysander's creative fundraising methods in the Greek cities allied to Sparta, Callicratidas approached Cyrus at Sardis, cap in hand. The young prince kept Callicratidas kicking his heels at the satrapal capital while he himself spent the day drinking. Deeply insulted, the new navarch stormed back to the coast, vowing, we are told, to reconcile the Greeks so the barbarians would again come to fear them (Xen. *Hell.* 1.6.6–8; Plut. *Lys.* 6.2). Unfortunately for Callicratidas' grand plans, the Spartan fleet was decisively defeated later in his term in a large naval engagement with the Athenians near the islands of Arginusae off the Asia Minor coast, and he was killed (Xen. *Hell.* 1.6.31). So crippling a reverse was the defeat at Arginusae that Sparta sent ambassadors to Athens to sue for peace, a proposal the Athenians rejected (Arist. [*Ath. Pol.*] 34.1). Seeing all their side's gains crumbling and worried for their own futures, Sparta's allies and Cyrus himself clamored for the return of Lysander. Since according to Spartan procedure no one was allowed to serve in a capacity such as that of navarch more than once, the problem was solved through a bureaucratic fiction: a non-entity named Aracus was named navarch and Lysander became his "secretary," though no one doubted where the real power lay (Xen. *Hell.* 2.1.7; Plut. *Lys.* 7.2–3).

The end was not long in coming. Delighted at having his old friend back again in Ionia (probably winter 406/5), Cyrus turned on the Persian tap again and promised much more. If his father the Great King was not forthcoming, he said that he would come up with the cash himself, even if it meant cutting up his solid gold and silver throne. Going even further, he entrusted his satrapy to Lysander when his father summoned him back to Persia for a consultation (Xen. *Hell.* 1.1.11–14; Plut. *Lys.* 9.1–3). Few would have missed the irony of the situation, with the effective governor of much of Persian-controlled Asia Minor a countryman of Leonidas and the heroes of Plataea, whose city had more recently declared war against Athens in the name of freedom for the Greeks, but few probably realized how accurately it foreshadowed the future.

Lysander kept his fleet busy while waiting for the reinforcements Cyrus had promised. He attacked Aegean islands, laid waste to Aegina and Salamis, just off the Attic coast, and met up with King Agis, who was doggedly harassing the Athenians from his stronghold at Decelea (Plut. *Lys.* 9.2–3). What thoughts went through Agis' mind when he witnessed the review Lysander put on for him of the naval forces at the *mothax's* personal disposal can only be imagined. Despite his show of strength, Lysander still felt unready to meet the Athenians in open battle, so upon learning of their approach he quickly removed himself and his fleet back across the Aegean. There he found the city of Lampsacus on the Hellespont unguarded. In a combined operation with allied land forces under a Spartiate named Thorax, Lysander captured and sacked the town. Hot on his heels, the Athenian fleet soon found out about Lampsacus and decided to sail into the Hellespont and beach their ships in a place where they could keep an eye on their enemies (Xen. *Hell.* 2.1.18–21; Plut. *Lys.* 9.4). Across from Lampsacus, the Hellespont flattens out and is lined with nondescript beaches. Today, rusting hulks of freighters litter the landscape; in antiquity, it was named "Goat Rivers" after the streams that flowed there – Aegospotami.

Day after day, the naval secretary embarked his men onto the ships at dawn and drew up his infantry in their battle lines on shore, refusing to react when the Athenians approached and only standing down at evening after he had verified that the Athenians themselves had disembarked (Xen. *Hell.* 2.1.22–4; Plut. *Lys.* 10.1–3). Alcibiades, unexpectedly visiting the Athenian camp from his nearby compound, advised his compatriots to move to a safer location closer to the city of Sestos but was brushed off (Xen. *Hell.* 2.25–6; Plut. *Lys.* 10.4–5; *Alc.* 36.4–37.1). The Athenian generals thus played right into Lysander's hands. The fifth day began as the others had. But this time, when the Athenians had disembarked and had dispersed to go foraging, shopping, cook a meal, or take a nap, Lysander did not stand his troops down. Instead, as he had already ordered, the surveillance ships sailed back at top speed once they saw the Athenians were ashore. When they reached the middle of the channel they raised a bronze shield as a signal for the rest of the navy to attack. Rushing across the narrow divide, Lysander caught the enemy by surprise (Xen. *Hell.* 2.1.21). Lysander's attack caused complete confusion; landing a force of infantry on shore, he soon captured the enemy camp and the vast majority of the surviving Athenian naval forces. Only one general, Conon, slipped through the Spartan net and sailed off with eight triremes to spend the next few years in the service of King Evagoras of Cyprus (Xen. *Hell.* 2.1.27–29; Plut. *Lys.* 11).

Now that Athenian power had been shattered, Sparta, or more accurately Lysander, was supreme in the Aegean. Lysander's ships uncontestedly controlled the straits of the Hellespont, through which Athens' vital grain supplies from the wheat fields of the Crimea passed. Lysander's hand was around Athens' throat. To ensure the now-blockaded city felt the pressure, he then toured the Aegean ordering all Athenians in every city to return to Athens on pain of death, thus increasing the number of mouths that had to be fed. He also made good on his promises to his cronies by installing them in power as ten-man juntas called decarchies under the protection of Spartan governors (*harmostai*) (Xen. *Hell.* 2.2.1–2; Plut. *Lys.* 13.2–4). With major Greek cities now in the hands of ruthless men whose allegiance was to him personally rather than to the city of Sparta, Lysander had begun to build his own private empire.

When he arrived in Attica again, he was joined by kings Agis and Pausanias. For the first time in over a century, two Spartan kings were in the field at the same time, a sign of the magnitude of the event. At a meeting of the kings, commanders, and allies, the two most prominent "hawks," Agis and Lysander, proposed wiping Athens off the map (Paus. 3.8.6). But they apparently had not bothered to consult with the ephors back in Sparta, where opinion was deeply divided on how to deal with a defeated Athens. Among those who opposed this extreme measure was probably Agis' political rival Pausanias. The ephors called a meeting where, to the Thebans' and Corinthians' disappointment, Athens was spared (Xen. *Hell.* 2.2.19–20).

Thwarted, and with Athens still stubbornly refusing to surrender formally, Lysander headed yet again back to his familiar territory of the eastern Aegean, where he continued his work of removing democracies and installing decarchies. It was a bloody business: many people lost their lives or became refugees as Lysander re-shaped the Aegean world to suit his ambitions. His siege of Samos succeeded and he gave the city over to oligarchic exiles. He also scored a couple of propaganda victories, returning the people of Aegina to their island, which he freed from Athenian control, and bringing the now-aging survivors of the horrific massacre perpetrated by the Athenians in 416 back to Melos (Xen. *Hell.* 2.2.9; Plut. *Lys.* 14.1–3).

Meanwhile, with the annihilation option off the table, negotiations dragged on as the Athenians tried to obtain the best terms possible. After several months, they accepted a decree of the ephors at the urging of Theramenes, who had the reputation of being a survivor. The Spartan terms were simple: if they desired peace, the Athenians were to demolish the Piraeus fortifications and the Long Walls, remove their settlers and garrisons from all cities that still remained under their control, confine their future activity to the territory of Attica, and allow exiles to return (Xen. *Hell.* 2.2.18–22; Plut. *Lys.* 3–6). This last provision was key to Lysander's plans for the governance of an Athens subservient to Sparta, as events would soon show. The great war between the two leading states of Greece finally ended on Munichion 16, 404, when Lysander sailed into the Piraeus with the returning exiles and the city's famous walls began to be razed, accompanied by flute music (Xen. *Hell.* 2.2.23; Plut. *Lys.* 15.4). Soon after, Lysander must have sailed off again, biding his time.

Post-war Athens was in turmoil. Already reeling from months of blockade, the city now had to deal with an influx of returning settlers, soldiers, and political exiles. Food was in desperately short supply, over-crowding unbearable. Given these factors alone, the practical obstacles to peace and order would have been almost insurmountable. But added to this was a heightened level of tension in the city as various oligarchic factions contended over how to effect the "regime change" the Spartan victors so obviously wanted. After the peace terms were accepted, Theramenes first attempted to establish a government accept-able to Sparta, but his agitation came to nothing. There was still some life left in the democracy after all. Theramenes' failure to establish a moderate oligarchy, however, provided some of the returned exiles with the opportunity to call upon Lysander to intervene (Arist. [*Ath. Pol.*] 34.3). In the fall of the year, in an assembly meeting called at the Spartans' behest, the Athenians voted to hand their government over to a provisional committee of thirty members, ten of whose members Lysander chose himself. Having established yet another government controlled by men beholden to him alone, Lysander then sailed off one final time, never to return to Athens (Xen. *Hell.* 2.3.1–3; Plut. *Lys.* 12.73–8).

Lysander's power and prestige were now at their height. The Aegean world was full of cities governed by his creatures, while he enjoyed the full backing of the ephors at home and a Persian prince abroad. The grateful Samian oligarchs renamed their major religious festival the *Heraia Lysandreia* in his honor, sacrificing and singing paeans to him as if to a god. Statues of him were erected by the Ephesians and the Acanthians; he had his own epic poet, Choerilus, on retainer. Lysander himself dedicated bronze tripods in the sanctuary of the Graces at Amyclae and two gold statues of Victory on Sparta's acropolis, each holding an eagle in commemoration of his victories at Notium and Aegospotami (Plut. *Lys.* 18; Paus. 3.17.4, 18.7–8). But he saved his most extravagant gesture for the panhellenic site of Delphi, a massive group of 37 bronze statues with himself in the front row being crowned by Poseidon, placed just inside the entrance to the sanctuary (Plut. *Lys.* 18.1; Paus. 10.9.7–9).

These developments must have caused concern to the authorities back in Sparta. Would Lysander, with his unparalleled preeminence and apparently widespread support throughout the Aegean, ever be content with a subordinate role again? Was he a threat to national stability? Lysander's role in the discussions of Athens' fate and his arrogant behavior had shown that he was not exactly the model of a Spartan consensus-builder. There were other reasons for worry. Lysander's right-hand man, Gylippus, the hero of Syracuse, had been caught trying to embezzle 30 talents of silver from the cash Lysander sent back from Asia (Diod. Sic. 13.106.8–9; Plut. *Lys*. 16.1–17.1). In 403/2 the kings Pausanias and Agis, in a rare show of unanimity, decided to rein Lysander in.

The colony of captains and bosuns from his fleet at Aegospotami that he had imposed on the city of Sestos as a punishment for their pro-Athenian leanings was withdrawn, and the original inhabitants allowed to return (Plut. *Lys*. 14.3). The ephors also abruptly abolished his system of decarchies. Henceforth, every city was to enjoy its "ancestral constitution" – a politically pliable term which could be made to refer to almost any type of government (Xen. *Hell*. 3.4.2). Athens was probably the first beneficiary of this change in policy, where the abuses of the committee of Thirty had fueled a democratic insurgency that had already succeeded in capturing the port of Piraeus (Xen. *Hell*. 2.4.1–10). Lysander, at the head of an army sent out from Sparta to impose order in Attica, was overtaken at Eleusis by Pausanias, whom the ephors had ordered to replace him in the field. Lysander was recalled and, after a short skirmish, Pausanias effected a settlement at Athens which abolished arbitrary rule and re-established the democracy (Xen. *Hell*. 2.4.28–32). Within Sparta, the huge amounts of cash now flowing into the city raised such grave concerns about social stability that the ephors introduced a prohibition on the private ownership of precious metal coinage (Plut. *Lys*. 17.1–6), which although short-lived cost the life of at least one high-profile Spartiate, the commander Thorax, who was executed after being found in possession of silver (Plut. *Lys*. 19.4).

Lysander may have been down but he was not out. An attempt to convict him of bribing the oracle of Zeus Ammon in Libya, which he had unexpectedly visited soon after his return to Lacedaemon, failed, despite denunciations directly from the Libyans themselves (Diod. Sic. 14.13.5–7; *FGrH* 70 F206). And almost immediately after the Athenian crisis had passed, Pausanias found himself on trial for his "leniency" towards the Athenians, with his behavior compared unfavorably to Lysander's more robust approach. At this point, Lysander may have helped garner Spartan support for Cyrus' attempt to unseat his elder brother as Great King of Persia, which involved the creation of a Greek mercenary army – Xenophon's famous Ten Thousand (Xen. *Hell*. 3.1). Another sign of Lysander's continuing influence followed upon the death of Agis in 400, when he skillfully devised a smear campaign against Agesilaus' half-nephew Leotychidas that succeeded in destroying Agis' heir's claim to the kingship, thus enabling his former lover to ascend the throne despite oracles which explicitly ruled out lame kings for Sparta (Xen. *Hell*. 3.3.1–4; Paus. 3.8.9).

The time seemed ripe for a comeback. The young king Agesilaus needed to legitimize himself with military glory and Lysander knew just the arena for it – Asia, where, he urged, the decarchies needed to be re-established (Xen. *Hell*. 3.4.2). Two years of campaigning there, prompted by a request from the Asiatic Greeks, had resulted in no significant gains, and now word had come that the Persians were strengthening their fleet in order to challenge Sparta's control of the Aegean (Xen. *Hell*. 3.4.1; Plut. *Ages*. 6.1). After a less than felicitous start, when Agesilaus' attempts to emulate Agamemnon by sacrificing at Aulis were disrupted by Boeotian cavalry, the king arrived in Ephesus with Lysander among his advisers (Xen. *Hell*. 3.4.3–4). But things did not work out as Lysander had planned, for Agesilaus was indisposed to be a cipher, and very soon a permanent break occurred between them. The reason was simple yet crucial, for, despite all the professions of equality, status was a desperately serious matter at Sparta, as Lysander would be reminded to his cost.

When Agesilaus brought Lysander to Ephesus as one of his advisers in 396, the locals already knew Lysander, and so addressed their petitions first to him, as a sort of power-broker. In retaliation, Agesilaus refused Lysander any military commands and either rejected outright any petition he thought his adviser supported or only partially granted it. When Lysander realized what was happening, he supposedly advised his old supporters to go directly to the king without approaching him beforehand. Most did, but people still tended to gather around him on his walks and in the gymnasia (Xen. *Hell*. 3.4.7–9). To a proud Spartan king, seeing Lysander surrounded by fawning crowds while he himself walked through the streets almost alone, like a private citizen, must have been intolerable.

Agesilaus inevitably prevailed in this status contest, crowning his victory with a petty insult: rather than appoint his former friend to a prestigious military or administrative post, he named Lysander his "carver" (*kreodaitês*), which may have been roughly equivalent to the modern rank of Quartermaster General (Plut. *Lys*. 23.11). The duties were hardly suited to the ambitions of a man like Lysander. He eventually prevailed upon Agesilaus to send him away from Ephesus on an ambassadorial mission to the Hellespont, where he had some success in inducing the disgruntled Persian leader Spithridates to defect to the Spartan side together with his troops. But with no other demands for his skills, Lysander returned home when his term expired (Xen. *Hell.* 3.4.10, 20).

Even now, the wily old warrior retained influence in Sparta. Circumstances seemed to play into his hands in 395, when a long-running territorial dispute between Locris and Phocis broke out into an open conflict, aggravated by Theban interference and Persian gold, that history would record as the opening of the Corinthian War (Xen. *Hell.* 3.5.1–5; Plut. *Lys.* 27). When the Phocians appealed to Sparta for military assistance, Lysander saw his chance. Still nursing a deep-seated grudge against the Thebans for their support of the Athenian insurgency during the days of the Thirty, Lysander so played on Spartan suspicions of Boeotian motives that the ephors readily decided to station a garrison in Thebes itself with Lysander as commander (Xen. *Hell.* 3.5.6; Plut. *Lys.* 28). While he approached Thebes from the north, his old adversary Pausanias would lead another army up from the Peloponnesus to a rendezvous point near the small, but strategically located city of Haliartus in Boeotia. Lysander arrived first, after sending a message to Pausanias that was intercepted and handed over to the Thebans, who quickly sent reinforcements to the endangered city (Xen. *Hell.* 3.5.7; Plut. *Lys.* 28.3–4). Running out of patience the next day sitting outside the walls waiting for Pausanias to arrive, Lysander made a foolish, and fatal, mistake. Through heralds he urged the citizens to surrender, and when they refused, he attacked. As he led his troops dangerously close to the walls, the Thebans, whose presence in the town he was evidently unaware of, burst out on the attack. Lysander and several of his men, including his personal seer, were killed while his army fled in disarray. When Pausanias arrived on the scene, he arranged a truce in order to recover Lysander's body, despite vociferous objections from the hardliners in his staff that Spartans should win Spartan bodies back from their enemies by force of arms or die in the attempt (Xen. *Hell.* 3.5.18–24; Plut. *Lys.* 29.1–2).

Even death did not remove Lysander completely from the Spartan political scene, for Pausanias paid the price for his contravention of Sparta's all-or-nothing ideology. After the debacle at Haliartus, the king found himself again on trial before the ephors, this time on the capital charges of failing to arrive at Haliartus on time and refusing to fight for Lysander's body. Old accusations concerning his handling of the Athenian crisis years before were also dug up. Seeing the writing on the wall, Pausanias did not wait for the inevitable death sentence, but fled to nearby Tegea, where he wrote political pamphlets until his death of disease some years later (Xen. *Hell.* 3.5.25).

Finally, a strange tale. Sometime after Lysander's death, when Agesilaus was looking for certain papers in Lysander's house, he came upon an interesting speech (Plut. *Lys.* 30). Written for his former friend by a top speechwriter, it proposed a radical reform of the Spartan constitution, namely the opening up of the kingship to election from all the Heraclid families. Further digging revealed that Lysander thought to bolster his argument for this revolutionary change by means of an elaborate charade involving a boy from Pontus whose mother claimed he was the son of Apollo; counterfeit oracles at Delphi, one of which would explicitly call for Spartan kings to be elected "from the best citizens;" and the bribing of priests there and at the other oracle sites of Dodona and Siwah in Libya. The full implications of Lysander's visit to the oracle of Zeus Ammon at the end of the war with Athens were now revealed. Without doubt, and with some justification, Lysander had thought that he would be the successful candidate under such a system. Luckily for Sparta's stability, though, the plan collapsed when, as Plutarch enigmatically put it, "Lysander never got his little play because of the timidity of one of his actors and co-conspirators, who when it came to the job, was frightened and got out of costume" (*Lys.* 26.6). Despite some questions about details of this story, for Lysander to have made this attempt is consistent with what we know of his character – he was indeed "the man who would be king."

8

Agesilaus and the Army

When the Eurypontid Agesilaus II became king in 400 B.C.E., thanks to Lysander's machinations, he could not have foreseen the complete ruin of Spartan power that would occur during his lifetime. In the space of some thirty years, his city went from being the undisputed power in the Aegean to lacking even the ability to control the most prized part of its own territory. Agesilaus' role in the process has been debated since antiquity. The subject of a hagiographical biography by his friend and supporter Xenophon and a more nuanced one by the Boeotian Plutarch, Agesilaus has few advocates among historians today. But it is doubtful whether any single individual would have been able to keep Sparta in the position it held in 400, and certainly not one lacking all Lysander's dark talents. Agesilaus was far from a second Lysander, though not since Cleomenes had a king been so in control of the domestic political scene as Agesilaus was throughout his reign. Agesilaus, however, lacked his Agiad predecessor's ability to translate dominance at home into coherent foreign policy and flexibility in realizing its goals.

Agesilaus was about forty years old when he succeeded Agis (Xen. *Hell.* 5.4.13) and, because he was not the heir apparent, had gone through the state-run citizen training (Plut. *Ages.* 1.2–4). This experience was supposed to have given him a feeling for the common man, but it also might have fixed in him a rigid conception of what was proper for Sparta. He was also congenitally lame in one leg; the disability did not bar him from the training, in which he did rather well (Plut. *Ages.* 2.2–3). The first recorded event of Agesilaus' reign was the discovery of Cinadon's conspiracy, foreshadowed by an omen while the new king was sacrificing (Xen. *Hell.* 3.3.4). The ephors' swift and ruthless suppression of it may have influenced his own actions when faced with other serious conspiracies in 369 (Plut. *Ages*. 32.6–11). But the most important event of his early reign was his crossing over to Asia Minor at the head of an army of 10,000, a surge of troops intended to bring Sparta's war against the Persians to a successful conclusion.

Agesilaus' two years in Asia Minor (396–394 B.C.E.) hinted at the shape of things to come. Efficiently showing Lysander who was now in charge, Agesilaus sidelined him. But, despite vague plans to march into the heart of the Persian Empire (Xen. *Ages*. 1.36; *Hell*. 4.1.41; Plut. *Ages*. 15.1), he made no lasting gains. Certainly, he defeated Persian forces several times, once penetrating as far east as Paphlagonia (Xen. *Hell*. 4.1.3). He achieved enough against Tissaphernes, Sparta's old (and undependable) ally, for the Great King to have his underling executed and replaced (Xen. *Hell*. 3.4.25), but captured no significant enemy strongholds and adapted little to new methods of warfare, contenting himself with ravaging the countryside. Agesilaus' traditional Spartan disdain for the sea moreover proved fatal, resulting in the defection of the strategic island of Rhodes in 396 to Conon at the head of a Phoenician fleet (Diod. Sic. 14.79.4–8), while his neglect of the threat the Thebans posed to his rear eventually resulted in his recall well before he had accomplished his mission. Relations between Thebes and Sparta had been steadily worsening for several years. The Thebans' open support for Thrasybulus and his insurgents during the rule of the Thirty in Athens had not helped. In the Aulis incident, the Thebans showed their disdain for Agesilaus' panhellenic pretensions, and their defeat of Lysander's army by Haliartus in 395 brought their split with Sparta out into the open, gaining them eager allies. The situation in Greece was rapidly deteriorating.

Laden with booty, Agesilaus returned via the northern land route (Xen. *Ages*. 2.1; *Hell*. 4.3.1). At Amphipolis, he received good news of a Spartan victory at the Battle of the Nemea River (Xen. *Hell*. 3.1) and later battled his way through a now-hostile Thessaly, where he inflicted a defeat on its renowned cavalry (Xen. *Ages*. 2.2–4; *Hell*. 4.3–8), to the borders of Boeotia. Agesilaus' next battle, at Coronea in August 394, was another welcome victory, especially since news of Conon's destruction of the fleet off Cnidus arrived just before the battle (Xen. *Hell*. 4.3.10, 15–21). Leaving a huge tithe to Apollo at Delphi, Agesilaus, though wounded, crossed over the Corinthian Gulf with his haul from Asia Minor but left insufficient forces behind to re-establish Spartan control over central Greece. He spent the next years campaigning in the Corinthia. Spartan successes such as the capture of Lechaeum harbor, Piraeum on the Perachora peninsula, and the destruction of Corinth's Long Walls (Xen. *Hell.* 4.4.7–13, 5.1–6) were tempered by the shredding of a regiment (*mora*) of Lacedaemonian hoplites by Athenian light-armed troops near Lechaeum in 390 (Xen. *Hell.* 4.5.11–17). The next year saw Agesilaus in western Greece, supporting the Achaean stronghold of Calydon against the local Acarnanians. The results were similar to those of his Asia Minor campaign, and his withdrawal after several months of fighting left the Achaeans dissatisfied. Still, the mere threat of his return in 388 was enough to induce the Acarnanians to join the Peloponnesian League (Xen. *Hell.* 4.6–7.1).

When the Corinthian War sputtered to an end in 387/6 on the heels of an Athenian defeat at the Hellespont (Xen. *Hell.* 5.1.25–9), the Spartans held the whip hand at the conference to ratify the peace deal dictated by the Persian King Artaxerxes. The King decided that all Greek cities in Asia Minor should belong to him and that all other cities, except only the Athenian possessions of Lemnos, Imbros, and Scyros, should be autonomous (Xen. *Hell.* 5.1.31). The King's Peace, as it is called, suited the interests of Sparta and of Agesilaus, who perhaps saw an opportunity to recover Sparta's old supremacy in the Peloponnese and to re-establish what he saw as its traditional hegemony in mainland Greece. With Persian support, Sparta now acted as the Peace's self-appointed policeman, broadly interpreting the autonomy clause to justify intervention in any state on nearly any pretext. Agesilaus enforced the provisions of the Peace by using the threat of armed force to break up the Boeotian League (Xen. *Hell.* 5.1.33). This action was, on the surface, justifiable, but not the destruction of Mantinea in Arcadia, for which Agesilaus was morally, if not materially, responsible.

Relations between Sparta and Mantinea were rocky at the time: although a member of the Peloponnesian League, Mantinea was a democracy in 385 and was cozying up to Argos. Mantineans had been reluctant to send troops during the recent war (Xen. *Hell.* 5.1.1–2). Indicative of the tension was that Agesilaus preferred to bring his army home through Mantinean territory at night after the Lechaeum disaster rather than risk the locals' ridicule by marching in daylight (Xen. *Hell.* 4.5.18). The new Peace now afforded Sparta the chance to settle this score, so envoys were sent to demand that the Mantineans pull down their walls. They refused; Sparta declared war (Xen. *Hell.* 5.2.3). Despite his personal involvement, Agesilaus begged off the command with the flimsy excuse that the Mantineans had provided signal service to his father Archidamus during the helot revolt of 465/4 B.C.E. Instead, his co-king Agesipolis did the unwelcome job well and with little loss of Spartan life. Realizing that he could not take the city by traditional methods like circumvallation and ravaging of the land, since the Mantineans possessed a large store of grain, he made the river Ophis flood so that the city's mudbrick walls began to dissolve, which quickly motivated the Mantineans to surrender. The Spartans then wiped the city from the map, demolishing its walls and breaking it up into its constituent villages in a sort of reverse synoecism. Leading pro-Argive politicians were allowed to go into exile, the government was turned over to aristocratic landowners, and Sparta was rid of a nuisance (Xen. *Hell.* 5.2.4–7).

Watching Mantinea's fate with interest was a group of exiles from Phlius, who now decided to use the Spartans' policy of scrutinizing their allies' past behavior to their advantage. In 384, they pleaded their case before the Spartans, who pressured the Phlians to restore them and their property (Xen. *Hell.* 5.2.8–10). After three years, however, settling the returned exiles' property claims caused so much friction that they again approached the Spartans for help. This unauthorized request for foreign intervention prompted a large fine from the Phlians. Agesilaus had all the excuse he needed. The ephors duly mobilized the troops and, despite opposition at home to antagonizing groundlessly a city with several times the population of Sparta, Agesilaus invaded Phlian territory and settled down for a siege (Xen. *Hell.* 5.3.10–16). By strictly rationing their food supply, the Phleians held out for much longer than expected. In fact, with Agesilaus devising no creative solutions to resolve it, the siege dragged on for twenty months, until the Phlians sued for peace directly to the authorities at Sparta. Petulant at this disregard for his powers as a king in the field, Agesilaus used his domestic supporters to block any deal and ensured that all decisions about Phlius' fate should be his alone. Armed with the ephors' authorization, he imposed a settlement eerily reminiscent of Lysander's for Athens – a commission of one hundred Spartan sympathizers empowered to draw up a new constitution and to execute anyone it wanted (Xen. *Hell.* 5.3.21–5).

Agesilaus' disdain for legality and public opinion is still better illustrated in a episode that has remained notorious since the fourth century. Two Spartan armies had been sent out in 382 in response to a request by northern Greek cities for protection against the expansionist designs of the city of Olynthus on the Chalcidic peninsula. The smaller advance force arrived quickly and began operations in Thrace, but one Phoebidas, who commanded the main body of troops that set out later, had other ideas. He diverged from the route through Boeotia and encamped outside Thebes, which was split, as were many cities, into rival pro- and anti-Spartan factions. The dominant anti-Spartans had just passed a provocative law forbidding Thebans from fighting with the Spartans against Olynthus. Aided by a leading member of the pro-Spartan faction, Phoebidas seized the Cadmea, the city's acropolis, when all the Theban women were congregated there to celebrate a religious festival. With their women held hostage, the Thebans surrendered, hundreds of anti-Spartans fled, and a Spartan garrison was imposed on the city (Xen. *Hell.* 5.2.25–31; Diod. Sic. 15.20.2). But when Leontiades, the Theban quisling who had betrayed his city to the Spartans, arrived in Lacedaemon to bring the good news, he was met with an unexpected storm of criticism from the ephors and most of the populace, who roundly condemned Phoebidas for his unauthorized action. The exception was, unsurprisingly, Agesilaus, who publicly articulated his policy: expediency was the only factor that counted in foreign relations (Xen. *Hell.* 5.2.32). The king's words had an effect, for though they imposed a huge fine on Phoebidas (perhaps paid by Agesilaus himself), the Spartans did not withdraw the garrison (Xen. *Hell.* 5.2.35; Diod. Sic. 15.20.2). Greek public opinion was shocked (Diod. Sic. 15.20.2), while the reception of Leontiades shows how ambivalent many Spartans were becoming about Agesilaus' aggressive "Sparta first" policy. Agesilaus had again allowed his simmering resentment of Thebes to shape his judgement. His hostility was so well known that it was thought, not without reason, that Phoebidas had acted under secret instructions from the king himself (Plut. *Ages.* 24.1; Diod. Sic. 15.20.2).

On the northern front, the massive defeat of a Spartan army in 381 under Teleutias, Agesilaus' half-brother, had been followed by successful campaigns under Agesipolis and, after his death of fever, his successor Polybiades, who brought the Olynthians to heel in 379 and enrolled them as subordinate allies in the Peloponnesian League (Xen. *Hell.* 5.2.37–3.12, 18–20, 26–7). With the north pacified, trouble broke out in 378 in the most expected of places, Thebes. In a daring, well-planned plot, democratic conspirators assassinated the ruling three-man junta and, supported by Athenian troops, expelled the Spartan garrison. A bloodbath ensued as the Theban people vented their anger against their oppressors, killing any of the pro-Spartans they could find and murdering their children (Xen. *Hell.* 5.4.2–14). The ephors' response upon learning the news was to call out the guard, though it was midwinter (Xen. *Hell.* 5.4.13–14). Agesilaus, whose ham-fisted approach to Thebes had been largely responsible for the dire situation, begged off on grounds of age: being over sixty, he was no longer eligible for conscription. Even Xenophon, normally careful to skate around overt criticism of his hero, found this specious, preferring instead to believe that Agesilaus did not want to be seen showing support for tyrants (Xen. *Hell.* 5.4.13). Instead, Cleombrotus, who had just succeeded his brother as Agiad king, dutifully led an army into Boeotia, his first field command. The campaign was perfunctory, to say the least, with little fighting and no attempt at all to capture Thebes. After about a fortnight outside Thebes, perhaps awaiting a diplomatic response, Cleombrotus withdrew his forces, leaving Sphodrias as harmost at Thespiae along with some of the allied troops. Because of the two kings' starkly different approaches, Spartan war policy was in such disarray that ordinary soldiers were unsure whether or not they were actually at war with Thebes (Xen. *Hell.* 5.4.14–18).

The harvest of Agesilaus' misbegotten Theban policy was beginning to ripen. The Thebans declared themselves a democracy, rapidly revived the Boeotian League along democratic lines, and prepared for the expected Spartan reaction (Diod. Sic. 15.28.1). They could expect no help from the Athenians, who were officially horrified at the revolution and so frightened of Sparta's reaction that they punished the two generals involved (Xen. *Hell.* 5.4.19). However, Athenians continued exploratory negotiations with states around the Aegean to form a new system of maritime alliances (Diod. Sic. 15.28.2–4). A series of Spartan missteps – this time not the fault of Agesilaus alone – would soon provide the impetus for the foundation of the Second Athenian Naval Confederacy as a counterweight to Sparta's hegemony in Greece.

Soon after Cleombrotus left him behind in Thespiae, Sphodrias launched a sneak attack on the Piraeus. Unable to get anywhere near his target overnight, he turned back after causing some damage in the Thriasian Plain (Xen. *Hell.* 5.4.20–1). His reasons for flagrantly violating the territory of a state with which Sparta was at peace were unclear – stories of bribery naturally abounded – but the effects of Sphodrias' abortive raid were dramatic. Livid at his duplicity, the Athenians immediately arrested the Spartan ambassadors who happened to be in town and dispatched envoys to Lacedaemon to make their displeasure absolutely clear. For their part, the Spartans, aghast at Sphodrias' actions, had already put him on trial *in absentia* and assured the angry Athenians that the death penalty was inevitable (Xen. *Hell.* 5.4.21–4). Agesilaus now showed that his consummate mastery of internal Spartan politics contrasted with an almost wilful ignorance of the consequences his decisions would have on the international scene.

Agesilaus' unexpected decision to vote for Sphodrias' acquittal on the grounds that Sparta could not afford to lose soldiers whose previous behavior had been so exemplary (Xen. *Hell.* 5.4.25–33) may have been acceptable at home but gave the Athenians justification for creating their own multilateral alliance to provide them with security against Spartan aggression. Domestically, Agesilaus had reasserted his dominance, deftly neutralizing what may have been an attempt to weaken his standing, but he had cynically revealed to all that Sparta's immediate advantage was his sole guiding principle in interstate relations.

In the same year, 378, hostilities between Sparta and Thebes developed into a full-scale war. A major reform in how the Peloponnesian army was levied now meant that the burden of supplying manpower was more evenly distributed among ten geographical areas, with allies being permitted to hire mercenaries to fulfill their obligations (Xen. *Hell.* 5.2.20–1; Diod. Sic. 15.31.1–2). Thus, it was at the head of a large army conscripted under the new system that Agesilaus, despite his earlier protestations about his age, marched into Boeotia, the younger Cleombrotus having lost the authorities' trust. Over several months of fighting, Agesilaus accomplished nothing of consequence, wasting most of his time in attempts to breach defensive works erected around the city. Unable to lure the Theban forces out into a pitched battle, he went home with his army at the end of the campaigning season (Xen. *Hell.* 5.4.38–41; Diod. Sic. 15.32–33.1). Agesilaus returned in 377 with similar results, although his ravaging did cause a food shortage at Thebes (Xen. *Hell.* 5.4.47–57). This was Agesilaus' last active command for seven years. On the return journey he suffered an attack of acute thrombophlebitis at Megara; its treatment resulted in a significant loss of blood. Carried back to Sparta, he spent the next several months on his sickbed (Xen. *Hell.* 5.4.58).

With Agesilaus still incapacitated in spring 376, Cleombrotus led the invasion force. He only half-heartedly attempted to force passage into Theban territory, thus signaling a significant shift in policy. For the next two years, Boeotia would be left in peace (Xen. *Hell.* 5.4.59, 63) while Sparta dealt with the threat posed by the Athenians' growing naval power, which that same year brought them victory over the

Peloponnesian fleet off Naxos, Athens' first autnomous naval triumph since the Peloponnesian War (Diod. Sic. 15.35). The change in focus was partly due to severe disaffection among Sparta's allies, who were tired of Agesilaus' obsession with Thebes and inability to prosecute his campaigns successfully (Plut. *Ages.* 26.6). There were also signs that Agesilaus no longer wielded overwhelming influence over Spartan foreign policy. Some realism had entered into their calculations, best exemplified by Sparta's refusal to send military aid to Pharsalus in Thessaly in 375 due to lack of manpower (Xen. *Hell.* 6.1.4–17). Gone were the days when Sparta could project its power anywhere in the Aegean.

Threats were multiplying on every side. Thebes was successfully consolidating its power over Boeotia and developing a formidable military machine (Xen. *Hell.* 5.4.46, 63, 6.1.1; Plut. *Pel.* 15). Against all odds, Athens was attracting new allies for its Naval Confederacy, including Thebes (*IG* II^2 43). In Thessaly, a newcomer to Greek power politics, Jason of Pherae, had exploited Sparta's incapacity to help Pharsalus to establish himself as the supreme leader (Xen. *Hell.* 6.1.18–19). In spring 375, the Thebans inflicted a morale-crushing defeat at Tegyra on a Spartan *mora* returning from Locris to its quarters in Orchomenus, killing two of their commanding officers (Diod. Sic. 15.37; Plut. *Pel.* 16–17). They also threatened Sparta's old ally Phocis, prompting the Spartans to dispatch a force under Cleombrotus to protect it (Xen. *Hell.* 6.1). A short respite in the crisis was afforded by the King's Peace, renewed at the demand of the Great King in 375, though in allowing the Athenians to retain their new Naval Confederacy, it simply recognized the facts on the ground (Diod. Sic. 15.38.1–3). Whether the Thebans were included in the Peace or not, they retained control over most of Boeotia.

When the Peace broke down in a matter of months, Spartans found themselves confronting an unstable alliance of Athens, Thebes, and Thessaly. Thebes' capture of Plataea and Thespiae in 373 put Theban relations with Athens under great strain, but the alliance held, for the moment (Diod. Sic. 15.46.4–6). By 371, however, Athenians were so nervous about the intentions of their ambitious ally that they joined in sending ambassadors to Sparta to hammer out another general peace agreement (Diod. Sic. 6.3.1–2). All went well until a dispute broke out at the signing ceremony between the Theban representative Epaminondas and Agesilaus, now back on the scene, over the touchy matter of autonomy. Epaminondas refused to sign for Thebes alone rather than for the Boeotians as a whole unless Agesilaus did the same as Sparta's representative. To Agesilaus' angry question whether he would allow Boeotian cities to be independent, Epaminondas asked the same question of Sparta and the Laconian cities. An intelligent politician, Epaminondas must have been prepared for Agesilaus' reaction: he struck Thebes off the treaty and soon declared war (Xen. *Hell.* 6.3.2–20; Plut. *Ages.* 28; Diod. Sic. 15.50.4). For the moment Thebes stood alone, as the rest of Greece implemented the terms of the new Peace. In the debate over what to do with Cleombrotus and the army, still in Phocis, Spartans rejected the advice of one Prothoos, perhaps an ephor, that they disband the army and forge a coalition specifically to deal with Thebes, in favor of immediate action (Xen. *Hell.* 6.4.2–3). Reluctantly, Cleombrotus marched his allied army of some 11,000 into Boeotia, where he encamped in sight of the Thebans and Boeotians in the territory of Thespiae, near a place called Leuctra (Xen. *Hell.* 6.4.4).

Cleombrotus was an unwilling battle commander; only by threats of dire punishment awaiting him should he not engage the enemy, did his "friends" persuade him to join battle with Epaminondas (Xen. *Hell.* 6.4.5). He was not alone in his ambivalence, for it was rumored that the Spartans drank until noon on the day of the battle to sharpen their courage (Xen. *Hell.* 6.4.8). When the battle lines were drawn, Cleombrotus chose a standard arrangement of Spartan hoplites in columns twelve deep on the right, with allied troops to the left. He unwisely positioned his badly trained cavalry in front of his hoplite phalanxes, to protect them and screen their movements. He took the usual commanding position on the right wing surrounded by his bodyguard of three hundred elite young troops. Epaminondas, on the other hand, threw the rule book away. Opposite the Spartans and their king he massed his 4,000 Theban troops on the left at an astonishing depth of fifty men, led by Pelopidas and the newly instituted Sacred Band. The Boeotians he lined up eight or twelve deep on the right facing the Spartans' allies. He countered the placement of the Spartan cavalry by putting the battle-hardened Theban horse in front of his own lines (Xen. *Hell.* 6.4.10–12; Diod. Sic. 15.55.1).

Cleombrotus sent his cavalry forward to engage the enemy while units from his left wing redeployed to his right to meet the Theban danger opposite. This maneuver was never completed. The Theban cavalry quickly repulsed the Spartan and pushed it back into the hoplite lines. Confusion broke out. Meanwhile, Cleombrotus' attempt to stretch his line to the right to outflank his enemy had opened up a gap between the Spartan and allied ranks that no one could now fill. The Thebans and Boeotians advanced, but not in the expected way. Epaminondas had got his troops to move forward as if they were a massive hammer, the head of which comprised the Theban columns. As the fifty-deep Theban phalanxes readied themselves to strike against Cleombrotus and his Spartans, the Boeotian troops advanced in a diagonal line with those on the right hanging back somewhat from those on the left. Pelopidas and the Sacred Band rushed forward from the Theban columns. Cleombrotus ordered the Spartans to counterattack, but many did not receive the order because of the confusion caused by the cavalry. Pelopidas' onslaught broke the Spartan front ranks, allowing Epaminondas to apply the full force of the Theban left in smashing through those behind. When the dust cleared, the Thebans were in control of the field and 1,000 Lacedaemonians lay dead, including Cleombrotus. Casualties among the Peloponnesian allies were relatively light since the Boeotians in their diagonal advance had scarcely engaged them. The disaffection of Sparta's allies was well known – some were even said to have been not displeased with the outcome – and Epaminondas clearly hoped to win them over by showing that Thebes' quarrel was with Sparta alone (Xen. *Hell.* 6.4.13–15; Diod. Sic. 15.55–6).

The news reached Sparta on the last day of the Gymnopaediae, while the men's chorus was performing. The ephors allowed it to finish before they announced the defeat and the names of the fallen. Xenophon tells us that the relatives of the dead walked about with smiles on their faces while those of the considerable number of survivors were dejected (Xen. *Hell.* 6.4.16). A politically convenient recurrence of Agesilaus' infirmity meant that the relief force was dispatched to Leuctra under his son Archidamus. That army never engaged the Thebans, as a truce was negotiated through the agency of Jason of Pherae (Xen. *Hell.* 6.4.17–19, 22–6). At Sparta, the survivors of Leuctra precipitated a constitutional crisis. Sparta had sent 700 citizens to the battle, where 400 had been killed, among them the 300-strong royal bodyguard of the best soldiers aged twenty to thirty (Xen. *Hell.* 6.4.15). Of the 300 survivors, many had fled the battle and so were guilty of cowardice. As "tremblers" (*tresantes*) they would normally have been subject to a range of social and economic sanctions, but Sparta could hardly afford to alienate so sizeable a chunk of its Spartiate population now that the total citizen body numbered only slightly over a thousand. Agesilaus, restored to health, was vested with supreme constitutional authority and announced that on this occasion alone, "the laws must sleep for a day" (Plut. *Ages.* 30.5–6).

But there were bigger problems than a few hundred less than enthusiastic hoplites. Leuctra shattered the illusion of Spartan invincibility. In 371/0 Mantinea dared to re-amalgamate under a democratic constitution, the Tegean oligarchy was forced out, and a federal league was founded to embrace all Arcadians (Xen. *Hell.* 6.5.3–9). To meet this new threat and to punish the Tegeans, Agesilaus led troops into Arcadia. True to form, he captured a minor city, laid waste some land, and returned to Laconia without any major engagement (Xen. *Hell.* 6.5.10–21). The Arcadians, however, were no longer willing to allow their land to be used as the Spartan army's dancing floor, and so approached the Thebans for help. This appeared in the form of a massive army of Thebans and their new Peloponnesian allies. As the Theban army marched south, perioecic communities began to defect (Xen. *Hell.* 6.5.25, 32). Epaminondas then struck straight down into the Eurotas valley, destroying fields and houses as he went. The unimaginable had happened. An invading army was in the Laconian land. So alarmed were the Spartans that they offered freedom to any helot who would take up arms against the invader. Six thousand answered the call, to the considerable unease of the remaining Spartiates. Two separate conspiracies were uncovered: one among the perioeci and inferiors, and another, more worrying, among full Spartiates. Agesilaus successfully repressed both, resorting to extra-judicial killing in the case of the Spartiate conspiracy (Plut. *Ages.* 32.6–11).

Despite the Spartans' fears, however, Epaminondas had no intention of destroying their city, just their military and political power. So, after ravaging the land around Sparta and down to the port of Gytheum, he took his army north and west into Messenia, where he inflicted a more damaging blow than burning Sparta's temples and dwellings could ever have been (Xen. *Hell.* 5.6.31–2). He liberated Messenia from Spartan rule and recalled the exiles to found their city anew (Diod. Sic. 15.66). Stripped of their most productive land and a large part of their helot workforce, Spartans would be forever reduced to the status of a second-rate power. In a second invasion of the Peloponnese later in 369 (Xen. *Hell.* 7.1.14–25; Diod. Sic. 15.69–70.1), Epaminondas managed to detach several more states from their alliance with Sparta. Even the Spartan victory in 368 over an allied army of Arcadians, Argires, and Messenians in the Tearless Battle, so named because supposedly no Spartan died, resulted simply in the Arcadians founding the city of

Megalopolis to be yet another obstacle to a resurgence of Spartan power (Xen. *Hell.* 7.1.28–32; Diod. Sic. 15.72.4).

Needless to say, Agesilaus and the Spartans never accepted the loss of Messenia. Spartans refused to be party to any agreement that recognized Messenian independence, explicitly or implicitly. Their intransigence alienated the Great King, whose 367 decree calling for the renewal of the Peace guaranteed Messenia's independence and effectively repudiated his alliance with the Spartans (Xen. *Hell.* 7.1.33–7). When Spartans allowed the Corinthians and any remaining allies who wished to make peace with Thebes in 365, they refused to renounce their claims on Messenia (Xen. *Hell.* 4.7–11), causing the final dissolution of the Peloponnesian League. For his part, Agesilaus spent many of his final years trying to gather funds to hire the now-necessary mercenaries that would enable Sparta to regain its lost possession. Mercenaries sent by Dionysius of Syracuse had comprised the overwhelming bulk of Archidamus' army in the Tearless Battle, which for the time being had revived Spartan confidence (Plut. *Ages.* 33.3–5). But Sparta could not rely simply on the generosity of strong men like Dionysius; money was needed, and so Agesilaus' own career as a mercenary began, with a discreet mission to the Hellespont sometime between 366 and 364; he returned richly rewarded for services rendered to the rebellious satrap Ariobarzanes and the dynast Maussolus of Caria (Xen. *Ages.* 2.26–7).

Agesilaus commanded a citizen army one last time, in 362. The Arcadian League had split into democratic and oligarchic camps, and each called on the appropriate outside power for support. On the side of democratic Tegea, Epaminondas led an expeditionary force into the Peloponnese and, when he learned that the Spartan army had left the city undefended as it marched to meet him, launched a lightning raid into Laconia. Splitting his forces, Agesilaus hastened back and was just able to deploy his men as Epaminondas attacked the city. After some street fighting, the Thebans withdrew to Arcadia. The two sides met near Mantinea. There, Epaminondas and his vast allied army won a resounding victory over oligarchic Mantinea, Sparta, Athens, and Elis, but his death in battle robbed Thebes of the ability to capitalize on his success (Xen. *Hell.* 7.5.27; Diod. Sic. 15.85–7). Wearied by war, the combatants drew up a Common Peace, the first without Persian involvement, to end the pointless interstate conflicts that had exhausted Greek resources for decades (Diod. Sic. 15.89.1–2). Like other recent treaties, it recognized Messenia, making it unacceptable to

Agesilaus and his still (inexplicably) powerful supporters, who effected yet another Spartan refusal to participate and kept the city in a state of war with its western neighbor (Plut. *Ages.* 35.3–5).

By 360, Agesilaus was in Egypt selling his services to one rebel against the Persian Empire before deserting him for another more likely prospect, all the time representing himself and the other mercenaries as an officially sanctioned Spartan military expedition (Plut. *Ages.* 36–9). He died on the coast of Libya on his way back to Sparta with his fee of 230 talents, a tiny fraction of his booty from Asia Minor in 394. His body encased in wax, Sparta's twenty-sixth Eurypontid king was brought home for burial in the family plot in Limnae (Xen. *Ages.* 2.30–31; Plut. *Ages.* 40.2–4). A competent but not brilliant general, he had spent his talents over the years in a single-minded effort to promote Sparta's interests, unfailingly choosing short-term benefits over long-term gain. His obsession with Thebes brought his city to disaster and ensured its continuing isolation. Domestically, Agesilaus built a reputation for liberality and loyalty, helping his friends profit whenever he could and sheltering them at all costs and in the face of clear evidence of their wrongdoing (Xen. *Ages.* 5.1–3). His political techniques at home were sophisticated, but Spartans paid dearly for Agesilaus' management of international relations, limited throughout his reign only to confronting Thebes.

At this point, with Sparta's dream of reconquering Messenia fading and the city's proud military tradition in tatters, we have an opportunity to trace the development of the Spartan army over time and to see what sort of military forces were available to Agesilaus during his reign. There are three traditional "fixed points" around which discussions of the army have centered – Herodotus' account of the battle of Plataea in 479, Thucydides' description of the battle lines drawn up at Mantinea in 418, and the data that can be gleaned from Xenophon's *Hellenica* and *Constitution of the Lacedaemonians* on the army of his own time, the first decades of the fourth century down to the battle of Leuctra in 371. No two authors use precisely the same terminology nor, in fact, do they seem at first sight to be describing exactly the same military structure.

Before the Persian Wars, matters are very hazy indeed. From the few surviving scraps of Tyrtaeus, we can infer that the Archaic army was organized in sections according to the three Dorian tribes, Hylleis, Dymanes, and Pamphyloi (F19 West[2], lines 8–9). It may have fought in hoplite phalanx formation, though this is far from clear, and certainly included light-armed soldiers (*P Oxy.* 3316, line 14). In the Battle of the Champions (*c.* 545) the first inconclusive phase involved the selection of 300 warriors from each side to fight it out in Homeric style. Although victory in the end had to be determined by a normal, full-scale battle, the Battle of the Champions shows how fluid combat formations could be, even at such a relatively late date (Hdt. 1.82).

Only with the battle of Plataea do we finally have some real troop numbers, as well as names for units and officers, though naturally none are beyond dispute. The Spartan force at Thermopylae the previous year – 300 Spartiates out of 3,100 Peloponnesians plus 1,100 Boeotians and maybe a total of 2,000 from Locris and Phocis – was anomalous for its size and unique in the (possible) absence of any perioecic troops (Hdt. 7.202–203.1). To meet the Persians in Boeotia, on the other hand, Herodotus writes that the ephors dispatched 5,000 Spartiate warriors, each accompanied by seven helots, for a total of 40,000 men. Next day, the astonished Athenian envoys were sent to meet them with an additional 5,000 elite perioecic troops (9.10.1, 11.3). When combined with warriors, both hoplite and lightly armed, from the other members of the Hellenic Coalition, the Greek army at Plataea totaled 110,000, according to Herodotus, including an oddly unarmed contingent of 1,800 Thespians (9.26.2–9.30). As often with ancient calculations of military strength, however, even this apparently straightforward set of numbers holds problems. Herodotus seems here to have forgotten about the 5,000 perioecic hoplites sent out after the Spartiates. Not just that – when they do reappear implicitly in his numbers for the Lacedaemonian and Tegean troops isolated later in the battle, they are joined by a hitherto completely unmentioned contingent of 5,000 light-armed troops (9.29.2, 31.2). Sparta thus fielded an army of 50,000 men at Plataea, of which only 5,000 – one in ten – were full citizens. The small (and declining) proportion of Spartiates in the Spartan army was a constant throughout the fifth and fourth centuries, symptomatic of an increasingly serious demographic problem as Sparta literally began to run out of Spartan citizens. The Spartiates at Plataea were organized into *lochoi* (9.53.2, 57.2), apparently under officers Spartans called *lochagoi* (9.53.2; cf. Thuc. 5.66.3–4; Xen. *Lac.* 11.4). Most historians believe that there were five Spartan *lochoi* at Plataea, each recruited from one of the five constituent communities (*ôbai*) of the city, because Herodotus identifies one of the *lochoi* as "the *lochos* of Pitane" (9.53.2).

In contrast to Herodotus' sketchy allusions, Thucydides offers a detailed analysis of the Spartan-led army at the Battle of Mantinea in 418 (5.66.2–67.1, 68.1–3). The Spartans had raised a full levy of their available troops (*pandêmei*) which they dispatched post-haste under King Agis' command into Arcadia to prevent Tegea and the rest of Sparta's still loyal allies from defecting to the Argives. Upon reaching Orestheion to wait for his allies, Agis ordered home one-sixth of the army, comprising the oldest and youngest, to provide homefront security (5.64). The army at Mantinea represented five-sixths of Sparta's total military assets. On the left wing were the Sciritae, a unit of perioeci who held this as a traditional privilege; next were the Brasideioi, the helot hoplites freed after their service in Thrace, and with them the Neodamodeis, the other newly liberated helot warriors. In the center were the Lacedaemonians arranged in *lochoi*, then Arcadians from nearby regions (Thuc. 5.67.1). On the right wing were the Tegeans and "a few" (*oligoi*) Lacedaemonians. Cavalry was stationed on both wings. Opposite these forces stood the Argives, Athenians, and their various allies in an army whose total manpower has been calculated at approximately 8,500 to 10,000.

The problem lies in Thucydides' numbers. Thucydides admits his inability to obtain accurate figures for the Spartans at Mantinea because the size of the Spartan army was concealed "as a matter of state secrecy" (*dia tês politeias to krupton*), an often quoted phrase (5.68.2). Yet he claims to have been able to reach an estimated total by calculating from the disposition of the Spartan forces that were present. He then proceeds to describe the organization of the army on that day: apart from the 600 Sciritae, seven *lochoi* fought, in each of which there were four *pentakostyes* ("fiftieths"?), each of them comprising four *enômotiai* ("sworn bands"). Four men fought in the front rank of each *enômotia*, and the *enômotiai* were, on average, eight ranks deep. Thus, concludes Thucydides, the front rank of the Lacedaemonian part of the army was 448 men strong, excepting the Sciritae on the left wing (5.68.3). From this, historians have deduced that the *lochoi* held about 3,584 men. With the Sciritae added, along with Agis and his 300-strong bodyguard of *hippeis*, forgotten here but mentioned later (Thuc. 5.72.4), the Spartan portion of the army totaled 4,485. Since Sparta's Arcadian allies probably could have contributed no more than 3,500 troops at the very most, the whole army would have been about 8,000 men strong. But Thucydides twice states that the Spartan army appeared to be and was actually larger than the enemy's (5.68.1, 71.2). The only way for this to be true is if the cavalry stationed on both wings and the "few" Lacedaemonians on the right numbered anywhere from 1,000 to 2,000 troops. Scholars therefore reject his numbers as being too small.

The most commonly accepted solution is that Thucydides made an error in military terminology. Instead of *lochoi*, he should have called the largest units *morai*, which are known to have existed at least from 403 B.C.E. onwards (Xen. *Hell.* 2.4.31). Each *mora* comprised two *lochoi*, one of Spartiates and one of perioeci. Not only does this expedient effectively double the number of Lacedaemonian soldiers at Mantinea, it also accounts for the curious absence of perioeci in Thucydides' narrative. A further benefit relates to the Spartan officers: in his account of how orders pass quickly down from the king, Thucydides mentions four ranks – *polemarchoi, lochagoi, pentekonteres*, and *enômotarchai* – but only three levels of unit (Thuc. 5.66.3–4), leaving the polemarchs with no troops to command. Although they might have been the equivalent of general staff officers, it seems better to consider them as commanders of *morai* in 418, as they were in the fourth century (Xen. *Lac.* 11.4). A simple textual emendation removes the objection that Xenophon in the *Constitution of the Lacedaemonians* (*Lac.* 11.4) states that there were four *lochagoi* for every *mora*.

The Brasideioi and Neodamodeis almost certainly fought in a single combined unit (Thuc. 5.67.1), which may have been called a *lochos*, but actually had a strength equivalent to a *mora*. This unit would not have been affected by Agis' orders that one-sixth of the army return home, because it would not have been structured along year-class lines, as were the other units. No Brasideioi were recruited after the Thracian campaigns, and Neodamodeis could hardly have been recruited from the helots strictly according to age-cohort. The Spartan troop-strength can then be calculated as follows: 600 Sciritae + *c*. 1,200 Brasideioi and Neodamodeis + *c*. 6,144 Spartiates and perioeci in 6 *morai* comprising 12 *lochoi* of *c*. 512 men each + 300 *hippeis*, for a total of *c*. 8,544, not including cavalry and the few Lacedaemonians on the wings. With the Arcadian troops added, Agis would have led an army of over 12,000, easily justifying Thucydides' claim that it was the larger.

If this solution is correct, then Spartans reorganized their army at some point after the battle of Plataea and before 418. A solid if not absolutely conclusive argument can be made that this reform took place before 425 B.C.E. because of certain features in Thucydides' account of the Spartans' reaction to the threat posed by Demosthenes' capture of Pylos. Thucydides tells us that the Spartans sent contingents of 420 hoplites in rotation onto the island of Sphacteria drawn by lot from all the *lochoi* (4.8.9), by which he is understood to mean that the lots were drawn among each *enômotia* in the *lochoi* rather than among individual soldiers. If, as is very probable, the Spartans at this time mobilized 35 out of the 40 available age classes from 20 to 59 years of age, the number 420 is best explained as the result of one *enômotia* of 35 men being drawn from each of 12 *lochoi*, implying an army of 6 *morai*, each made up of 2 *lochoi*. That perioeci were already brigaded with Spartiates in the same *morai* can be deduced from Thucydides' statement that of the 292 survivors from the last detatchment only 120 were full Spartan citizens (4.38.5).

After Thucydides, various references in Xenophon's *Constitution of the Lacedaemonians, Anabasis,* and *Hellenica* give us a relatively detailed idea of the shape of the army. Despite some difficulties, the picture that emerges is sufficiently clear. The largest unit was the *mora*, of which there were six (*Hell.* 6.1.1), each commanded by a *polemarchos* (*Hell.* 4.4.7). Each *mora* contained two *lochoi* (*Hell.* 7.4.20), each under a *lochagos* (*Lac.* 11.4, see above), which in turn comprised four *pentekostyes* (*Anab.* 3.4.22), whose officers were called either *pentekostêres* (*Hell.* 3.5.22, 4.5.7) or *pentekonterês* (*Anab.* 3.4.21). In each *pentakostys* were four *enômotiai* (*Hell.* 6.4.12) under the direction of four *enômotiarchai* (*Anab.* 3.4.21). This last calculation involves preferring Thucydides' clear statement that there were four *enômotiai* in each *pentekostys* (5.68.3) over Xenophon's equally bald assertion that there were sixteen *enômotiai* in each *mora*, implying only two per *pentekostys* (*Lac.* 11.4).

The Spartans had acquired military capabilities of other kinds as well. Their first true cavalry force came into being in 425 as a response to the threat posed by Athenian raiding after their capture of Cythera and the promontory near Pylos (Thuc. 4.55.2). Apparently organized in parallel with the hoplites into six *morai* (Xen. *Lac.* 11.4) under *hipparmostai* (Xen. *Hell.* 4.5.12), the total number of cavalry troopers is unknown but was probably somewhat more than 600, the approximate number present in five cavalry *morai* at the Nemea River in 394 (Xen. *Hell.* 4.2.16). The cavalry was the junior service, as the commander of a cavalry *mora* was subordinate to his infantry equivalent, the polemarch (Xen. *Hell.* 6.5.12). Surprisingly, the pro-Spartan Xenophon, though a horseman himself, had little time for the Spartan cavalry (*Hell.* 6.4.11).

The Spartan navy that is attested as early as the sixth century (Hdt. 3.54.1) and essentially won the long war against Athens was just barely part of the military establishment. The city's concentration on infantry, with all the social and institutional biases attending that choice, meant that the maritime service was undervalued. Moreover, apart from captains and marines, the crews were all helots or mercenaries and thus unlikely to have gained much credit in the eyes of Spartiates, despite their evident success (Xen. *Hell*. 7.1.12). We know of only two Spartan naval ranks, and those only because Lysander held them – *nauarchos* or navarch, the supreme naval commander, and *epistoleus* or secretary (Xen. *Hell*. 2.1.7; Plut. *Lys*. 7.2–3). The annual post of navarch could only be held once in a lifetime, which may have been intended to thwart the overly ambitious but, as we have seen, potentially deprived Sparta of much-needed military expertise. That only a small handful of Spartan royals ever deigned to command the fleet is a sign of the low esteem in which naval operations were held.

Sparta's reputation depended upon the hoplites, renowned for their discipline in formation combined with the ability to execute flawlessly what seemed to other Greeks to be complicated maneuvers. The orderliness of the Spartan ranks was result of two factors – the inculcation of obedience that began with entry into the system of citizen training and never really ended, and the depth of rank in the army itself. The Spartan army hierarchy was quite remarkable. The Athenian army, for instance, after the reforms following Marathon, had only three officer ranks: the generals, taxiarchs, and the commanders of *lochoi* within each *taxis*. An Athenian *lochos* may have consisted of 100 men, it has been estimated, over double the size of the *enômotia* at its maximum capacity. And the Spartan enomotarch was not actually the most junior officer, for under him the file leaders themselves were in charge of the men lined up behind them (Xen. *Lac*. 11.5), numbering from five to fourteen. Thucydides had a point when he wrote that almost all the Spartan army consisted of officers commanding officers (5.66.4). Orders passed swiftly down this chain of command, enabling the army to shift from marching to battle formation with impressive speed – a maneuver Xenophon assures us the professional arms trainers claimed was extremely difficult – and to face attacks from the sides and rear (*Lac*. 11.8–10).

Marching in step, while perhaps known to other Greeks, was particularly associated with the Spartan army. Famously, their troops at Mantinea advanced towards the Argive army with a slow rhythmic pace to the sound of many flutes, not for a religious reason, as Thucydides explains to his readers, but in order to maintain a steady pace and to prevent the ranks from breaking up, which tended to occur in large armies (5.70). Plutarch also referred to the awe inspired by a Spartan advance (*Lyc.* 22.4–5). Greeks had long regarded dancing, either solo or in a choral group, as an eminently effective way of learning both evasive movements to escape from harm on the battlefield and coordinated motion as a unit (Pl. *Leg.* 796c, 803e, 813e; Athen. 14.25 [628F]). Spartan dances, such as the Pyrrhiche – a lively dance with shield and spear – and the choruses of the Gymnopaediae, Hyacinthia, and others were widely known.

Xenophon thought the choruses and gymnastic competitions of the young men at Sparta worth hearing and seeing (*Lac.* 4.1–7); they were manifestly an important part of the city's training of its future citizens. The military advantages gained from a practical knowledge of music and dance are apparent in incidents such as at Amphipolis in 422, when Brasidas' practiced eye noticed, from the uncoordinated movement of their heads and spears, that the Athenians outside the walls could not withstand a direct assault (Thuc. 5.10.5).

8.1 The "Round Building," now identified as the Chorus, site of the Gymnopaediae dances

During the fifth century, the Spartan army appears to have become more and more standardized in dress and armament. Like all other Greek armies of the time, Spartan weaponry would have included at a minimum a sword and a short thrusting spear. From early on, all Spartan warriors were famous for growing their hair long – the mark of a free man, as Aristotle (*Rhet.* 1367a) would have it. But evidence for the other elements in the ancient, and modern, image of the Spartan soldier as an almost faceless unit in a massive killing machine comes from later in the century. The large circular shield that gave the hoplite his name was the characteristic armament of the Greek heavy infantry in the Classical period. Like their counterparts in other cities, Spartans in the later sixth and early fifth centuries most likely carried individual emblems on their shields as a means of personal display. The famous lambda insignia is first mentioned only at the time of the Peloponnesian War (Eupolis Fr. 359 Kock). Spartans were not alone in branding their army in this way; they lulled the Argives into complacency before the Long Walls of Corinth in 392 by carrying shields emblazoned with sigmas taken from a Sicyonian unit they had just defeated (Xen. *Hell.* 4.4.10).

The earliest mention of the *phoinikis*, the crimson garment that served as the Spartan military uniform, is in Aristophanes' *Lysistrata* (1136–40), produced in 411, though referring to the aftermath of the earthquake of 465/4 B.C.E. That it was actually a cloak, as some ancient and most modern authors have thought is confirmed by archaeological evidence, namely the remains of prominent Spartiates buried in the Kerameikos after the clash between King Pausanias and the democratic insurgents in 403 B.C.E. (Xen. *Hell.* 2.4.33).

The skeletons show signs of having been wrapped tightly from head to toe in a long garment which was fastened by pins at the shoulders. This, combined with the near-total absence of grave goods (one body was buried with a single alabastron), fits so nicely with Plutarch's statement (*Lyc.* 27.2) that Spartan war dead were customarily buried without any grave goods, crowned with olive, and wrapped in the *phoinikis* that it seems almost certain that a cloak formed at least part of the military dress known as "the crimson."

Head coverings were also standardized. Artifacts from the early fifth century, small lead figurines found in the sanctuary of Artemis Orthia, and the so-called "Bust of Leonidas" depict hoplites wearing helmets of different shapes and designs. By the end of the century, these had been replaced by conical felt hats (*piloi*) that were indistinguishably

8.2   The Tomb of the Lacedaemonians in Athens

uniform. In addition, Spartan hoplites wore light chest protection of quilted linen or leather instead of bronze cuirasses. The evidence for standardization raises the question of procurement. How did individual Spartans acquire their weapons and armor? Historians incline towards a central distribution agency, especially since we know that the state replaced and repaired the equipment of soldiers on campaign (Xen. *Lac.* 11.2). In such a system, the perioeci would logically have provided the craftsmen to manufacture the articles to Spartan specifications.

Spartan military efficiency was also evident in the swift mobilization of troops. The overnight call-up of 5,000 Spartiates along with 35,000 helots before Plataea may strain credulity (Hdt. 9.10.1), but the Spartans clearly had a streamlined system of conscription that made the Athenian practice of the general and taxiarchs selecting troops individually for each campaign look very clumsy indeed. Rather, the Spartans called up hoplites by age in eight blocks of five years each from twenty to fifty-nine. When the ephors "showed the guard," they designated which units were to be sent out and which age groups would man them (Xen. *Lac.* 11.2; *Hell.* 6.4.17). Each Spartiate would have been permanently assigned to a *lochos*, making mustering simple.

Theoretically, each Spartan hoplite would have been the only representative of his year class in every *enômotia*, so that the number of men in each would have corresponded exactly to the number of year classes mobilized. Such a system would have been unworkably rigid, however, so historians have concluded that each group of five men did not necessarily contain one man from each of the block's five year classes. Only in the first two blocks, representing the year classes from twenty to twenty-nine, can there have been a realistic chance of filling the one-man, one-year-class requirement, because of the high mortality rate among Spartiate warriors. And, as the first ten year classes (*ta deka aph' hêbês*) were commonly sent out as shock troops at the beginning of a battle (Xen. *Hell.* 2.4.32, 3.4.23, 4.5.14, 5.4.40; *Ages.* 1.31.6), they were not immune from heavy losses themselves.

These young men were also eligible for distinction as members of the 300-strong crack unit called the *hippeis* or "knights," who actually fought as hoplites, not on horseback. Their most prestigious duty was to act as bodyguards for each king while he was on campaign, with the task usually assigned to one-third of their number (Hdt. 6.56). While the rest of the *hêbontes* were brigaded throughout the *lochoi*, the *hippeis* had the extraordinary privilege of forming a separate corps outside the military chain of command. At Mantinea, Leuctra, and other occasions when the Spartan state ordered full mobilization, the entire corps would have been present, with catastrophic results at Leuctra (Xen. *Hell.* 6.4.15). The *hippeis* also acted as the domestic security service, as in the Cinadon crisis (Xen. *Hell.* 3.3.9). The *hippeis'* loyalty and discretion in carrying out such sensitive assignments was due to their special status in the Spartan military hierarchy. On campaign the *hippeis* and *hippagretai* answered directly to the kings, at home to the ephors. The ephors chose their three commanders, called *hippagretai*, directly every year from among men over thirty. Each *hippagretes* then chose one hundred of the best *hêbontes* to form a contingent of *hippeis*, publicly announcing his reasons for accepting some and rejecting most (Xen. *Lac.* 4.3–4). Sparta's culture of praise and blame would have been on full display on these occasions. The story of Pedaritus (Plut. *Lyc.* 25.4), who went away smiling after being rejected for the *hippeis* because, as he said, it meant that the city had three hundred men better than he, is the exception proving the rule. The rejected were encouraged to keep a close watch over the behavior of the chosen in hopes of catching them acting improperly, and the two sets of *hêbontes* frequently came to blows whenever they happened to meet (Xen. *Lac.* 4.6).

The army was the Spartans' pride and joy. Unsurprisingly, they credited Lycurgus with its foundation. Herodotus (1.65.5) reports that Lycurgus was responsible for the military institutions of his own time, in particular, the *enômotiai*, the *sussitia* (the common messes, which had some as yet unclear connection with the army), and the mysterious *triakades* ("thirds"). Curiously, over a hundred years later and after at least one major structural reform, Xenophon also considers Lycurgus the founder of the military institutions of his day (*Lac.* 11.1–4), including the *morai*, which most historians regard as the cornerstone of the later fifth century new-style army.

Unlike the Athenians, Spartans buried their warrior dead in the lands where they fell. It was a matter of pride, for Spartiate graves served as tangible signs of their city's ability to project its power. At Sparta, families commemorated their dead relatives with simple memorials bearing their names followed by the famous, suitably laconic, inscription "in war." As a consequence, one of the most familiar apophthegms, that attributed to a Spartan mother saying, as she bids her warrior son farewell, "(Come back) with it or on it," meaning his hoplite shield, cannot have been from a Spartan source, since dead warriors were not brought home (Plut. *Mor.* 241f).

Throwing away one's shield was an offense commonly punished throughout Greece, but Sparta has always been notorious for severely penalizing soldiers considered to be cowards, or "tremblers" (*tresantes*). Writers ancient and modern have catalogued the punishments inflicted upon any Spartiate falling short of the city's demanding code of honor. However, many of the penalties listed in our earliest source, Xenophon's *Constitution of the Lacedaemonians* (*Lac.* 9.4–6), were socially, not legally rooted. For example, people were ashamed to eat or exercise in the company of a coward; cowards were left out of the ball teams and assigned the most demeaning positions in dances; young men did not give way to them in the streets nor accord them seats at public events. Moreover, the term "trembler" itself was applied only to one man, Aristodemus, the sole survivor of Thermopylae (Hdt. 7.231–2), who redeemed himself by dying bravely at Plataea (Hdt. 9.71.2). The legal penalty imposed was evidently a form of *atimia* (loss of citizen rights) that varied according to circumstances and was of a specific duration, as in the case of the 120 ex-POWs from Sphacteria, who were stripped of the right to hold office and carry out financial transactions for a period of time until being restored to full Spartiate status (Thuc. 5.34.2). In the other notable instance of Spartan *atimia*, Plutarch reports that king Agesilaus called for the laws to sleep for a day during the crisis over how to treat the survivors of the Leuctra disaster (Plut. *Ages.* 30.5–6). Taking all the evidence together, the harsh treatment of "tremblers" could well have been more notorious to outsiders as a concept than to Spartans as a commonly inflicted punishment.

9

From Archidamus III to Nabis

Upon Agesilaus' death in 360/59, Archidamus III became king and continued his father's policy of absolute intransigence regarding Messenia. Sparta's weakness, however, was exemplified by her non-involvement in the conflict between Athens and several powerful allies in the Second Naval Confederacy (357–355). On the other hand, the Sacred War (356/5–346), in which Sparta and Athens supported the Phocians, who had seized Delphi and the sanctuary of Apollo, against Thebes and the rest of the Amphictyonic Council, presented an opportunity to retaliate against the Thebans for engineering the levying of a huge fine for the seizure of the Cadmea in 382, doubled when the Spartans could not pay (Diod. Sic. 16.29.2–3). That the Thebans' attention would be distracted from the Peloponnese was a welcome collateral benefit.

When war broke out, the belligerents could have had no idea that their ambitions and rivalries, particularly Sparta's petty irredentism, would soon become irrelevant. For years, Philip II had been consolidating control over Macedon and the Greek cities along the north coast of the Aegean. When Thessaly split over the city of Pherae's support for Phocis as a consequence of the Sacred War, the Thessalian League called on Philip for aid; he became its military leader. After two unwonted defeats by the Phocian army in 354, Philip returned with a vengeance the following year, annihilating the Phocians at the Battle of the Crocus Field; as a reward, he became Thessaly's supreme leader (*tagos*). Meanwhile, as Thebes continued the fight with the Phocians in central Greece, the Spartans made their expected move against Megalopolis in 351, having prepared the ground with a proposal to restore ancestral territories to their "legitimate" owners (Dem. 16.4, 11). Archidamus' proposal fell flat and the raids achieved nothing, as the Thebans sent reinforcements to their Arcadian allies.

In 346, Philip intervened directly in the Sacred War, on the Theban side. Faced with his overwhelming military might, the Phocians capitulated. Their cities were broken up; they were to repay all the money taken from Apollo's treasury; and their votes on the Amphictyonic council went to Philip. Honored by being made president of the Pythian games for that year (Diod. Sic. 16.60.2) and controlling both Thessaly's and Phocis' votes, he was now the single most powerful force on the Amphictyonic Council. Ominously, one of his first pronouncements in that capacity was to call on the Spartans to renounce their claims to Messenia (Dem. 6.13). In answer, they renewed the struggle, which soon drew in both the Arcadians and Argives. Philip countered with military aid to Sparta's enemies. By now, even the patience of Sparta's long-time allies the Athenians was at an end, and so they now made peace with Argos, Achaea, and Messenia. Sparta's diplomatic isolation was almost complete.

Even the prospect of meeting Macedon on the battlefield at Chaeronea (338) did not tempt the Spartans away from their navel-gazing. Their complacency would be short lived, however, as Philip decided soon after his victory to deal once and for all with the Spartan nuisance to Peloponnesian peace and security. In the winter of 338/7, the Macedonian army invaded Laconia, part making its way all the way down to Gytheum (Polyb. 9.28.8; Paus. 3.24.6, 5.4.9; *IG* IV² 128, lines 57–9). His point made as to Sparta's ability to mount an effective defense, Philip withdrew, but not before cutting off large chunks of Laconia and distributing them to his grateful Peloponnesian allies. Argos received the long-desired Thyreatis (Paus. 2.38.5). Arcadia and Messenia profited handsomely too (*FGrH* 115 F238, 243, 244; Tac. *Ann.* 4.43). Spartan territory was now confined essentially to the old heartland of the Eurotas valley, plus the Malea and Taenarum peninsulas. Needless to say, Spartans saw no point in joining Philip's League of Corinth nor in subscribing to his son's panhellenic crusade to wreak vengeance on the Persian Empire. Alexander never forgot the snub: the inscription over the spoils from the Battle of Granicus (334), his first major victory over the Persians, alluded pointedly to the Spartans' absence (Plut. *Alex.* 16.18).

Spartan foreign policy in these years was at least consistent. However, other Greeks may have viewed Alexander's history-changing victories in the east, Spartans saw his campaign against the Persians as yet another opportunity to regain Messenia and humble Arcadia. By 333 Agis III, who had succeeded upon Archidamus' death in southern Italy in 348 (*FGrH* 115 F232), was acting as the Persians' agent in Greece, stirring up trouble behind Alexander's lines. The high-water mark was undoubtedly his winning over of Crete to the Persian cause, where he gathered together a sizeable army of mercenaries for his attempt to challenge Macedonian power in Greece (Arr. *Anab*. 2.13.4–6; Curt. 4.8.15). In 331, he took advantage of Alexander's regent's involvement in Thrace to forge an anti-Macedonian coalition and marched on Megalopolis. Alerted by Agis' defeat of a Macedonian commander, Antipater abandoned the Thracian conflict to hurry south. The two large armies met near Megalopolis, and Agis was soundly defeated and killed (Diod. Sic. 17.63.2). In the wake of the battle, Antipater extracted fifty hostages from among Sparta's elite, a severe blow considering the city's continuing acute manpower problem (Plut. *Mor*. 235b). "A battle of mice" was Alexander's comment on the news – harsh, but apt (Plut. *Ages*. 15.4). Spartan saber-rattling would never again disturb the sleep of the powerful.

Surprisingly (or perhaps not) after Alexander's death in Babylon, Sparta did not join the more than twenty Greek cities attempting to throw off the Macedonian yoke in the Lamian War (323–322). Spartans probably saw the rebellion's failure and Athens' subsequent fate as justifying their choice. Better to cultivate one's own garden – as apparently some Spartiates were now doing in defiance of the Lycurgan prohibition (Arist. *Pol*. 2.2.11 [1264a]). Those of less settled ways could always seek their fortunes in the expanding mercenary market, for which Laconia was a major supplier through the center at Taenarum (e.g. Diod. Sic. 17.108.7). Spartans might also have seen these adventurers' military projects as a useful means of promoting their city's interests while maintaining a high degree of deniability. This was just as well, for Thibron's attempt to reduce Libya in 323–322, although reinforced by 2,500 mercenaries from Taenarum, led to his defeat by Ptolemy and his torture and crucifixion at Cyrene (Diod. Sic. 18.19.2–21). Also a failure was Acrotatus' expedition to the west in 314 to support Gela, Messina, and Agrigentum against Syracusan, designs, which ended with him being hounded out of Sicily back to Laconia by his erstwhile allies, disaffected by his Spartan arrogance (Diod. Sic. 19.70–71.5).

A physical sign of the Spartans' profound psychological change was their realization, prompted by Cassander's pillaging of the Peloponnese in 317, that the city needed a wall (Justin 14.5–7). This belated concession to reality probably took the form of a palisade and ditch arrangement along the north and west sides of the city, which faced the normal route into the Eurotas valley from the north (Paus. 1.13.6). The reign of Areus I (309–265/4) would herald more changes, as this king accelerated the trend towards a Hellenistic-style monarchy. He presided over the first Spartan minting of coins in order to pay mercenaries. The later issues carried his name, along with an image of Heracles, now the emblem of choice for Spartan kings in preference to the traditional but dualist symbolism of Castor and Pollux. Statues of Areus, including one equestrian representation, were erected at Olympia (Paus. 6.12.5, 15.8; *Syll.*³ 433). At Sparta, a grandiose personification of the Eurotas sculpted by one of Lysippus' pupils was erected (Pliny *HN* 34.78). The new conception of his position is evident in Sparta's relations with other cities, where documents mention Areus separately from the Spartans (e.g. *Syll.*³ 434/5, lines 27, 29–30). As Heraclids, the two kings had traditionally been considered somewhat aloof from the rest of the body politic, but now only a single king appears. On the ground, the growth of small farms in the marginally productive area northwest of Sparta in the third century may indicate the increasing dependency of small landholders on the wealthy city elite who had acquired the Eurotas valley's more productive land.

Though Areus was a minor at his accession, with his uncle Cleonymus as his regent, he easily survived Cleonymus' challenge to his kingship when he came of age and must have shared in the Spartan authorities' relief when Cleonymus acceded to the Tarentines' request in 303 to serve as commander against the Lucanians and Romans (Diod. Sic. 20.104.1–2; Paus. 3.6.2–3). The expedition was a mixed success. Cleonymus intimidated the Lucanians into making peace but subsequently alienated the Tarentines and ended up as a minor warlord on Corcyra, with a well-deserved reputation for brutality (Diod. Sic. 20.104–5). Cleonymus' military expertise was evidently more important to the Spartans than any qualms they may have had over his behavior, as he was sent in 292 on an official mission to prepare Thebes' defenses against Demetrius Poliorcetes (Plut. *Dem.* 39.2–3). Two years before, after roundly defeating the hapless Archidamus IV at Mantinea, Poliorcetes had led yet another invasion of Laconia (Plut. *Dem.* 35.1–2), so the Spartans needed every experienced military man they could find, regardless of his trustworthiness.

In 281, taking advantage of Macedon's weakness, the Spartans attacked the Aetolians, who were controlling Delphi at the time.

Leading the army as it advanced into central Greece was Areus, in his first recorded command. It was not a happy debut: the Aetolians inflicted a shattering defeat, slaying over 9,000 men, and when the Spartans tried to regroup later to continue the war, their own allies refused, their suspicions about Spartan motives still lively (Justin 24.1). Cleonymus was more successful in the Peloponnese, conquering Troezen (Polyaen. 2.29.1) and menacing the Messenians so greatly that they dared not send troops to help resist the Gallic invasion of central Greece in 279 (Paus. 4.28.3). He also advanced Spartan interests on Crete (*IC* II xi 1), until the irrevocable split with Areus occurred in 273/2.

The ostensible reason was the very public affair Cleonymus' much younger wife Chilonis was having with Areus' son, Acrotatus. Deeper political forces may have been at work: Cleonymus' choice of a wife from the other (Eurypontid) house was perhaps part of an attempt to gain influence and wealth through the land Chilonis controlled, again in order to challenge Areus for the kingship, especially given the king's mixed military record. If so, he was outplayed, for Acrotatus' open cuckolding heaped public insult on him in a society where such things still mattered profoundly. At wit's end, Cleonymus left for Epirus to ask its king Pyrrhus, the rising military power, for help. Seeing this as a golden opportunity to conquer the entire Peloponnese, Pyrrhus invaded Laconia with his entire army, including elephants. The Spartans were caught by surprise, deceived by Pyrrhus' declaration that he was in the Peloponnese to expel Macedonian garrisons and to enroll his sons in the Spartan citizen training system. With Areus away fighting on Crete, Cleonymus' friends and helots were so sure of his triumphant return that they decorated Cleonymus' house and prepared a dinner for him and Pyrrhus. But Pyrrhus met uncommonly fierce resistance to his attempts to breach the city's defenses, directed in part (we are told) by some of Sparta's redoubtable *grandes dames*. The siege was eventually relieved when a Macedonian army arrived from Corinth and Areus returned with 2,000 soldiers (Plut. *Pyrrh.* 26.8–30.6). Forced to withdraw to defend the city of Argos, Pyrrhus died there in street fighting against the Macedonians and Spartans, led by Areus (Plut. *Pyrrh.* 34.1–7). The Spartan-Macedonian alliance was short lived. By 268, the city was allied to Athens and Ptolemy of Egypt in the last great push to free Greece from Macedon – the Chremonidean War (*Syll.*[3] 434/5). But the allies were no match for Macedonian military might. Areus never succeeded in pushing past the Macedonian garrison guarding the

Isthmus and died in his third attempt in 265/4. His son Acrotatus fell fighting by Megalopolis soon after, and Athens capitulated in 263/2.

In the following years, Sparta was quiescent under the Agiad regent and then king, Leonidas II (252–235), Cleonymus' son by an earlier union. His many years spent at the glittering Seleucid courts must have broadened his outlook and made the Spartan hankering after past military glories appear rather ridiculous by comparison (Plut. *Agis* 3.6, 11.4). But the Spartan mirage was powerful, nowhere more so than in the city of its creation, and Leonidas had the misfortune, for his later reputation, to reign when some tried to turn that hankering into reality. Reform was certainly needed. Sparta's army was a shell: most of the troops on any active campaign were mercenaries whose wages stretched Sparta's meager resources to the limit. Laconia's security was a joke. The numerous incursions since Leuctra had perceptibly affected people's lives. The inhabitants of Geronthrae were forced to huddle together on their acropolis for protection and rebuild its walls on their Bronze Age foundations. The citizen training system had finally collapsed a few years before and with it much of the glue holding Sparta's social fabric together. The common messes still existed but had become elite dining clubs.

The cause, as historians have long understood, was the chronic shortage of citizens at Sparta (*oliganthrôpia*), evident as early as the Battle of Plataea and reaching crisis proportions long before Leonidas' reign. Being a Spartiate was never an inalienable right; it was a privilege that demanded strenuous effort to retain. Cowardice, real or perceived, could result in temporary reduction in status. More serious was failure in the training system or an inability to keep up contributions to the common mess, both of which resulted in permanent degradation to the status of inferior (*hupomeiôn*). Land was at the root of this crisis: Sparta's unusual inheritance system allowed females to inherit land in their own right, which encouraged marriage alliances to increase estates the husband's family controlled. On the other hand, partible inheritance caused iandholdings to shrink into ever smaller portions as estates were divided among heirs. Heavy Spartiate casualties in Sparta's many wars would have meant that some families lost control of their property if no male heirs could be found. All these factors contributed to a gradual concentration of land in the hands of a few, coupled with increasing rates of demotion from Spartiate status as many holdings became too small to produce the required mess contributions. By the mid-third century, Plutarch claimed, of the no more than 700 men with Spartiate status only 100 owned land. Outside this small circle was a poverty-stricken mob with few legal rights and little enthusiasm to fight to defend the privileges of the rich (Plut. *Agis* 5.6–7).

Onto this volatile scene stepped the young Eurypontid king Agis IV, who during his brief, tragic reign (244–241 B.C.E.) set forces in motion that shook his city and continue to reverberate in Spartan history down to the present. With the exuberance of youth – he was only twenty when he became king – Agis adopted all the trappings of what he thought was the traditional Spartan lifestyle, rejecting the innovations that had crept in over the past decades (Plut. *Agis* 4). Upon attaining power, he made it clear that he intended a two-pronged reform program comprising debt cancellation and land redistribution. The bill introduced in 243/2 by his supporter, the ephor Lysander, called for debts to be cancelled and all land in Laconia to be divided up into two classes of allotment (*klêros*), those in the Eurotas valley and immediate environs going to Spartiates and the rest to the perioeci. The Spartiate citizen body would be enlarged to 4,500 by enrolling suitable perioeci of the hoplite class and those foreigners (actually mercenaries already under contract to the city) who were free men and in the prime of life. With everything in place, large common messes would be instituted and all would live the lifestyle (*diaita*) of their forefathers (Plut. *Agis* 8). Though packaged as a return to the ways of Lycurgus and Spartan virtue, Agis' reforms may not have been altogether inspired by romantic nostalgia. The young king reportedly recognized that Sparta did not have the resources to compete with the Successor kingdoms (Plut. *Agis* 7.2), which was certainly true; the bills for the mercenaries in Sparta's armies must have been crippling. A return to some form of compulsory citizen militia might at least provide essential security for Laconia.

After much political wrangling, the bill, vigorously opposed by Leonidas as mouthpiece of the vested interests, passed in the Assembly but was narrowly defeated in the Gerousia (Plut. *Agis* 9–11.1). This the reform party did not take lying down. Lysander indicted Leonidas on charges of having violated a supposedly Lycurgan law forbidding citizens from living abroad and fraternizing with foreign women. Witnesses were easily found and, probably to no one's surprise, when Lysander and the ephors spent the night looking for a sign in the heavens that a king had done wrong – in a ritual never before attested – they saw one, a comet (Plut. *Agis* 11.2–4). Sensing the tide turn against him, Leonidas fled to the protection of the temple of Athena Chalcioecus on the acropolis. He was quickly deposed and his son-in-law Cleombrotus declared king in his stead (Plut. *Agis* 11.5). The reform party now faced a problem: Lysander's term as ephor had ended, and the new ephors for 242/1 were not sympathetic. The two kings, perhaps influenced by Lysander and other powerful reformists, decided on radical action and forcibly removed the ephors from office, replacing them with their own men, including Agis' uncle Agesilaus as eponymous ephor. Leonidas was escorted out of Laconia to exile in Tegea (Plut. *Agis* 12).

Then Agis committed two fatal errors. First, he allowed himself to be dissuaded from implementing the two core elements of his program simultaneously. The blame for this rested with Agesilaus, according to Plutarch, or more accurately his source Phylarchus, a fervent propagandist for Agis and his spiritual heir Cleomenes III. Rich in land but heavily indebted, Agesilaus, like probably many others, supported only the cancellation of debts (Plut. *Agis* 13.1–2). Secondly, after implementing only that part of his reforms, Agis left, leading an army composed of a large number of his young supporters north to support Aratus, general of the Achaean League, against an incursion by Aetolian League forces. In the meantime Agesilaus, with the ingenuity that still marks the Greek bureaucrat, found a series of excuses to delay redistributing land although the people desired it and the king ordered it (Plut. *Agis* 13.3–4).

Aratus had probably paid little attention to Sparta's internal affairs, but would now have heard disturbing reports of the aspirations among the dispossessed that the Spartan army's astonishingly well-behaved march through the Peloponnese had engendered and the corresponding unease among Achaea's well-to-do (Plut. *Agis* 14). Like the Spartans in the 460s, Aratus dealt with his ideologically unreliable ally by sending him home with the excuse that the Aetolians could do little harm, as almost all the crops had already been gathered in (Plut. *Agis* 15). Although Phylarchus put a positive spin on the dismissal, he could not disguise the fact that Sparta was in turmoil when Agis returned (Plut. *Agis* 15.3). Agesilaus, now with his own private bodyguard, had illegally added a month to the year to lengthen his term and was spreading rumors that he would be ephor for a second year. Agesilaus' behavior had so alienated the populace, especially the poor who had expected land redistribution to become a reality, that his enemies were emboldened to bring Leonidas back from exile. With his return, the reform movement collapsed. Agesilaus fled the country; Agis claimed asylum at Athena Chalcioecus and Cleombrotus at the sanctuary of

Poseidon Taenarius in town (Plut. *Agis* 16). Entreated by his daughter Chilonis, who had shared his exile, Leonidas let his son-in-law Cleombrotus leave Laconia accompanied by Chilonis, her children, and an unknown number of supporters of reform. He then replaced the remaining ephors with his own men and tried to entice Agis out of the sanctuary (Plut. *Agis* 17–18.3). Finally, as he was returning from a secret visit to the bathhouse, Agis was betrayed by Amphares, an erstwhile friend who held a grudge against his mother, Agesistrata. Leonidas surrounded the prison with mercenaries – a sure sign of the king's continuing popularity among some sectors of the population – and swiftly had a kangaroo court made up of ephors and anti-reform members of the Gerousia condemn Agis to death. With him died Agesistrata and Archidamia, his grandmother, either because of Amphares' vindictiveness or because they were too powerful and dangerous to live (Plut. *Agis* 19–20).

Along with the female supporters of Cleomenes III, these women are the latest and most prominent embodiment of the stereotypical Spartan woman – self-confident and empowered. Agesistrata, for instance, "wielded a lot of power in the city due to her mass of hangers-on, friends, and debtors, and was active in many public affairs," and Archidamia is described, when she is about to be executed, as "already an extremely old woman who had lived her life with the highest repute among the female citizens" (Plut. *Agis* 7.7, 20.3). Generally speaking, Spartan woman are considered almost modern compared to their shuttered sisters elsewhere in Greece. Ancient texts paint a consistent picture of females enjoying considerable economic, social, and sexual freedom. Not that this was an admirable aspect of Spartan life: to Aristotle, "the licence concerning women" (*Pol.* 2.6.5 [1269b]) was shocking evidence of Lycurgus' failure as a lawgiver. Sparta's women were notorious. They competed in footraces and trials of strength (Xen. *Lac.* 1.4); they paraded publicly nude or wore such revealing chitons they were called "thigh flashers" (*phaineromerides*) (Ibycus F58 Page); they were devious (Hdt. 6.52.2–3); and they had a reputation for forthright speaking even in front of men (Hdt. 5.51, 7.239.3–4). Their morals were loose: ex-king Demaratus assured his mother when asking her for the truth about his parentage that if she had been with other men before Ariston, his official father, she would be in the company of many others (Hdt. 6.68.3). Spartan wife-sharing, according to Xenophon, was doubly advantageous – wives could run two households and husbands gained extra sons without breaking up the family's wealth, not to mention the eugenic advantages of such practices "opposite to the others" (Xen. *Lac.* 1.9).

The reality is more complicated. References to the sexual licence and almost masculine aggressiveness of Spartan women first appear in Athens during the Peloponnesian War, when writers such as Euripides (*Tr.* 983–7; *Andr.* 147–53) and the pro-Athenian Herodotus cast their Spartan female characters in terms appropriate to non-Greek women, who likewise display unnerving intelligence while being obsessed with sex. In addition, Spartan practice is not completely unparalleled. The Athenians even allowed men to conceive citizen children with women other than their wives to combat a shortage of males towards the end of the Peloponnesian War (Athen. 13.556a–b). Young girls ran naked in the Arkteia festival at Brauron in Attica, as a series of ritual vases shows. It is tempting thus to regard the Spartan races as ritual as well, although most historians prefer to see them as belonging to a female version of the training system for Spartiates. Conversely, nothing suggests that Sparta was any different from other cities in the degree of control men exercised over women's lives. Husbands chose sexual partners for their wives, and fathers picked husbands or guardians for their daughters, the king fulfilling this function if the father died without making a decision (Hdt. 6.57.4). Public display of wealth was severely restricted. Spartan women were forbidden to wear ornaments or gold and could not grow their hair long (Herac. Lemb. 373.13 Dilts).

Their ability to own land did set Spartan women apart, however, and must have afforded them a certain amount of "soft" power. Recent research has shown that, as at Gortyn on Crete, females could inherit real property just like their brothers, albeit in a smaller proportion. With Spartan citizenship dependent on fixed amounts of produce from land, acquiring a wife with her own estates would have been an attractive proposition. As the shortage of citizen males (*oliganthrôpia*) became acute in the fourth century, women thus controlled increasing amounts of land. Aristotle complains that in his day women controlled 40 percent of the citizen-owned land in Laconia (*Pol.* 2.6.11 [1270a]). An intriguing indication of the influence women might have wielded behind the scenes earlier in the century is the execution in 379 of Chryse and her sister, the former beauty Xenopeitheia, whose son Lysanoridas, commander of the Spartan forces in Thebes, was exiled for losing control of the city (Athen. 13.609b). Lysanoridas compounded his misfortune by being a personal enemy of Agesilaus, who possibly considered his mother and aunt such threats to his own position that they had to be eliminated.

The final years of Leonidas' near-monarchical rule were uneventful, apart from a horrific Aetolian invasion deep into Laconia perhaps in 240, during which considerable numbers of helots and perioeci were captured and the sanctuary of Poseidon on Taenarum pillaged (Polyb. 4.34.9, 9.34.9–10; Plut. *Cleom.* 18.3). Leonidas consolidated his power by forcibly (and illegally) marrying Agis' young widow Agiatis to his own underage son Cleomenes so as to gain control over her father's considerable estates, to which she was the heir (Plut. *Cleom.* 1.1). If we are to believe Phylarchus, who attributes Cleomenes' conversion to the reformist cause to his wife's reminiscences of her ex-husband, this was a mistake.

Whatever the cause, when he came to the throne upon Leonidas' death in 235 Cleomenes took up Agis' mantle. But he was enough his father's son not to shrink from the ruthless use of violence to attain his goals. He allowed the murder of Agis' brother Archidamus, whom he himself had recalled from exile and restored to the kingship, probably because he considered the Eurypontid a potential rival (Plut. *Cleom.* 2–3). Like Agis, he presented his radical measures as a return to the ways of Lycurgus. Unlike Agis, he was effective in changing Sparta: some of his reforms survived his fall to become permanent aspects of Spartan public life. The ephors, whose power over the state had been much enhanced by Leonidas' inactivity, posed Cleomenes' most immediate problem. He therefore spent the first years of his reign building up a military reputation, helped on several crucial instances by Aratus' odd reluctance to exploit tactical advantages (Plut. *Cleom.* 3.4–6.5). At the same time, he increased his support among the elite at home (Plut. *Cleom.* 7.1) and when all was in place in 227, set his plans for a coup d'état in motion. He removed many potential opponents by the simple expedient of enrolling them in an expedition into Achaea and leaving them to garrison captured towns. Then he quickly returned with mercenaries and supporters to Sparta, where he sent an assassination squad to liquidate the ephors while they were having dinner; only one escaped (Plut. *Cleom.* 7.4–8.2). After sending 80 leading citizens into exile, Cleomenes justified his actions before the Assembly the next day. Using king Pausanias' old argument, he maintained that the ephorate was not founded by Lycurgus but came into being because of the Messenian War to assist the kings. But as time passed, the ephors had illegally arrogated powers to themselves and now stood in the way of those, like Cleomenes, who desired to see again in Sparta "the most beautiful and divine state of affairs." He regretted the bloodshed, but, after all, had not Lycurgus surrounded himself with an armed retinue? (Plut. *Cleom.* 10).

Cleomenes now implemented his reforms. He cancelled debts. Land was pooled, then redistributed in allotments of equal size (*klêroi*) among the citizen body, which was expanded to 4,000 by the inclusion of deserving perioeci and foreigners (Plut. *Cleom.* 10.6–11.3). Recent scholarship confirms that Cleomenes' land policy lies at the root of the popular misconception that Classical-period Spartans were apportioned equal lots of land by the state which were inalienable and reverted to the state upon death. Actually, land at Sparta before Cleomenes was privately owned since as far back as evidence is available. Aristotle reported that Tyrtaeus mentioned agitation for land redistribution in the *Eunomia* (*Pol.* 5.6.2 [1306b–1307a]). Alcaeus attributed the pithy aphorism, "Wealth makes the man. No poor man is noble or honorable" (Campbell F25), to the Spartan Alcidamus. Both Herodotus and Thucydides refer to wealthy Spartans in the sixth and fifth centuries (e.g. Hdt. 6.61.3, 7.134.2; Thuc. 1.6.4). Every Spartiate was expected to own land sufficient to produce the fixed amounts of foodstuffs he was required to contribute monthly to his common mess (Plut. *Lyc.* 12.2), but there is no evidence of restrictions on owning land above that minimum. Indeed, extensive tracts of land would have been required to produce feed for the four-horse chariot teams that certain Spartans successfully entered at the Olympics and other festivals in the Classical period. By the time of Cleomenes, however, equality of land ownership had become integral to the image of Sparta elaborated by philosophers (Pl. *Leg.* 737e) and political thinkers, so it was only logical that the king would present his radically new idea of equal ownership of land as a return to Lycurgan precepts.

The image of Sparta's legendary lawgiver was essential to the ideology of Cleomenes' program, if not to its reality. Both Cleomenes and Agis before him must have viewed their city's humble international position as inextricably linked to its domestic troubles. Everyone knew that Sparta's power had grown as long as she had lived by the rules laid down by Lycurgus (Xen. *Lac.* 1.1–2). For Spartans to regain their former eminence, they had to be led back to the way of life that had made them great. Considering the circumstances of the third century B.C.E., though, there could be no real return to the Lycurgan code, whatever that had been. In fact, Cleomenes introduced profound innovations into Sparta's political institutions while professing to be turning the clock back. He limited the Gerousia's power severely by reducing tenure from life to a single year and by creating an official called the *patronomos* ("guardian of tradition") to replace the ephors. He made a mockery of the dyarchy by appointing his own brother Eucleidas as his co-king instead of a member of the Eurypontid house. On the other hand, he revitalized the army by exchanging the hoplite's traditional but long outdated spear (*doru*) for the fearsome fifteen-foot long Macedonian *sarissa* (Plut. *Cleom.* 11.2). With a well-equipped core of 4,000 citizen warriors, Cleomenes could begin to reclaim Sparta's rightful position as *hêgemôn* of the Peloponnese and perhaps even of Greece. But that core needed to be maintained or even expanded with highly motivated Spartans who had been trained up to the standards of the armies of Plataea and Mantinea.

Sparta's own citizen training system, the first in Greece to be under state control (Arist. *Pol.* 7.1.3 [1337a]), famously used to produce warriors of such caliber but had fallen into desuetude earlier in the third century. A set of maturation rituals of a type commonly found in many societies that emphasize the otherness of youths growing from boys into men while putting them through a series of harsh testing rites had taken on the form of a system that prepared Spartan youths to become citizens, which at Sparta meant spending a lot of time either at or training for war. In the Classical period, young Spartans passed through three age grades on their way to full participation in public life: children (*paides*), teenagers (*paidiskoi*), and young men (*hêbôntes*) (Xen. *Lac.* 2.1–4.7). The Spartans entered the *paides* grade at age seven, the usual age at which Greek boys began their education and left at about fourteen. From fourteen to twenty years of age, they underwent strenuous training and contests as *paidiskoi*, until they became *hêbôntes* at twenty and began their military careers. Supervising the training was the *paidonomos*, a state magistrate with wide disciplinary powers over all Spartiates (in varying degrees) under the age of thirty, whose principal duties included "gathering the boys," probably for contests (Xen. *Lac.* 2.2).

Paides and *paidiskoi* would have been recognizable from their short hair, bare feet, the single outer garment they were required to wear whatever the season, and the sickles they carried with them. Sickles were also typically dedicated by victors in contests held at the sanctuary of Artemis Orthia, the patron deity of the Spartan training throughout its history. We know very little about most of the contests during the Classical period: the single epigraphical testimony from the fourth century refers unhelpfully to "the gatherings of boys" (*IG* V.1 255). One exception exists – a ritual in which one group of youths tried to steal cheeses from Artemis' altar while another group warded them off with whips (Xen. *Lac.* 2.9). Xenophon explained it as Lycurgus' way of teaching Spartan youth to endure short-term pain for long-term glory, but it is better regarded as a violent rite of passage marking the transition from the *paidiskoi* to the *hêbôntes* age grade. Youth also had an important role in Sparta's most famous festivals, such as the Gymnopaediae, where choruses drawn from various age categories performed over several days in the *choros* near the agora (Xen. *Hell.* 6.4.16; *FGrH* 595 F5), and the three-day Hyacinthia held at the Amyclaeum, during which Spartan youths performed music, sang, danced, and rode richly caparisoned horses (*FGrH* 588 F1).

Although we know nothing about the specific content of the training, it was demonstrably based upon continual testing and competition. Plato mentions mass unarmed combat and the endurance of pain (Pl. *Leg.* 1.633b). Some elements bear the mark of ritual activity, such as the requirement at certain times for young Spartans to sleep outdoors by the Eurotas on beds of reed they had gathered themselves without the use of blades (Plut. *Lyc.* 16.13). Rations were kept meager in order to keep the boys slim, according to Xenophon (*Lac.* 2.5), but this practice is also found in rituals surrounding childhood elsewhere. Endurance, obedience, self-control, and modesty were the qualities this testing was supposed to inculcate – qualities of a good citizen as well as of a soldier. To enforce discipline, the youths were grouped within each age grade into squadrons, called *ilai*, each commanded by the fiercest boy (Xen. *Lac.* 2.11). In his absence, the behavior of young Spartans was monitored, not just by the *paidonomos*, but by any adult Spartan, so that the boys never lacked an authority figure (Xen. *Lac.* 2.10).

To other Greeks as well as to moderns, the strangest aspect of Spartan training was the part played by theft. Apart from the ritual theft of cheese at Artemis Orthia, boys were expected to steal food to supplement their rations, with the targets being the "gardens" (*kêpoi*) close to town and the common messes (*sussitia*) where adult Spartiates were expected to eat regularly (Xen. *Lac.* 2.6–7; Plut. *Lyc.* 17.5–6). Xenophon justified the practice as ideal for teaching boys military skills such as staying awake at night, sending out scouts, and laying ambushes, but such activity is again a common indicator in many societies of the outsider status of youths undergoing lengthy rites of passage to adulthood. At Sparta the practice was regulated, not unexpectedly, with only certain items permitted to be stolen (Xen. *Lac.* 2.6; *Anab.* 4.6.14) and corporal punishment meted out to culprits caught in the act of stealing badly (Xen. *Lac.* 2.8).

Although hedged about by customs that emphasized his position outside adult Spartan society, a youth would have had a vital link to that world through his lover or "inspirer" (*eispnêlas*), who would have introduced him into his own common mess, where he would reply to questions put to him in a sort of catechism (Xen. *Lac.* 2.12–14, 3.5). The lovers may also have been responsible for teaching certain practical skills and ethical conduct, as was common in the aristocratic education of the Archaic period. Education in the modern sense of the teaching of basic literacy, history, and similar subjects seems to have been a private matter: nothing indicates that Sparta differed so radically from other cities as to incorporate these elements in its citizen training. There was also the opportunity to hear lectures by visiting scholars such as Hippias of Elis, although he complained that Spartans were only interested in ancient history in general and moral instruction, not in more trendy subjects like astronomy and geometry (Pl. *Hipp. Maj.* 285d, 286a).

In becoming a *hêbôn*, a Spartan became a Spartiate, eligible for entry into a common mess (*sussition*), and entered the first ranks of the army. As we have seen, those in the ten year classes up to age thirty, the *hêbôntes*, formed the Spartan army's shock troops. From them were chosen the 300 elite *hippeis*. *Hêbôntes* were still subordinate to the *paidonomos*, who had the power to arrest them; punishment, however, was the prerogative of the ephors. The young warriors' collective identity continued to be emphasized in choruses and athletic competitions, which Xenophon recommended as "definitely worth hearing and seeing," and they might be picked for teams in ball games amongst the adult Spartiates (Xen. *Lac.* 4.2, 9.5). During the years spent as *hêbôntes*, some were chosen for the Crypteia, a mysterious institution shrouded in secrecy and contradiction in our sources (e.g. Arist. F611.10 Rose; Plut. *Lyc.* 28.1–7; Schol. ad Pl. *Leg.* 633b–c). According to a recent study, though, the authorities sent young men into the countryside, bereft of all home comforts and armed only with daggers, to hunt helots as a means of reducing the pent-up aggression characteristic of the *hêbôntes* as a group. The murders of helots, selected supposedly at random, confirmed the superiority of the Spartiates as a whole and within that group marked out potential leaders. The Spartan elite was also replenished annually by the appointment of a select five of the *hippeis* from among those who had reached thirty years of age to serve as special agents (*agathoergoi*) for sensitive missions even outside Laconia (Hdt. 1.67.5). At the same time, all the former *hebontes* were finally eligible to hold civic office (Xen. *Lac.* 4.7).

The Spartan training system's elaborate multi-year structure must have became increasingly difficult to maintain as the number of boys eligible for citizenship declined. Admitting a few foreigners as *trophimoi* and allowing boys from families that had lost their Spartiate status to enter the system as *mothakes* under the patronage of boys from wealthy citizen families were stopgap measures (*FGrH* 81 F43) insufficient to reverse the decay. By the end of the reign of Areus II, the Spartans probably no longer trained their youth in the traditional way. Agis IV purposed to revive the ancestral training (Plut. *Agis* 4) but did not get the chance.

When he turned to the education and training (*paideia kai agôgê*) of the youth, Cleomenes consulted an outside expert, the Stoic Sphaerus of Borysthenes, who wrote two books on Sparta and whose lectures on educating ephebes and young men Cleomenes had attended as a teenager (Plut. *Cleom.* 2.2, 11.4). As Plutarch stresses, Sphaerus was jointly responsible for most of the new training system. The *paides* and *hêbôntes* grades were eliminated and the remaining seven years (14–20) divided up into annual age grades with names that combined traditional Laconian age designations and concepts familiar from other Hellenistic training systems. The training probably consisted of a heavy dose of instruction in athletics and combat skills, leavened by participation in choral and musical events at religious festivals. The mass combats mentioned by Plato almost certainly continued, since we have eyewitness accounts from the Roman period. On the whole, however, the Spartan training would probably have resembled similar systems in other Greek cities, which also endeavored to produce citizen warriors thoroughly indoctrinated with the appropriate civic values. Even the ritual at Artemis' altar was transformed: now, instead of trying to steal cheeses, boys entering the seventh age grade were whipped in a test of their endurance as they stood by the altar until only one remained standing. The importance Cleomenes placed on his revived training (*agôgê*) can be measured in the attention he lavished on the sanctuary of Artemis Orthia. He placed her cult figure on a series of silver tetradrachms and very likely rebuilt the temple. The Crypteia lived again, but with the disappearance of the *hêbôntes* class now became a specialized corps of scouts in the army (Plut. *Cleom.* 28.2). As a complement to the training, Cleomenes and Sphaerus also revived the common messes, though whether they put Agis' ideas for large, 300-member *sussitia* into practice (Plut. *Agis* 8.1–3) or revived the Classical-period 15-man messes is unknown (Plut. *Lyc.* 12.1).

Over the next half-decade, Cleomenes' Sparta seemed poised to challenge the Achaean League and realize its goal of supremacy in the Peloponnese but, as events proved, Spartan military success was ephemeral. Still, it began spectacularly enough with the capture and looting of Megalopolis, followed by a change of constitution at Mantinea and an Achaean rout at Dymae (Plut. *Cleom.* 12, 14). The Achaeans then pursued a two-track diplomatic policy: on the one hand, they half-heartedly attempted to bring Cleomenes to the conference table, and on the other they approached Antigonus Doson, king of the much-feared Macedonians, to intervene against the Spartans. The open breach came when the Achaeans apparently changed the conditions of a peace conference at Argos, so angering Cleomenes that he declared open war on the League (Plut. *Cleom.* 15.2–17.2). The reforms at Sparta, particularly the cancellation of debts, had captured the imagination of many in the Peloponnese, especially those unhappy about an Achaean alliance with Macedon. The high-water mark was reached in 225 when Cleomenes occupied the lower city of Corinth and engineered the submission of the old enemy Argos, a feat that had eluded even his namesake Cleomenes I (Plut. *Cleom.* 17.4–19.3). Sparta seemed unstoppable.

Rapidly, however, Sparta's mini-empire collapsed as Peloponnesians realized that Cleomenes had no intention of exporting his reform program but simply wanted to reassert Spartan dominance. In 224, Argos successfully revolted, and Antigonus quickly occupied Corinth once Cleomenes had withdrawn (Plut. *Cleom.* 19.4–20.1; Polyb. 2.53.2–54.7). In the next campaigning season, Sparta's remaining allies melted away as Arcadia fell in the face of Macedonian armed might. Cleomenes retreated to Sparta where he made some difficult decisions for the security of his city, sending his mother and his children to Egypt as hostages in return for continued financial aid from Ptolemy III. Nevertheless, payments evidently stopped, and so Cleomenes was compelled to offer freedom to helots willing to pay the not inconsiderable sum of five minae each for the privilege of fighting for Sparta (Plut. *Cleom.* 21.4, 22.3–23.1). Six thousand answered the call, raising a total contribution of five talents for the war effort. In 223/2, Cleomenes made a show of force, ravaging the Argive plain up to the city's walls and destroying Megalopolis (Plut. *Cleom*. 23.2–26.2), but Antigonus would not succumb to provocation.

Cleomenes' resources were fast running out. Confined to Laconia, he would have had increasing difficulties funding his mercenary troops, still a sizeable component of his forces. Antigonus in contrast had Macedon's vast resources to draw on as well as the support of the regional power, the Achaean League. All he needed was to gather his troops; Sparta's defeat was simply a matter of time. The end came in the summer of 222 near the town of Sellasia in northern Laconia, where the outmaneuvered Spartan army was almost completely wiped out (Plut. *Cleom*. 28; Polyb. 2.65–9). Cleomenes fled the field and, after instructing the undoubtedly terrified Spartans to receive Antigonus peacefully, set sail from Gytheum to Egypt, from where he perhaps hoped to launch an insurgency (Plut. *Cleom*. 29–31; Polyb. 2.69.11). In the event, he met his death a few years later in Alexandria after a heroic but quixotic attempt to rouse the populace against the dissolute Ptolemy IV Philopater, who succeeded his father in 221 B.C.E. (Plut. *Cleom*. 33–9).

Antigonus Doson spent only a few days in Sparta before hurrying north to deal with incursions into Macedonian territory by neighboring tribes (Plut. *Cleom*. 30; Polyb. 2.70.1, 5.9.9). While in the city, he restored the citizen body to its old order (*patrion politeuma*), likely by restoring exiles, disenfranchising perioeci and helots, and ensuring that men of conservative persuasion controlled the important offices. Under Macedonian hegemony, Sparta still possessed most, if not all, of Cleomenes' social reforms. The *patronomos* still existed, the *syssitia* and the reformed training system still functioned. But his political reforms were overturned: the ephorate was restored and, most importantly, the kingship was abolished. The unbroken line of kings who traced their ancestry back to Heracles himself was now at an end.

Despite the humiliation of Sellasia, some in Laconia (it is easy to guess who) were so pleased with Antigonus' settlement that they declared him their benefactor (*euergetês*) and raised him to the level of savior (*sôtêr*) following his death several months after his departure (Polyb. 5.9.10; *IG* V.1 1122). Sparta remained under a Macedonian governor until 220 (Polyb. 20.5.12), after which political life swiftly degenerated to a level of chaos that became as notorious as the state of affairs that supposedly preceded Lycurgus' reforms many centuries before (Polyb. 4.81.12–14; Strabo 8.5.5). Political violence came out into the open. Some supporting the Aetolians, others the Macedonians, the ephors –

now indisputably the supreme power in Sparta – had their political opponents cut down in public or were themselves butchered wholesale (Polyb. 4.22.5–12, 35.2–5, 81.5). An attempt by the ephors to revive the dyarchy in 219 after news reached them of Cleomenes' death led to a predictable outcome: their choice for the Eurypontid kingship, one Lycurgus, who may have prevailed through bribery, simply bided his time until he could exile his co-king, the under-aged Agesipolis, two years later and rule alone (Polyb. 4.35.8–14; Livy 34.26.14). Early in his reign, Lycurgus himself was forced to flee Sparta during the briefly successful coup of Chilon, who played on grievances among the Spartan general population about the concentration of land ownership resulting from the abolition of Cleomenes' reforms. When the crowd turned ugly at his rallying speech in the agora, however, probably because he supported the victors at Sellasia, he left for self-imposed exile in Achaea (Polyb. 4.81.1–11). In 219, Lycurgus had provoked Macedon by launching campaigns to recover territory lost to Argos and Achaea (Polyb. 4.36, 60.3). The new Macedonian king, Philip V, inevitably responded in 218 by crossing into Laconia with his army. Philip's invasion was the most destructive yet: the Macedonian army reached as far as Capes Taenarum and Malea, marching through the Laconian land at will, pillaging and burning as it went. In gestures emblematic of the Spartans' impotence, he pitched camp at the Amyclaeum and the Menelaeum, which commanded a view over the city. Despite Lycurgus' best efforts, Philip withdrew in safety after spending little over a week in Laconia (Polyb. 5.18–24). Years of unrest followed Lycurgus' death in 215/4. His young son Pelops succeeded to the throne, but actual power may already have been wielded by one Machanidas, who by 209 was Sparta's supreme leader (Polyb. 10.41.2; Diod. Sic. 27.1). Machanidas met his end in battle two years later near Mantinea at the hands of a man who would prove Sparta's nemesis, Philopoemen, newly elected General of the Achaean League. Philopoemen then loosed his soldiers on a defeated Laconia for days of unhindered pillage (Polyb. 11.18).

Soon after Machanidas' death, a Spartan leader finally arose with strength of mind and military prowess to match Cleomenes. Nabis, son of Demaratus (reigned 205–192 B.C.E.), has been vilified by a completely hostile historical tradition derived ultimately from Polybius, who wore his Achaean sympathies on his sleeve and consistently referred to Nabis as a tyrant (e.g. Polyb. 13.6.1–3, 16.13.1). Unlike his predecessor, Nabis was fated not to have his own Phylarchus. As had become the practice in Spartan politics, he exiled his opponents (Livy 36.35.7), confiscated their property, enfranchised slaves, perioeci, and mercenaries, redistributed land, and sought to make Sparta a military power again (Polyb. 13.6.1–6, 16.13.1; Livy 34.26.12, 31.11). Nabis' aggressive policy of wealth distribution was enough to earn him the title of "tyrant" and the undying hatred of conservatives like Polybius (13.6–7). He strengthened the city's defenses with a defensive ditch and palisade system, later complemented by proper mudbrick walls capped with terracotta tiles (Livy 34.27.3; *IG* V.1 885). The urban water supply was safeguarded with the construction of Sparta's first covered aqueduct (*SEG* 50 406). With soaring ambition, he built a navy which Polybius naturally interpreted as a pirate fleet (13.8.1; Livy 34.32.18). Like Areus I, Nabis evidently pursued a Hellenistic, rather than purely Spartan, model of kingship, styling himself as Sparta's king, minting coins with his portrait, having his title stamped on tiles (*IG* V.1 885), and being addressed as a monarch in documents from other states (*Syll.*³ 584). Despite the lip service paid to "Lycurgan ideals" (Livy 34.31.16–18), Nabis' Sparta had assumed a thoroughly Hellenistic aspect. The rich adorned their houses with artworks reflecting the most cosmopolitan tastes, while their ruler lived in a sumptuous palace worthy of a Hellenistic dynast (Livy 35.36.1; Plut. *Philop.* 15.6).

At first, Nabis proved remarkably adept at negotiating the treacherously shifting political sands of late third-century Greece, made even more dangerous by the increasingly assertive position of Rome, the new western power. Nabis' aims would have been familiar to any Spartan leader over the previous century and a half, for Messenia and Achaea still dominated foreign policy. Even so, Sparta and Messene appeared on the same side for a brief period in 205, as secondary signatories (*adscripti*) to the Romans in a treaty with Philip V, because of their shared hostility to Macedon (Livy 29.12.14). When one war ceased, however, Nabis began another in 201 by invading his putative ally Messene (Polyb. 16.13), which provoked hostilities with Achaea that continued to the end of his life. The outbreak of the Second Macedonian War the next year folded this local conflict into a larger struggle that had profound geopolitical consequences. Since the Achaean and Aetolian Leagues sided with Rome against Macedon, Nabis preferred to sit on the sidelines until Philip made him a proposition he could not refuse: temporary control of Argos, which Philip expected him to defend until the conflict ended (Livy 32.38.2). Once in power at Argos, the hometown of his wife Apia, Nabis won great popular support by redistributing the land and canceling debts (Livy 32.38.9) and soon made it clear that he had no intention of relinquishing the city. In 197, at a conference held at Mycenae, Nabis defected to the side of the Roman commander Titus Quinctius Flamininus, whose terms demanded troops to fight against Philip and peace with Achaea (Livy 32.39.6–10).

After Flamininus followed his victory with the famous announcement at the Isthmian Games of 196 guaranteeing freedom for the Greeks, Nabis' continuing occupation of Argos became an embarrassment to the Romans (Livy 33.32.1–6). When the senatorial commission mandated with the imposition of peace terms reported he had designs on becoming tyrant of Greece, Nabis found himself the focus of unwelcome Roman attention (Livy 33.44.8–9, 33.36). Playing on innate fear and hostility towards Nabis among the Greek propertied classes, Flamininus quickly amassed a huge invasion force and attacked Laconia by land and sea (Livy 34.22.4–26.14). He himself laid siege to Sparta while his brother Lucius dealt with the coastal cities; some of them joined the Romans freely, others under compulsion (Livy 34.29.1). When the port of Gytheum fell under a joint assault by Roman, Rhodian, and Pergamene forces, Nabis sued for peace.

The terms were harsh. Among other things, they required Argos and other possessions to be relinquished, slaves to be returned to their owners, and exiles to be restored; they also limited the navy to a couple of light transport ships and imposed a huge indemnity (Livy 34.35.3–11). The most devastating result of Nabis' defeat, however, was that the cities which had surrendered to the Romans were not returned to Sparta but made a quasi-protectorate of the Achaean League. Spartans refused to accept the loss of these maritime perioecic cities and tried repeatedly to reconquer them over the next decades. In fact, an attempt in 192 to regain Gytheum led to Nabis' death and Sparta's downfall.

Although he captured Gytheum in the early stages of the conflict, Nabis was later defeated by Philopoemen, the popular Achaean general, and confined to the city as the Achaeans ravaged the Eurotas valley for a month (Livy 34.36–9). Later, when an Aetolian force came to Sparta on the pretext of offering him aid, Nabis welcomed them, only to be treacherously murdered by an Aetolian as he was participating in a parade outside the town (Livy 35.35). Using the confusion that followed Nabis' death as a pretext, Philopoemen entered Laconia and persuaded (or threatened) the "leading citizens" to have Sparta join the Achaean League (Livy 35.37.1–3; Plut. *Philop*. 15.4).

By the end of Nabis' reign, Sparta was a transformed and much weaker state, especially because of the crippling loss of territory and forced membership in the Achaean League. On the other hand, the perioecic cities, finding themselves unexpectedly independent, began to develop ties among themselves and soon formed the League of Lacedaemonians, initially as a means of preserving their newly granted autonomy. The members of the Lacedaemonian League almost certainly included helots, who followed the perioeci in deserting Nabis for the Romans (Strabo 8.5.5). As a result, helotage as an institution disappeared with the fall of Nabis, who is sometimes credited erroneously with its deliberate abolition. But there was a bright spot. In accordance with the Achaean policy of internal autonomy for members, Sparta entered the League with all laws intact, including those of Nabis, which meant that many of the reforms introduced by Cleomenes, particularly his revived citizen training system, continued to function.

10

From the Achaean League to the Roman Empire

Sparta was not docile as an Achaean city. Almost immediately, factional strife broke out. In 189, after a series of coups and counter-coups, an anti-Achaean government came to power. Still irritated by the loss of the perioecic towns, the Spartans could not tolerate the occupation of Las by pro-Achaean exiles. Upon hearing that the Spartans had attacked Las, the Achaeans voted that they had broken the treaty of 195, obliging Nabis not to interfere with the cities formerly under his power. Both Achaeans and Spartans sent embassies to the Senate, which declined to intervene in the League's internal affairs (Livy 38.30–2). Considering this a *carte blanche*, Philopoemen marched again into Laconia in 188. Once encamped near Sparta, he demanded the leaders of the anti-Achaean faction be handed over to him in return for a pledge to spare the city and to give his prisoners a fair trial. But when the people he wanted entered the camp, they were set upon by pro-Achaean Spartans in Philopoemen's army; seventeen were killed. The next day, the other sixty prisoners were put to death after a perfunctory trial (Livy 38.33.6–11; Plut. *Philop.* 16.4; Paus. 8.51.3).

Philopoemen then took his revenge on Sparta, ordering the walls pulled down, the mercenaries and helots in the citizen body exiled, and the current exiles restored (Livy 38.34.1–3; Paus. 8.51.3). His most significant measures, however, were constitutional, obviously based on a conviction that any remaining vestiges of institutional exceptionalism at Sparta had to be eliminated. To that end, he imposed an Achaean framework onto Spartan institutions: the ephors and the Guardians of the Laws (*nomophulakes*), a Cleomenean magistracy, were combined into a *synarchia*, a joint committee with probouleutic and executive powers common in League cities, and a council (*boulê*) was instituted that consisted of the *synarchia* and Gerousia. At least two other offices now appear – the *engdotêr/ekdotêr*, in charge of publishing legislative acts, and the *epidamiourgos*, who had jurisdiction over public funds (*IG* V.1 4, 5). But the Spartan citizen training that had been so successful under Cleomenes and apparently continued to produce good soldiers for Nabis could not be allowed to continue. Philopoemen replaced it with a training system more in keeping with Achaean norms. As Pausanias put it, Philopoemen forbade the Spartan youths to exercise according to the laws of Lycurgus and forced them to exercise according to Achaean rules (Paus. 8.51.3). This particular aspect of his brutal treatment of Sparta was controversial in antiquity – Livy admitted, in a summation apparently derived from Polybius, that none of Philopoemen's actions was said to have caused as much hardship to the Spartans as the removal of the Lycurgan discipline (Livy 38.34.9).

Despite chronic internal unrest over the restitution of various sets of exiles' property, often played out before the Senate (e.g. Polyb. 23.4.9), Spartans lived for over forty years under this Achaean-style constitution. The Lycurgan myth nonetheless remained so strong that Livy anachronistically called Sparta "famous not for the grandeur of its buildings, but for its discipline and customs" when L. Aemilius Paullus, victor over the Macedonians at Pydna, visited in 168/7 (Livy 45.28.4). However, only after the Achaean War in 146, fought partly over the question of Sparta's right to secede from the League, did Spartans obtain permission from the Romans to readopt what they considered their ancestral laws and customs (Plut. *Philop.* 16.9; Paus. 8.51.3). Rome also awarded the Spartans reparations of 200 talents from the Achaeans (later cancelled) and, for their services, the status of a free city (*civitas libera*) (Strabo 8.5.5; Paus. 7.16.10). The Spartan cause would not have been harmed by the Romans' belief in their descent from the Spartans and the perceived similarity between the Roman and Spartan constitutions (Polyb. 6 *passim*; Strabo 9.2.39; *FGrH* 87 F59).

Sparta presumably shared in the relative prosperity following the destruction of Corinth (e.g. *IG* V.1 1390, 1432, 1433). On the other hand, the perioecic towns were still independent and showed no signs of pining for their old dependent status. The League of Laconians appointed *proxenoi* in other cities, even at Sparta, to look after its interests (*IG* V.1 961, 965, 1112, 1113, 1226) and occasionally minted festival coinage. It also had a vestigial bureaucracy and a treasury, perhaps located at one of the League's main cult sites, Cape Taenarum (*IG* V.1 1226–1227). Apart from one period in the later first century

B.C.E., relations between the member cities of the League and their old master were generally amicable. Economics played some part in this relationship since Sparta's main port was always Gytheum (Strabo 8.3.12, 5.2).

The first century was a time of trial for Greece. Athens did not recover from Sulla's ravages for a century. On the other hand, far from allying themselves to the Pontic king Mithridates against Rome in 90–85 (App. *Mithr.* 29), Spartans may been part of the Peloponnesian contingent Sulla later took with him to Italy to fight the Marians (App. *BC* 1.79). Such requisitioning of men and materiel would soon ravage Laconia (App. *BC* 1.102). An inscription from Gytheum bearing witness to the terrible hardship brought about by the stationing of troops during M. Antonius Creticus' war against piracy around 70 B.C.E. honors the brothers Cloatii, two Roman carpetbaggers (*negotiatores*) resident in Laconia, for reducing interest paid by the city on its borrowings from an outrageous 48 percent compounded to a merely usurious 24 percent simple interest (*IG* V.1 1146). Laconian cities were not alone in being preyed upon by *negotiatores*: groups of these businessmen were active throughout the Peloponnese during the first century B.C.E. (e.g. *IVO* 335; *IG* IV 605, V.1 1434, V.2 215, 268). Notwithstanding sporadic attempts to eliminate or at least control their rapacity, these Roman entrepreneurs grew wealthy on the resources of a defenseless land. That Sparta itself suffered under the yoke of official sanctions is evident from an honorific inscription for a man who came to the city's rescue when it could not meet an extortionate tax assessment probably also imposed by Creticus (*IG* V.1 11; Cic. *Verr.* 1.60, 2.80).

The age of the civil wars was one of shifting loyalties, as each city maneuvered to protect its interests. Sparta was no exception; in the war between Caesar and Pompey, like most Greek states, it sent archers to fight for Pompey (Caes. *BC* 3.4.3). In 44 B.C.E. Caesar and Antony, however, were well enough disposed to the Spartans to award them the Dentheliatis, a perennial bone of contention between Sparta and Messenia. Faithful to the dictator's memory because of this, Sparta ran the risk of being left to the tender mercies of the republican troops had Brutus prevailed at Philippi, where two thousand Spartans lost their lives fighting for Octavian (Plut. *Brut.* 41.8, 46.1). During the Perusine War, Livia sought refuge at Sparta with her husband and child, with which they had close ties because of the Claudian family's vaunted Spartan ancestry (Suet. *Tib.* 6; Cato *Origines* F51). As the civil wars entered their final phase, Sparta became merely a pawn. According to the provisions of the treaty of Misenum (39 B.C.E.), Antony and Octavian ceded Sardinia, Sicily, and the Peloponnese to Sextus Pompey as his fiefdom for five years (Vell. Pat. 2.77.2; App. *BC* 5.72), causing another round of oppressive requisitioning as Antony attempted to squeeze as much as possible out of his holdings before yielding them to Sextus (App. *BC* 5.77). But Pompey never ruled the Peloponnese, for Octavian and Antony declared that he had contravened the treaty, thus rendering it invalid (App. *BC* 5.80).

One particular measure Antony took when governing Greece had important consequences for Sparta's later history. He ordered the execution of a Spartan named Lachares, whom the Athenians had earlier honored as benefactor (*IG* II² 3885), for "piracy" (Plut. *Ant.* 67.3), likely meaning harassment of Antony's Egyptian grain ships from a base on Cythera. Unsurprisingly, when tensions between Octavian and Antony erupted into war, Lachares' son Eurycles committed himself to Octavian's side, dispatching a force of Spartan ships to fight at Actium. In return, the appreciative victor granted Sparta the presidency of the new Actian games at Nicopolis (Strabo 7.7.6; Plut. *Ant.* 67.2–3). Eurycles himself was handsomely rewarded, installed in power at Sparta, given control over the cities of the Lacedaemonian League, and granted Roman citizenship, a coveted prize (*SEG* 29 383). Eurycles' position as leader (*hêgemôn*) and his power (*epistasia*) at Sparta rested solely in his formal friendship (*amicitia*) with Augustus (Strabo 8.5.1, 5.5) though in the absence of evidence we cannot be certain that Eurycles did not attempt to legitimize his power by holding constitutional office. After all, he issued coins with the legend "in the time of Eurycles" on them, while advertising his all-important links to the imperial family on some obverses. A Spartan letter sent by the ephors and the city to Delphi in the early 20s B.C.E., however, suggests that the post-Cleomenean constitution was still functioning during Eurycles' hegemony (*IG* V.1 1566).

Augustus' *amicitia* afforded great power and influence. It was also a weakness, since it depended on a single man. When Augustus visited Sparta in 22/1 B.C.E., Eurycles' enemies, the traditional Spartan aristocracy, saw their chance. However, in Eurycles' trial before Augustus, the prosecutor, seeing his case failing, foolishly alluded to Roman interference in Sparta's internal affairs by quoting a famous speech of his ancestor Brasidas in which Thucydides has the general solemnly promise to follow a policy of non-intervention in the cities of Macedon (Plut. *Mor.* 207f; Thuc. 4.86.4–5). Incensed, Augustus packed him off temporarily to prison and made it quite clear he was not about to withdraw his support from his friend. On the contrary, he honored the city and reaffirmed his confidence in Eurycles by attending a common mess and awarding the old perioecic towns of Cardamyle and Thuria to Sparta and Cythera to his friend as a personal fief (Strabo 8.5.1; Dio Cass. 54.7.2; Paus. 3.26.7, 4.31.1).

Eurycles had been able to use Augustus' friendship to surmount this difficulty. The next time he would not be so lucky, as he cast the net of his ambitions well beyond Laconia and the Peloponnese. Eurycles now made the serious mistake of involving himself in the politically sensitive Middle East, when he meddled in the affairs of Kings Herod of Judaea and Archelaus of Cappadocia (Jos. *AJ* 16.301–10; *BJ* 1.513–31). Eurycles' pretext for his visit was probably the kinship (*syngeneia*) between Spartans and Jews, an idea that had gained currency by the end of the first century B.C.E. Herod the Great himself must have been at least partly motivated by this idea to bestow benefactions on Sparta (Jos. *BJ* 1.425). Concocted to assert the primacy of Jewish culture in terms comprehensible in the Hellenistic age, the kinship link had been invested with a plausible history going back to a letter supposedly sent by King Areus I in which he claimed to have discovered that the Spartans and Jews were brethren (1 *Macc.* 12.19–23). Later, the renegade high priest Jason purportedly intended Sparta to be his place of exile in 168 (2 *Macc.* 5.9). The high point was an embassy supposedly sent by the Hasmonean Jonathan to Sparta about 144 to renew the ties binding the two peoples. To Herod and his colleagues, a visit by a Spartan leader was thus nothing out of the ordinary. Eurycles, however, was intent on nothing but gain (Jos. *BJ* 1.513), and by playing one court faction off against another contributed substantively to the execution of Herod's son Alexander. After enriching himself at his hosts' expense, and after being honored for it by a naive Herod, he returned to Greece around 7 B.C.E. (Jos. *AJ* 16.300–10). Once home, Eurycles seems to have indulged himself in the same sort of interference in his neighbors' affairs as had proved so profitable in the east (Jos. *BJ* 1.531).

Augustus' patience was exhausted; the next time Eurycles was accused before the emperor, he was exiled (Strabo 8.5.5). Eurycles' death in exile sometime before 2 B.C.E. stilled the unrest, while his son Laco, who succeeded him in power at Sparta, preferred a quieter life. It was at this time that Augustus decided to separate the perioecic towns from Sparta once again and reconstitute the old Lacedaemonian League as the League of Free Laconians (*Eleutherolakônes*), a name which emphasized their independence from Sparta. Despite this, Laco maintained his family's prominence in the Eleutherolaconian League: the League erected a statue in his honor and Gytheum honored him as "Guardian of the nation and our city's bulwark and salvation" (*SEG* 11 623; *IG* V.1 1243). And so, apart from a short period during which Laco was disgraced in the tumult after the fall of Tiberius' powerful praetorian prefect Sejanus (Tac. *Ann.* 6.18), the Euryclids ruled at Sparta until the exile under Nero of Laco's feuding sons, Spartiaticus and Argolicus, signaled the end of the dynasty's grip on power (Stob. *Flor.* 4.40.9; cf. Plut. *Mor.* 487f–488a).

Beyond the vicissitudes of Eurycles' descendants, there is little to say of Sparta's role in the history of the first decades of the first century of our era. Under Tiberius, Spartans had their hopes dashed of recovering the Dentheliatis as the Senate confirmed a previous ruling under either Augustus or Tiberius that had awarded the land once again to the Messenians (Tac. *Ann.* 4.43). Later, Spartan boys may have been among the chorus of noble boys from Greece whom Gaius was on his way to hear when he was assassinated (Dio Cass. 59.29.6). After his accession, Claudius rewarded them with Roman citizenship, perhaps accounting for the considerable number of Spartan Tiberii Claudii attested later (Dio Cass. 60.7.2). Nero's reign saw one famous visit and a notorious absence. According to the third-century writer Philostratus, the sage and wonder-worker Apollonius of Tyana came to Sparta and cajoled Spartans into a vigorous revival of the Lycurgan discipline (Philostr. *VA* 4.27). Notwithstanding the slight possibility that the traditional training may have been allowed to lapse during the regime of the luxury-loving Spartiaticus (Stob. *Flor.* 4.40.9) and be revived after his fall, inscriptions clearly show that the heyday of Spartan archaism occurred a century after Apollonius' visit, while the first references to Lycurgus do not appear until the reign of Nerva (e.g. *IG* V.1 294, 309, 500, 554). The emperor Nero avoided Sparta and Athens during his tour of Greece in 67 C.E., not out of fear of the Furies at Athens nor distaste for the (non-existent) Lycurgan discipline at Sparta (Dio Cass. 63.14.3), but because neither city held games that were part of the "circuit" (*periodos*), victory in which bestowed the much coveted title of "circuit victor" (*periodonikês*) (Dio Cass. 63.8.3). As Sparta was not honored with the emperor's presence, neither did the city benefit significantly from his great gift. Since Sparta was already a free city, Nero's liberation of Greece, announced at the Isthmian Games in imitation of Flamininus, would have had little effect, though Spartans doubtless profited from the concomitant remission of taxes (Suet. *Nero* 24.2; *Syll.*[3] 814). Nothing is known of Sparta's fate in the turmoil after Nero's suicide, a period called by contemporaries "years of most harsh and uncertain circumstances" (*Syll.*[3] 796a). The *stasis* apparently ceased when Vespasian repealed Nero's grant upon gaining power (Paus. 7.17.4; Philostr. *VA* 5.41). But the new emperor did not repeal earlier grants of liberty, so that Sparta could continue as an ostensibly free city (Pliny *HN* 4.5).

The fall of the Euryclids under Nero marked the end of an era, and political life, dominated by various elite families, soon came to resemble that of other cities in the eastern empire. Symbolic of the change from one-man rule to the status of a normal provincial city was the fate of Eurycles' impressive marble theater. Only under the Flavians did public catalogs of magistrates and careers of prominent notables begin to be inscribed on the eastern retaining wall. The theater's unique feature, a scene building that could be rolled in and out of sight as needed, was removed, its stone rails either removed or covered over, and the

10.1   The early Roman theater on the acropolis

10.2   Inscriptions on the east parodos wall of the theater

Doric colonnade flanking them methodically smashed into tiny pieces. In its place, the Spartans erected a Roman-style scene building in 78 C.E. with financial support from Vespasian (*IG* V.1 691). The emperor also attempted to settle the continuing dispute over the Dentheliatis by having Sparta's western boundary surveyed, setting it on the contentious territory's eastern side (*IG* V.1 1431).

Another visitor to Sparta, albeit an unwilling one, was king Antiochus IV Epiphanes of Commagene, who spent a luxurious exile there after being forced from his throne in 72 C.E. (Jos. *BJ* 7.240). The marriage of one of his daughters to Spartiaticus' son Laco gave the presumably rehabilitated Euryclids an extensive network of relationships with the remaining royal houses of the east. In the 90s Sparta received yet more exiles, this time from Athens, as Hipparchus, Herodes Atticus' tyrannical grandfather, lived at Sparta following his condemnation by Domitian (Philostr. *VS* 547). Herodes' father, Atticus, participated in the *agôgê* and in the 130s held the patronomate, which had long ago replaced the ephorate as the city's eponymous magistracy (*IG* V.1 288). Herodes himself later went through the *agôgê* (*IG* V.1 45) and owned estates and a sumptuous villa in the Thyreatis, although what connection his ownership had with his Spartan ties remains unclear.

The late first century C.E. also saw the beginning of a great renaissance of Greek culture now known as the Second Sophistic, after a rhetorical style characterized by the widespread use of themes from the Archaic and Classical periods. The archaism of the Second Sophistic was paralleled in the civic culture of the time, when urban elites, especially in Greek-speaking areas, embraced an insistent and pervasive sense of the past, using their local histories as a means of legitimizing their own positions and, more generally, of framing the world around them. Foremost among the early actors in this movement was Plutarch, who, as we have seen, contributed significantly to the legend of Sparta. Plutarch's knowledge of Sparta was not completely secondhand: he visited the city to conduct research in the archives and see the sights, two of which he later mentioned, the Endurance Contest and the lance of Agesilaus (Plut. *Ages.* 19.10–11; *Lyc.* 18.1). Considering Plutarch's admiration for things Spartan and his promotion of the ideal of Sparta, his depiction of the city's ancient glory may perhaps have reinforced the archaizing trend at Sparta.

This trend first manifested itself at Sparta in the "renewal" or foundation of the Leonideia games at some point in Trajan's reign. These games, open only to Spartans, were presented as a revival of the funeral games for the hero of Thermopylae (*IG* V.1 18, 19; Paus. 3.14.1). As nostalgia for the great age of Greece increased over the next years, so did Sparta's prestige. The emperor Hadrian was instrumental in returning Sparta to her former position as the second city of Greece. He supported a decision by the Delphic Amphictyony to divide Thessaly's surplus votes among Athens, Sparta, and the other cities "so that the council might be common to all Greeks" (*FdeD* 3.4 302 col. 2, lines 5–6). In a letter sent to Cyrene, preserved only fragmentarily, the emperor referred to the Cyreneans' Dorian heritage and may have encouraged them to train their youth in the Laconian way (*SEG* 28 1566). He visited Sparta twice, in 125 and in 128/9, the second time holding the eponymous patronomate (*IG* V.1 32a, 486; *SEG* 11 492). In terms of raising Sparta's profile, however, Hadrian's most important act was his foundation of the Panhellenion in 131/2 C.E. All cities of "true" Greek culture and their colonies were eligible for membership in this panhellenic league; many took up the offer. Especially in Asia Minor, numerous cities claimed Spartan foundation or descent, with varying degrees of plausibility. Sparta, responding warmly to Hadrian's interest, sent her own representatives to the Panhellenion at Athens (*IG* V.1 47; *SEG* 11 499, 501); the number of altars dedicated to Hadrian at Sparta attests to his cult's particular veneration there (*IG* V.1 381–405).

When Gaius Julius Eurycles Herculanus died in 136/7, apparently without a male heir, the Euryclid line came to an end. In life, he had pursued a respectable career in the imperial service while giving his home city benefactions, including a gymnasium (Paus. 3.14.6); at Corinth, he also built a set of magnificent baths (*IG* V.1 1172; Paus. 2.3.5). In death he was no less generous. According to an unpublished inscription recording Hadrian's gift of Cythera to Sparta, Eurycles must first have bequeathed the island to the emperor, who thereupon returned it to Spartan control. At the same time, Eurycles endowed the city with funds to institute the Euryclea games in his memory and had a stoa dedicated at Mantinea to the divine Antinous, Hadrian's dead toyboy (*IG* V.2 281).

During Hadrian's reign, Sparta's profile was raised by the prominence of one particular public institution. Although the *agôgê*, Sparta's citizen training system, had undergone two lengthy periods of desuetude and revival by the second century C.E., it was now presented as an unsullied survival from the earliest days of the city's history. The *agôgê* was so important to the Spartan self-image that the eponymous magistrate, the *patronomos*, shouldered some of its expenses, for which benefaction he might be praised for his "patronage of the Lycurgan customs" (*IG* V.1 543, 544). The patronomate's association with the supposedly ancient training system attracted several cultivated foreigners to assume the office (e.g. *IG* V.1 32a, 71b). Boys were divided into groups with names redolent of hoary antiquity, such as *mikkichizomenoi* and *hatropampaides*, and competed in contests in dancing, singing, and hunting calls (e.g. *IG* V.1 278, 314), complemented by more typically "Spartan" activities like mass hand-to-hand combat at a place called the "Plane Tree Grove" (*Platanistas*) (Paus. 3.14.8–10) and, of course, the Endurance Contest. So famous became "The Whipping," as it was also known, that a single reference was enough to conjure up an image of Sparta (e.g. Hor. *Carm.* 1.7.10–11; Stat. *Theb.* 8.436–37; Maxim. Tyr. 23.2d). An anachronistic pastiche of the old Laconian dialect was the *agôgê's* official language, appearing on victory inscriptions and probably used in the singing competitions. A spectator at one of the events of the Spartan *agôgê* in the Roman period would thus have seen old Sparta in the full vigor of its youth, competing in age-old contests and speaking the language of Lycurgus and Leonidas – a living, tangible corollary to Cicero's astonishing description of the Spartans of his own time as "the only people in the whole world who have lived now for more than seven hundred years with one and the same set of customs and unchanging laws" (Cic. *Flacc.* 63). However questionable the validity of their claims to an unbroken continuity between the Classical discipline and the ephebate of their own day, later Spartans forged a formidable instrument to assert their status as a distinct society within the Greek half of the Roman Empire.

The second century was a time of prosperity and prestige, but also of increasing social inequality. Large villas lavishly decorated with mosaics were built in the city, and huge estates enclosed her countryside, increasing the concentration of population in Sparta as smallholders were forced out in favor of cash crops. Sparta's mainland territory was still confined mainly to the central Eurotas valley but, thanks to Hadrian, the city now enjoyed the income from the busy port of Corone in Messenia (*IG* V.1 34, 36b) and, in addition to Cythera, the small island of Caudus (mod. Gavdos) off the south coast of Crete (*IG* V.1 494). What little we know of Sparta's history during the Antonine period confirms the picture of a prosperous, unexceptional provincial town. Embassies were occasionally sent to emperors to petition for favors or decisions in disputes (*IG* V.1 36b, 37a, 508; *SEG* 11 492, 493, 501). We know of a quarrel between the Eleutherolaconian League and Sparta, presumably over boundaries or port duties (*IG* V.1 37a). Spartans sometimes called in foreign judges, or might help to settle disputes abroad (e.g. *IG* V.1 39; *SEG* 11 461, 472, 491). A community of Christians is attested in the second half of the century (Eus. *HE* 4.23.2). All in all, life seems to have been peaceful.

Sparta was largely untouched by greater events until the 160s. In 163–166 C.E., young Spartans enrolled in Lucius Verus' campaigns against the Parthians, or "Persians," as the Spartans still preferred to call them (*IG* V.1 816, 818; *SEG* 11 486). Later, in 175, one of Verus' Spartan veterans had to forsake the safety of Sparta to fight in a force sent to suppress the revolt of Avidius Cassius, governor of Syria (*SEG* 11 486). By then, the economic situation had worsened, with predictable results. In the 160s the city may even have suffered a short period of internal unrest, perhaps connected with increased Roman taxes to fund Marcus Aurelius' border wars, when no one could be found to serve as *patronomos* (*SEG* 11 486, 501). Two catastrophes of the late 160s, a plague brought back by veterans of the Parthian wars and a raid by the Costoboci into Greece, were almost certainly contributing factors (Paus. 10.34.5). The period immediately afterwards saw Greece in such a state that the brothers Quintilii were sent to Greece as *correctores*, with wide powers of financial regulation.

In the decades around the turn of the century, interest in Spartan culture was pervasive through the Roman Empire. The archaistic revival at Sparta was at its height. The Euryclea Games were accorded the status of sacred games, perhaps by Commodus, elevating them to panhellenic importance (*FdeD* 3.1.89). Young Spartan men who joined Caracalla on his procession through the east to fight the Parthians were grouped into a "Pitanate *lochos*," partly an allusion to the (in)famous division of the Classical Spartan army which may (or may not) have fought at Plataea (Herodian 4.8.1–3; cf. Hdt. 9.53; Thuc. 1.20.4) and partly an attempt to trump Alexander (Plut. *Alex*. 16.18). The memorials of five Spartans who participated in this campaign have been identified, portraying them equipped as members of the domestic security force (Papaefthimiou nos. 16–20).

The empire's unsettled circumstances had their effect on Sparta in the third century. The general trend to increased official Roman intervention in cities' internal affairs can be documented at Sparta. At least four *correctores* were active in connection with the city, including one who financed the repair of a bridge over the Eurotas (*IG* V.1 538). Straitened finances probably underlie the sharp decrease in public inscriptions, including lists of magistrates and inscribed careers, in the reign of Alexander Severus. The latest victory dedication at the sanctuary of Artemis Orthia has been dated to shortly after 225 (*IG* V.1 314); interestingly, it exhibits none of the archaistic mannerisms of earlier dedications and is written in ordinary Attic *koine*. In 267, Laconia was again invaded, for the first time in over four centuries, this time by the Herulians who raided Sparta during their devastating incursion into Greece (Syncell. 719.9).

Soon after the sack, the sanctuary of Artemis Orthia received a small amphitheater to seat spectators at the Endurance Contest, which incorporated many dedications set up by victors in the other contests of the *agôgê*. Restoration work at the city's theater also indicates an economic revival in the time of Diocletian and Constantine. A few years later, the scene building was restored again and dedicated to Constantius and Galerius (*SEG* 11 850). By the early fourth century, then, Sparta had regained a certain measure of prosperity, though other evidence suggests that the city had lost its dominant position in

10.3   Remains of the temple and amphitheater at the sanctuary of Artemis Orthia

Laconian economic life. Of the copies of Diocletian's price edict found in Laconia, no fragments come from Sparta or its immediate neighborhood, signifying that it had ceased to be a commercial center. The cult of Artemis Orthia would draw visitors until the double shock of the Edict of Theodosius and the invasion of Alaric. The young Libanius, for instance, took time out from his studies at Athens in the late 330s to see the festival of "the Whips" (Liban. *Or.* 1.23). In 359/60, the proconsul Ampelius ordered more restorations at the theater and was praised by the panegyrist Himerius for his work "from the Gates to the innermost recesses of the Peloponnese" (*SEG* 11 464, 851; Him. *Or.* 31.11). Later in the fourth century, Sparta suffered from the serious earthquake in 365, followed by repairs by the proconsul Anatolius (*SEG* 11 773). The new order also flexed its muscles: Christians burnt two bronze statues in the sanctuary of Athena Chalcioecus on the acropolis (Liban. *Ep.* 1518).

The capture of Sparta by Alaric's Gothic forces in 396 was a turning point (Zosim. 5.6.5). While physical evidence of destruction is slight, the walls surrounding the acropolis, so prominent a feature today, were probably first built around this time, when the Spartans again realized their aging defenses were inadequate. Into the construction of the new circuit went statue bases, inscribed stelae, and blocks from now-superfluous public buildings, as Sparta was transformed into a medieval city. It survived in a considerably shrunken state, essentially the old acropolis and agora areas, until the remaining Spartans fled to the Mani peninsula and the coastal slopes of Parnon when the Slavs invaded during the sixth to the ninth centuries. The Byzantines attempted to restore the city under the name *Lakedaimonia,* but by the fourteenth century it lay abandoned, serving as a marble quarry for the city of Mistras, built on an eastern outcrop of Mount Taygetus. Not until 1836 was the sown land again the site of a city, settled by this time by the inhabitants of Mistras, dislodged by the Greek war of independence.

Bibliography

Abbreviations

I use the following abbreviations for journals and series.

AA = *Archäologischer Anzeiger*
ABSA = *Annual of the British School at Athens*
AD (Chron.) = *Archaiologikon Deltion* (Chronika)
AE = *Archaiologikê Ephêmeris*
AION (filol) = *Annali dell' Istituto universitario orientale di Napoli, Dipartimento di studi del mondo classico e del Mediterraneo antico, Sezione filologico-letteraria*
AJP = *American Journal of Philology*
AMuGS = Antike Münzen und Geschnittene Steine
BCH = *Bulletin de Correspondance Hellénique*
BEFAR = Bibliothèque des Écoles françaises d'Athènes et de Rome
CJ = *Classical Journal*
CPC = Copenhagen Polis Centre
CQ = *Classical Quarterly*
GFA = *Göttinger Forum für Altertumswissenschaft*
GRBS = *Greek, Roman, and Byzantine Studies*
JHS = *Journal of Hellenic Studies*
JRS = *Journal of Roman Studies*
Op. Ath. = *Opuscula Atheniensia*
PAE = *Praktika tês en Athenais archaiologikês Etairias*
P&P = *Past and Present*
REA = *Revue des Études Grecques*
RHR = *Revue de l' Histoire des Religions*
ZRG = *Zeitschrift der Savigny-Stiftung für Rechtsgeschichte. Romanistische Abteilung*

Collections

Alcock, S. and N. Luraghi, eds. *Helots and Their Masters in Laconia and Messenia: Histories, Ideologies, Structures.* Washington and Cambridge, Mass., 2003.

Cartledge, P. *Spartan Reflections.* London, 2001.

Cavanagh, W. and S. Walker, eds. *Sparta in Laconia.* London, 1998.

Figueira, T.J., ed. *Spartan Society.* Swansea, 2004.

Powell, A. and S. Hodkinson, eds. *The Shadow of Sparta.* London and New York, 1994.

Powell, A. and S. Hodkinson, eds. *Sparta: New Perspectives.* London, 1999.

Powell, A. and S. Hodkinson, eds. *Sparta: Beyond the Mirage.* London, 2002.

Powell, A. and S. Hodkinson, eds. *Sparta and War.* Swansea, 2006.

Sanders, J., ed. *Philolakôn: Lakonian Studies in Honour of Hector Catling.* London, 1992.

Toynbee, A. *Some Problems in Greek History.* Oxford, 1966.

Whitby, M., ed. *Sparta.* New York, 2002.

Background and Origins

Aravantinos, V.L., L. Godart, and A. Sacconi. *Thèbes. Fouilles de la Cadmée I. Les tablettes en Linéaire B de la Odos Pelopidou.* Pisa and Rome, 2001.

Chapin, A. and L. Hitchcock. "Homer and Laconian Topography: This Is What the Book Says, and This Is What the Land Tells Us," in S. Morris and R. Laffineur, eds. *Epos: Reconsidering Greek Epic and Aegean Bronze Age Archaeology*, Aegaeum 28. Liège and Austin, 2007, 255–62.

Coulson, W. "The Dark Age Pottery of Sparta," *ABSA* 80 (1985) 29–84.

Dickinson, O. *The Aegean from Bronze Age to Iron Age.* London and New York, 2006.

Eder, B. *Argolis, Lakonien, Messenien vom Ende der mykenischen Palastzeit bis zur Einwanderung der Dorier.* Vienna, 1998.

Finkelberg, M. *Greeks and Pre-Greeks: Aegean Prehistory and Greek Heroic Tradition.* Cambridge, 2005.

Grove, A. and O. Rackham. *The Nature of Mediterranean Europe: An Ecological History.* New Haven and London, 2001.

Hall, J. *Ethnic Identity in Greek Antiquity.* Cambridge, 1997.

Hall, J. *Hellenicity: Between Ethnicity and Culture.* Chicago and London, 2002.

Literary Sources

Bruce, I.A.F. *An Historical Commentary on the "Hellenica Oxyrhynchia."* Cambridge, 1967.

Calame, C. *Les choeurs de jeunes filles en Grèce archaïque.* 2 vols. Urbino, 1977.

Cartledge, P. and P. Debnar. "Sparta and Spartans in Thucydides," in A. Rengakos and A. Tsakmakis, eds. *Brill's Companion to Thucydides.* Leiden and Boston, 2006, 559–88.

David, E. "The Pamphlet of Pausanias," *P&P* 34 (1979) 94–116.

de Blois, L. "Plutarch's Lycurgus: A Platonic Biography," in K. Vössing, ed. *Biographie und Prosopographie. Historia* Einzelschrift 178. Stuttgart, 2005, 91–102.

Dewald, C. and J. Marincola. *The Cambridge Companion to Herodotus.* Cambridge, 2006.

Dillery, J. *Xenophon and the History of His Times.* London and New York, 1995.

Gostoli, A. *Terpandro.* Rome, 1990.

Humble, N. "The Author, Date and Purpose of Chapter 14 of the *Lakedaimonion Politeia*," in O. Tuplin, ed. *Xenophon and His World. Historia* Einzelschrift 172. Wiesbaden, 2004, 215–28.

Lipka, M. *Xenophon's Spartan Constitution: Introduction, Text, Commentary.* Berlin and New York, 2002.

Marasco, G. *Commento alle biografie plutarchee di Agide e di Cleomene,* 2 vols. Rome, 1981.

Meier, M. "Tyrtaios fr. 1^B G/P bzw. fr. °14 G/P (= fr. 4 W) und die große Rhetra – kein Zusammenhang?" *GFA* 5 (2002) 65–87.

McKechnie, P.R. and S.J. Kern, eds. *Hellenica Oxyrhynchia.* Warminster, 1988.

Momigliano, A. "Per l'unità logica della *Lakedaimonion Politeia* di Senofonte," in *Terzo Contributo alla storia degli studi classici e del mondo antico* I. Rome, 1966, 341–5.

Ollier, F. *Le mirage spartiate,* 2 vols. Paris, 1933–43; repr. 1973.

Page, D.L. *Poetae Melici Graeci.* Oxford, 1962.

Rawson, E. *The Spartan Tradition in European Thought.* Oxford, 1969.

Rebenich, S. *Xenophon: Die Verfassung der Spartaner.* Darmstadt, 1998.

Tigerstedt, E.N. *The Legend of Sparta in Classical Antiquity,* 2 vols. Stockholm and Uppsala, 1965–74.

van Wees, H. "Gute Ordnung ohne Große Rhetra – Noch einmal zu Tyrtaios' *Eunomia*," *GFA* 5 (2002) 89–103.

West, M.L. *Iambi et Elegi Graeci ante Alexandrum Cantati* II, 2nd edn. Oxford, 1992.

Archaic and Classical History

Badian, E. "Towards a Chronology of the Pentecontaetia down to the Renewal of the Peace of Callias," in *From Plataea to Potidaea: Studies in the History and Historiography of the Pentecontaetia.* Baltimore, 1993, 73–108.

Bolmarcich, S. "The Date of the 'Oath of the Peloponnesian League,'" *Historia* 57 (2008) 65–79.

Bommelaer, J.-F. *Lysandre de Sparte: Histoire et traditions,* BEFAR 240. Athens and Paris, 1981.

Braun, T. "Chrêstous Poiein," *CQ* n.s. 44 (1994) 40–5.

Cartledge, P. *Sparta and Lakonia: A Regional History 1300–362 BC.* London, 1979.

Cartledge, P. "Sparta and Samos: A Special Relationship?" *CQ* n.s. 32 (1982) 243–65.

Cartledge, P. *Agesilaus and the Crisis of Sparta.* Baltimore, 1987.

Cartledge, P. "Spartan Justice? Or 'The State of the Ephors?'" *Dike* 3 (2000) 5–26.

Cawkwell, G. "The Decline of Sparta," *CQ* n.s. 33 (1983) 385–400.

Cawkwell, G. "Sparta and Her Allies in the Sixth Century," *CQ* n.s. 43 (1993) 364–76.

Cawkwell, G. *The Greek Wars: The Failure of Persia.* Oxford, 2005.

Corsano, M. "Sparte et Tarente: Le mythe de fondation d'une colonie," *RHR* 196 (1979) 113–40.

de Ste. Croix, G.E.M. *The Origins of the Peloponnesian War.* London, 1972.

Finley, M. "Sparta," in *The Use and Abuse of History.* London, 1975, 161–77.

Fornara, C. "Some Aspects of the Career of Pausanias of Sparta," *Historia* 15 (1966) 257–71.

Jacoby, F. "Chrêstous Poiein (Aristotle fr. 592R)," *CQ* 38 (1944) 15–16.

Kagan, D. *The Outbreak of the Peloponnesian War.* Ithaca and London, 1969.

Kelly, T. "Did the Argives Defeat the Spartans at Hysiai in 669 B.C.?" *AJP* 91 (1970) 31–42.

Klein, S. "Cleomenes: A Study in Early Spartan Imperialism," Diss. University of Kansas, 1973.

Krentz, P. "Fighting by the Rules: The Invention of the Hoplite Agon," *Hesperia* 71 (2002) 23–39.

Lang, M. "Scapegoat Pausanias," *CJ* 63 (1967) 79–85.

Larsen, J. "Sparta and the Ionian Revolt: A Study of Spartan Foreign Policy and the Genesis of the Peloponnesian League," *CQ* 27 (1932) 136–50.

Larsen, J. "The Constitution of the Peloponnesian League I," *CQ* 28 (1933) 257–76.

Larsen, J. "The Constitution of the Peloponnesian League II," *CQ* 29 (1934) 1–19.

Lazenby, J. "Pausanias, son of Kleombrotos," *Hermes* 103 (1975) 235–51.

Lazenby, J. *The Spartan Army*. Warminster, 1985.

Lazenby, J. *The Peloponnesian War: A Military Study*. London and New York, 2004.

Lehmann-Haupt, C. "Pausanias, Heros Ktistes von Byzanz," *Klio* 17 (1922) 59–73.

Lévy, E. *Sparte. Histoire politique et sociale jusqu'à la conquête romaine*. Paris, 2003.

Lewis, D. *Sparta and Persia*. Leiden, 1977.

Lippolis, E. "Le testimonianze del culto in Taranto greca," *Taras* 2 (1982) 81–135.

Loomis, W. "Pausanias, Byzantium and the Formation of the Delian League," *Historia* 39 (1990) 487–92.

Luraghi, N. "Becoming Messenian," *JHS* 122 (2002) 45–69.

Mari, M. "Il 'culto della personalità' a Samo, tra Lisandro e Demetrio Poliorcete," in E. Cavallini, ed. *Samo: Storia, Letteratura, Scienza. AION* (filol) 8. Pisa and Rome, 2004, 177–97.

Nafissi, M. "Pausania, il vincitore di Platea," in C. Bearzot and F. Landucci, eds. *Contro le "leggi immutabili." Gli Spartani fra tradizione e innovazione*. Milan, 2004, 53–90.

Ruzé, F. and J. Christien. *Sparte: Géographie, mythes, et histoire*. Paris, 2007.

Hellenistic and Roman History

Bowersock, G. "Eurycles of Sparta," *JRS* 51 (1961) 112–18.

Cartledge, P. and A. Spawforth. *Hellenistic and Roman Sparta: A Tale of Two Cities*. London and New York, 1989.

Gruen, E. *Heritage and Hellenism: The Reinvention of Jewish Tradition*. Berkeley, 1998.

Kennell, N. "Nerôn Periodonikês," *AJP* 109 (1988) 239–51.

Kennell, N. "IG V, 1, 16 and the Gerousia of Roman Sparta," *Hesperia* 61 (1992) 193–202.

Spawforth, A. "Sparta and the Family of Herodes Atticus: A Reconsideration of the Evidence," *ABSA* 75 (1980) 203–20.

Texier, J. *Nabis*. Paris, 1975.

Material Culture

Alcock, S., A. Berlin, A. Harrison, N. Spencer, and D. Stone. "Pylos Regional Archaeological Project, Part VII. Historical Messenia, Geometric through Late Roman," *Hesperia* 74 (2005) 147–209.

Bonias, Z. *Ena agrotikon ieron stis Aigies Lakônias*. Athens, 1998.

Boss, M. *Lakonische Votivgaben aus Blei*. Würzburg, 2000.

Catling, H.W. "Zeus Messapeus near Sparta: An Interim Report," *Lakônikai Spoudai* 10 (1990) 276–95.

Catling, H.W. "Zeus Messapeus at Tsakona, Laconia, Reconsidered," *Lakônikai Spoudai* 16 (2002) 67–99.

Cavanagh, W., J. Crouwel, R.W.V. Catling, and G. Shipley. *The Laconia Survey*, 2 vols. London, 1996–2002.

Cavanagh, W., C. Mee, and P. James. *The Laconia Rural Sites Project, ABSA* suppl. 36. London, 2005.

Crouwel, J., M. Prent, T.S. MacVeagh, G.-J. van Wijngaarten, C. Sueur, J. Fiselier, J. de Waele, J. van der Vin, R. Cappers, S. Mulder, T. Carter, E. Langridge-Noti, and L. van Dijk-Schram. "Geraki, an Acropolis Site in Lakonia: Preliminary Reports (1994–2005)," *Pharos* 3–14 (1995–2006).

Davis, J., ed. *Sandy Pylos: An Archaeological History from Nestor to Navarino*, 2nd edn. Princeton, 2008.

Dawkins, R., ed. *The Sanctuary of Artemis Orthia at Sparta*. Society for the Promotion of Hellenic Studies suppl. 2. London, 1921.

Grunauer-von Hoerschelmann, S. *Die Münzprägung der Lakedaimonier*. AMuGS vol. 7. Berlin, 1978.

Kaltsas, N. "Hê archaikê oikia sto Kopanaki tês Messênias," *AE* (1983) 220–1.

Kourinou, E. *Spartê: Sumbolê stê mnêmeiakê topographia tês*. Athens, 2000.

Lo Porto, F. "Topografia antica di Taranto," in *Taranto nella civiltà di Magna Grecia*. Naples, 1971, 343–83.

Matthaiou, A., E. Zavvou, and A. Themos. *Kattade edoxe tois Lake-daimoniois: Epigraphes dêmosiou charaktêra apo tê Spartê tou 5ou aiôna p.c.* Athens, 2006.

McPhee, I. "Laconian Red-figure from the British Excavations in Sparta," *ABSA* 81 (1986) 153–65.

Nafissi, M. "Distribuzione della ceramica laconica," *Studi sulla ceramica laconica*. Rome, 1986, 149–72.

Papaefthimiou, W. *Grabreliefs späthellenistischer und römischer Zeit aus Sparta und Lakonien*. Munich, 1991.

Pelagatti, P. and C.M. Stibbe. "La ceramica laconica a Taranto e nella Puglia," in G.P. Caratelli, ed. *Taranto e il Mediterraneo*. Taranto, 2002, 365–403.

Raphtopoulou, S. "Taphes tês epochês tou sidêrou stê Spartê," in *Praktika E' Diethnous Sunedriou Peloponnêsiakôn Spoudôn*, vol. 2. Athens, 1996–7, 272–82.

Ratinaud-Lachkar, I. "Insoumise Asiné? Pour une mise en perspective des sources littéraires et archéologiques relatives à la destruction d'Asiné par Argos en 715 avant notre ère," *Op. Ath.* 29 (2004) 73–88.

Salapata, G. "Lakonian Votive Plaques with Particular Reference to the Sanctuary of Alexandra at Amyklai," Diss. University of Pennsylvania, 1992.

Stibbe, C. *Das andere Sparta*, trans. H. Prost. Mainz, 1996.

Stroszeck, J. "Lakonische-rotfigure Keramik aus den Lakedaimoniergräbern am Kerameikos von Athen (403 v. Chr.)," *AA* 2006.2 101–20.

Themelis, P. "Anaskaphê Messênês," *PAE* 142 (1987) 73–104; 143 (1988) 43–79; 146 (1991) 85–128.

Themos, A., H. Zavvou, S. Raphtopoulov, and Ch. Flouris. "Annual Reports of the E' Ephoreia Proistorikôn kai klasikôn archaiotêtôn," *AD* (Chron.) 47 (1992)–52 (1997).

Waywell, G. and J. Wilkes. "Excavations at the Ancient Theatre of Sparta 1995–1998: Preliminary Report," *ABSA* 94 (1999) 437–55.

Zavvou, H. "Eurêmata tês Mesoelladikês kai prôimês Mukênaikês epochês apo tê Spartê," paper delivered at "Mesohelladika: The Greek Mainland in the Middle Bronze Age," International Conference, Athens, March 8–12, 2006 (forthcoming).

Institutions

Andrewes, A. "The Government of Classical Sparta," in E. Badian, ed. *Ancient Society and Institutions: Studies Presented to Victor Ehrenberg on his 75th Birthday*. Oxford, 1966, 1–20.

Carlier, P. *La Royauté en Grèce avant Alexandre*. Strasbourg, 1984.

Ducat, J. *Les Hilotes. BCH* suppl. 20. Paris, 1990.

Ducat, J. *Spartan Education: Youth and Society in the Classical Period*, trans. E. Stafford, P.J. Shaw, and A. Powell. Swansea, 2006.

Forrest, W.G. "Legislation in Sparta," *Phoenix* 21 (1967) 11–19.

Hall, J. "Sparta, Lakedaimon and the Nature of Perioikic Dependency," in P. Flensted-Jensen, ed. *Further Studies in the Ancient Greek Polis*. CPC Papers 5. *Historia* Einzelschrift 138. Stuttgart, 2000, 73–90.

Hansen, M. "The Perioikic *Poleis* of Lakedaimon," in T. Nielsen, ed. *Once Again: Studies in the Ancient Greek* Polis. CPC Papers 7. *Historia* Einzelschrift 180. Stuttgart, 2004, 149–64.

Hodkinson, S. "Servile and Free Dependants of the Classical Spartan 'oikos,'" in M. Moggi and G. Cordiano, eds. *Schiavi e dependenti nell' ambito dell' "oikos" e della "familia."* Pisa, 1997, 45–71.

Hodkinson, S. "The Imaginary Spartan *Politeia*," in M. Hansen, ed. *The Imaginary Polis*, Symposium, January 7–10, 2004. CPC Acts 7. Copenhagen, 2005, 222–81.

Kennell, N. *The Gymnasium of Virtue: Education and Culture in Ancient Sparta*. Chapel Hill, 1995.

Luther, A. "Der Name der Volksversammlung in Sparta," in A. Luther, M. Meier, and L. Thommen, eds. *Das frühe Sparta*. Munich, 2006, 73–88.

Meier, M. *Aristokraten und Damoden: Untersuchungen zur inneren Entwicklung Spartas im 7. Jahrhundert v. Chr und zur politischen Funktion der Dichtung des Tyrtaios.* Stuttgart, 1998 (www.gfa.d-r.de/5-02/meier.pdf).

Meier, M. "Zwischen Königen und Damos. Überlegungen zur Funktion und Entwicklung des Ephorats in Sparta (7.–4. Jh. v. Chr.)," *ZRG* 117 (2000) 43–102.

Millender, E. "Spartan Literacy Revisited," *Classical Antiquity* 20 (2001) 121–64.

Millender, E. "Νόμος Δεσπότης: Spartan Obedience and Athenian Lawfulness in Fifth-Century Greek Thought," in E. Robinson and V. Gorman, eds., Oikistes: *Studies in Constitutions, Colonies, and Military Power in the Ancient World Offered in Honor of A.J. Graham, 33–59.* Leiden, 2002.

Ogden, D. "Crooked Speech: The Genesis of the Spartan Rhetra," *JHS* 114 (1994) 86–102.

Rhodes, P.J. "The Selection of Ephors at Sparta," *Historia* 30 (1981) 498–502.

Richer, N. *Les Ephores: études sur l'histoire et sur l'image de Sparte (VIIIe–IIIe siècle avant J.C.).* Paris, 1998.

Richer, N. "Les Hyacinthies de Sparte," *REA* 106 (2004) 389–419.

Schütrumpf, E. "The Rhetra of Epitadeus: A Platonist's Fiction," *GRBS* 28 (1987) 441–57.

Shipley, G. " 'The Other Lakedaimonians': The Dependent Perioikic Poleis of Laconia and Messenia," in M. Hansen, ed. *The Polis as an Urban Centre and as a Political Community.* CPC Acts 4. Copenhagen, 1997, 189–281.

Thommen, L. *Lakedaimonion Politeia: Die Entstehung der spartanischen Verfassung. Historia* Einzelschrift 130. Stuttgart, 1996.

Thommen, L. *Sparta: Verfassungs- und Sozialgeschichte einer griechischen Polis.* Stuttgart and Weimar, 2003.

Wade-Gery, H.T. "The Spartan Rhetra in Plutarch, *Lycurgus* VI," in *Essays in Greek History.* Oxford, 1958, 37–85.

Westlake, H.D. "Reelection to the Ephorate," *GRBS* 17 (1976) 343–52.

Wheeler, E. "Hoplomachia and Greek Dances in Arms," *GRBS* 23 (1982) 223–33.

Index

procedure, 101, 107–8; kings and, 54, 55, 95, 96, 99, 104; in legislative procedure, 108, 110; Lycurgus and, 16, 101–4, 169–70; in Macedonian settlement, 176–7; mobilization of troops by, 106, 138, 140, 155; Pausanias (regent) and, 72, 73, 105; Peloponnesian League and, 104, 105, 129; powers of, over magistrates, 104; prohibition of precious metal coinage by, 131; *see also* Assembly; Gerousia/Gerontes

Ephorus of Cyme, 13; on destruction of Helos, 32; on helots, 16, 76, 79–80; on pamphlet of king Pausanias, 103; on perioeci, 88

epistoleus (secretary) of navy, 127, 152

Eretria, 61

Erineus: *see* Dorians: homeland of

Erythrae, 124

Euboea (island), 117; *see also* Carystus; Eretria

Eucleidas (king of Sparta), 171

Eunomos (king of Sparta), 94

Euripides, 168

Eurotas river, 5, 162, 172, 192; at Taras, 37

Eurotas valley: exploitation of, 40, 162; landscape changes in, 7; in late Bronze Age, 4, 25; settlements in, 30, 42, 81; topography of, 6–8; *see also* agriculture

Euryclea Games, 190, 192

Eurycles, C. Julius (leader of Sparta), 184–6, 187–8

Eurycles Herculanus, C. Julius, 190

Eurypontids, 29, 94, 95

Eurysthenes: *see* Procles and Eurysthene

Eurystheus, 20–1

Eurytus, 78

Evagoras (king of Cyprus), 128

Flamininus, Titus Quinctius, 179

Gaius (emperor of Rome), 186

Galerius (emperor of Rome), 192

Gargaphia spring, 67

Geraki: *see* Geronthrae

Geronthrae: conquest of, 32; "Dorianization" of, 88; excavations at, 9, 24, 32, 90; in Hellenistic period, 164

Gerousia/Gerontes, 109–11; Assembly and, 99, 112; Cleomenes III and, 171; as deliberative body, 111; election of, 17, 109; eligibility for, 109; ephors and, 106, 167; in Great Rhetra, 46, 48–9, 109; in judicial procedure, 106, 109, 167; kings and, 11, 96–7, 104, 110; in legislative procedure, 110–11, 165; in Philopoemen's settlement, 182; in Tyrtaeus' *Eunomia*, 44; *see also* Assembly; ephors/ ephorate

Gorgo, 57, 66

Gortyn, 32

Great Rhetra, 45–9; in legislative procedure, 110–11; Plutarch on, 16, 45–7; Rider to, 46, 49; Tyrtaeus' *Eunomia* and, 10, 45

Greek language, 28–9, 31

Gylippus, 85, 124, 131

Gymnopaediae festival, 144, 153, 172

Gytheum: Cleomenes III and, 176; Epaminondas and, 145; Laco and, 186; Nabis and, 179; *negotiatores* at, 183; Philip II and, 160; Romans and, 179; as Spartan port/naval base, 117, 182